MW00603730

Ordinary Women
Extraordinary Service

This book is dedicated to the daughters, granddaughters and great granddaughters of the Extension professionals and volunteers, the ordinary women, whose extraordinary service is represented in this book and whose spirit and dedication we salute. This is a great legacy for the next generations. May they continue the tradition.

Ordinary Women
Extraordinary Service

to family, community, and North Carolina

Written and Compiled by

Wilma Hammett, Jan Christensen, Joan Gosper

Designed by

Vickie Guin

Family&
Consumer Sciences
FOUNDATION NC State
University

NC State University
A&T State University
COOPERATIVE
EXTENSION
Empowering People • Providing Solutions

A Special Project of the
North Carolina Family and Consumer Sciences Foundation
and the
North Carolina Extension and Community Association Foundation

Copyright 2011

North Carolina Family and Consumer Sciences Foundation

North Carolina Extension and Community Association Foundation

Cover Photos

North Carolina State University Libraries Archives

Communication Services, NCSU

Harnett County Extension Family and Consumer Sciences

Perquimans County Extension Family and Consumer Sciences

The North Carolina Family and Consumer Sciences Foundation and the North Carolina Extension and Community Association Foundation support educational programs of Family and Consumer Sciences and Extension and Community Association volunteers statewide. The Foundations operate under the auspices of the North Carolina Agricultural Foundation, Inc.

FCS and ECA programming operates through North Carolina Cooperative Extension, fulfilling the land-grant missions of North Carolina State University and North Carolina A&T State University. North Carolina Cooperative Extension Centers in all 100 counties and with the Eastern Band of the Cherokee work with citizens to develop new agribusiness ventures, improve health and family life and sustain the environment.

Women have always been the heart and soul of the family and the home. As nurturers they have an unlimited capacity to want to make life better for their family. In 1911, Jane Simpson McKimmon created the home demonstration program, a "rural women's college," with ever-broadening activities where women could learn together and create a strong camaraderie for neighbor and community. The concept was simple. Give women an opportunity to learn skills that would provide ample food for the family, yet also provide additional income-income that could provide necessities for the entire family, educate the children, and buy conveniences to make life easier. The result was an improved living standard for all.

Home Demonstration evolved into Home Economics and now Family and Consumer Sciences (FCS), but whatever the name, it has a rich history of significant contributions to this state's well being for over 100 years. The herculean effort during WWI to help everyone grow and preserve food for their families in those hard times and during the flu epidemic in North Carolina in 1918 to organized their network of home demonstration club women into nursing and food distribution squads to help the sick are perfect examples. At one point, there were 75 soup kitchens serving over 100 people a day for a two-to-four week period, an effort unmatched by any other state.

Foreward

There are many programs and services we take for granted today that were started or supported by Home Demonstration. Two are: school hot lunch programs and libraries and bookmobiles. Their program to improve children's diets in the 1930s was implemented by the home demonstration club women who made and delivered hot lunches to rural schools. That effort was the forerunner of school cafeterias.

In the 1950s the club women led the way in fighting illiteracy in this state. They were determined that North Carolina would not be at the bottom of the list, so they lobbied county commissioners and raised money to make books more available in rural areas through local libraries and bookmobiles. By 1957, all but six counties had bookmobiles, more than any other state in the nation. That literacy effort continues today. Extension and Community Association (ECA) clubs across the state buy books for daycares, schools, libraries, and individual children, and often tutor children in their communities. They also provide over $175,000 each year in scholarship and loans to college students, helping them get the education they want and need to improve their lives.

Farmers markets and local foods are not new. The idea originated with Home Demonstration Curb Markets in the 1920s. Jane Mckimmon introduced the concept to women and girls: Produce more than the family needs and sell the rest to supplement family income. By the early 1940s there were 55 home demonstration curb markets in the state with an income of almost $1,200,000 for farm families.

During World War II, there was no stronger proponent for helping to win the war through salvage efforts and the sale of war bonds than home demonstration club women who raised more than half of the $4,000,000 needed for the renovation of the US Army hospital ship Larkspur.

There is no better tribute to the club womens' desire for learning than the Jane S. McKimmon Center that the women helped build with their "butter and egg" money. Their $100,000 check in 1966 provided the seed money and they did not stop there. They lobbied the NC legislators to provide the additional funding to build a continuing education center, one that serves as a model for other universities today.

Today Family and Consumer Sciences views the family, in all its diverse forms, as the cornerstone of a healthy society. Their mission is to improve the well-being of the family through programs that educate, influence public policy, and help families put research-based knowledge to work every day

FCS today, as it was in 1911, is relevant to the needs of families and offers a wide variety of nationally recognized programs that organizations in other states purchase for their own use.

Its network of agents, ECA volunteers, and campus faculty throughout the state is both efficient and effective. Their knowledge as well as their leadership and organizational skills often bring multiple organizations and agencies together to develop solutions on issues facing families today. Their programs help families manage and cope with challenges including financial instability, deployment, or care for elderly parents and addresses important issues such as obesity, money management, food safety, and energy conservation.

It has often been said that people are our greatest asset. I say not just people, but the Extension FCS professionals and ECA volunteers. The women professionals, who today still do their jobs because they truly believe that what they teach makes a difference in the lives they touch everyday; and the ECA volunteers, who give back to their communities, not for personal gain, but for the difference they can make to bring that community closer to its fullest potential.

I applaud these women and say "thank you" from the bottom of my heart. They do more than help people dream; they provide solutions for everyday living, helping make dreams realities. Today, North Carolina families face unprecedented challenges and need this Family and Consumer Sciences program and ECA volunteers just as much as the rural families did in 1911.

The stories on each of the pages in this book are a testament to the spirit, dedication, and leadership of women from the past and the present. That leadership and your extraordinary service have made this great state what it is today and will continue to help its families prepare for a better tomorrow.

Susan W. Woodson

First Lady, NC State University

The "history book" committee is the group that made this project come together. They include: Ada Dalla-Pozza, Jerry Hardesty, Nancy Young, Dr. Sarah Shoffner, Frances Turner, Jeannie Leonard, Jan Christensen, Joan Gosper, Dr. Judy Mock, Sue Counts, Wanda Denning, and Carol Cox. Special thanks goes to the "library team" of Joan, Carol, Wanda, Judy, and Jan who literally gave up their summer and fall to help sort the materials from the counties, review information in boxes in the NCSU Special Collections archives, and select stories for the county pages. Wanda and Carol provided details and information about the ECA organization when we "Raleigh folks" had questions. I have learned so much from them and my respect for the ECA organization has grown because of them.

The Foundations office has been the "foundation" of this project. Devona Beard and her team of students helped organize the county materials for the committee, keeping records of what had been received. However, the book would not be a reality had it not been for the fundraising efforts at the state and county level. Kay Saville, Maurene Rickards, and Sharon Rowland have truly taken this fundraising project "over the top" at the state level raising more than 20 percent above the set goal. Thanks also to those counties who met or exceeded their fundraising goals. I hope this book will help the whole state see what an asset you are to your county. Thanks to Susan Brame, Crystal Green, and Devona Beard for organizing all the donor information for the book. The creative talent of Sarah Ray has shone brightly in this project, in the promotional materials that visualize the concept of the book so perfectly even before we put it on paper. I continue to be awed by her talents and skills.

Acknowledgements

Thanks to FCS and the ECA Foundation Boards of Directors who have been incredibly supportive of this project and who have added to my own enthusiasm for it. A special thanks to those members like Ken Powell, Ed Emory, Jerry Hardesty, Ralph Warren, Cathy Wilkins, Murray Nixon, Ray Harris, Wanda Denning, Doris Davis, Joyce Klutz, Sue Counts, Leigh Guth, and Sylvia Churchwell, who helped identify potential donors and made personal visits.

Of course, without the efforts of the ECA members in the counties, the FCS agents, and specialists at NCSU and NC A&T, this book would not be the great story that it is. Thanks to all who submitted histories, success stories, and pictures. Without those we would not have this great story to tell! We especially appreciate the support of Extension administration including Dr. Joe Zublena, Dr. Ray McKinnie, Dr. Marshall Stewart, Dr. Carolyn Dunn, Dr. Celvia Stovall, and Dr. Thelma Feaster and the district directors. A special thanks also to Geri Bushel who was my communications link to the agents.

Researching information for a book is not an easy task. Joan Gosper was our electronic search guru. Jennifer Baker, Research Services Associate, Special Collections Research Center, NCSU Libraries was so accommodating to our requests and even suggested additional resources for us. Another valuable resource person was Kim

Cumber at The North Carolina State Archives. She directed us to the some resources that "filled in some gaps" for the early years and found some old pictures for the first chapter as well as some additional pictures of Jane McKimmon that we have used.

A special thank you goes to the Charles Winston family who gave us a box of his grandmother, Jane McKimmon's, papers that have been a treasure trove for us as well as several pictures that we have included in the book.

If I were handing out awards for this project, the winner would be University Communication Services. Mark Dearmon and all the staff have truly bent over backwards to help us with this project. They have been our technical experts, answering questions and assisting us in every way possible, allowing us to "invade" their space and interrupt their work, and have been so gracious to us while we worked.

Of course a book cannot happen without the writers. Jan Christensen and Joan Gosper have done a tremendous job in capturing all the material and writing so the reader wants to read the next page and the next chapters. Vickie Guin, the graphic designer, has created more than we envisioned this book could be. It is so beautiful, both inside and out. Not only is she a fantastic designer, she has been such a joy to have on our team. Her easy-going manner and her patience with us have been superb.

A book does not happen without editors and proof readers. Thanks to Dr. Carolyn Lackey, Dr. Judy Mock. Dr. Sarah Shoffner, Sarah Nixon, Murray Nixon, Cathy Wilkins, Beth Williams, Wanda Denning, and Carol Cox who have been our "fresh sets of eyes".

Thanks to all the groups who provided pictures for us in addition to the ECA clubs throughout the state and the FCS agents. Pictures throughout the book add to its interest. Picture credits include the following: Lee Pantas, www.cherryorchardstudio. com for the print and ink drawing of the Smith-McDowell House; North Carolina State University Archives, Special Collections; The North Carolina State Archives, Department of Cultural Resources; Agricultural Communications, NCSU; Communication Services, NCSU; Owen Balance's Studio, Raleigh, NC; Bryant Portrait Studio, Rocky Mount, NC; *Raleigh Times* newspaper, Raleigh, NC; *The Newton Observer*, Newton, NC; and Dave Lowe, Taylorsville, NC.

Last, but not least, thanks to my husband, Larry, who encouraged this effort even though it took me "on the road." He did not mind when all the book materials, folders, pictures, and scrapbooks were stored in our dining room, and would keep busy while I spent time on the computer organizing the volume of materials, pictures, and emails.

Dr. Wilma S. Hammett
Chair, History Book Committee

Contents

$\mathscr{O}$rdinary Women Extraordinary Service highlights 100 years of the Family and Consumer Sciences program which began as Home Demonstration and the work of the Extension and Community Association which began as Home Demonstration Clubs. The stories here are based on recollections of ECA members and agents, current reports from all 100 counties in the state and the Eastern Band of the Cherokee as well as the book committee's limited search of materials archived at the DH Hill Library at NC State University and the North Carolina State Archives. Some counties have compiled their history and have a wealth of materials and information. However, due to floods, fires, and lack of foresight, some valuable stories and pictures have been lost.

The history book committee was charged with developing a coffee table book that would make anyone who picks it up want to look at the pictures and read the stories, both past and present. We have enjoyed seeing the book come to "life". Readers will see that each chapter or decade features stories of how the program has impacted an individual, a family, or a community. We have included some state impacts, but as we put all the information together we saw how the program has affected individuals. The stories show the true value of both the program and its volunteers and the difference they have made and are making in the lives they touch every day. For every story, there are thousands more we did not have space to include.

As you read each chapter you will see that for 100 years, Extension professionals have provided families with unbiased, research-based information. Extension has not only the expertise, but a network of county agents and volunteers who care about the people in their communities and want to make a difference in their lives. Extension professionals at the state and county level are innovators in addressing and solving problems. They are collaborators and consensus builders gathering groups with common interests together, to find solutions to problems. More often than not, Extension professionals are the leaders of those coalitions.

Extension volunteers have a "get it done" attitude. Since their beginning in 1913 as home demonstration clubs, they have helped shaped today's North Carolina. Their accomplishments are many and their spirit is unflappable. Today they continue to give back to their communities. They are teaching others, providing financial assistance to numerous college-bound students, and are using their skills to assist individuals and groups who need a helping hand. Only a fraction of that service is highlighted in these pages.

Enjoy the stories and see what a difference ordinary women (and some men) can make ~ they are truly extraordinary!

Introduction

Jane McKimmon
in her own words

I did not like housekeeping or anything pertaining to foods and cookery as a girl. It was my sister who had a turn for these things, and I had my head stuck in a book. I never thought my life's work later would lead me into anything as practical as home economics.

I found that teaching people how to cook, sew, or improve the home was not dependent upon what was recognized as standard equipment. Much could be done through the exercise of good hard common sense and the ability to recognize usable substitutes in the things at hand.

I was told by a good sociologist friend not to be disappointed if adults did not prove to be interested in the home demonstration program. But this pronouncement was wrong. By 1916 farm women had taken the bit in their teeth and were running away with the Extension home demonstration club organization. They were hungry for the new experience of learning to do things through seeing them done; for the chance to produce an income that would furnish them with things they had so long desired; and for an outlet through which they could express themselves and get recognition from others for what they had done. All of these were things that satisfied fundamental urges, and I believe they furnish a solid foundation upon which a successful work for any group of human beings may be built.

Home agents did a fine piece of work through the years in making the farm family realize that it is the garden, the hen, the pig, and the cow which make the difference between good health and poor and between an empty larder and a well-supplied table.

The thing that gave every daughter of Eve personal satisfaction was what she learned about selecting patterns, making new dresses, and remodeling old ones. These things changed not only her appearance but her attitude toward life as well.

Can't read? Just give that sturdy backbone of our nation a chance. Provide it with books and a good electric light and watch the results.

I became State Home Demonstration Agent, not because of my love of home economics, but because of my love for people.

In 1911, Jane S. McKimmon was named State Home Demonstration Agent for the NC Agricultural Extension Service. She started girls' tomato club work in North Carolina.

Under McKimmon's leadership, the first home demonstration clubs were founded in 1913. During her tenure, she saw county programs expand from the original 14 to all 100 counties.

In 1925, she became Assistant Extension Director, as well as State Home Demonstration Agent.

In 1927, the Jane S. McKimmon loan fund was established by the home demonstration agents in her honor.

Mrs. McKimmon attended Peace Junior College and N.C. State where she received her B.S. degree in 1927 and her M.S. degree in 1929. In 1933, because of her outstanding leadership in adult education for farm women, the University of North Carolina conferred upon her an honorary degree of L.L.D.

Tribute

In 1935, she was appointed by Gov. John Ehringhaus to the Rural Electrification Committee and also to the Rural Electrification Authority which followed. Gov. Thomas Bickett appointed her to direct the food conservation program established in World War I. Gov. J. Melville Broughton appointed Mrs. McKimmon to the State Council of National Defense during World War II.

Jane McKimmon was the first woman in the United States to receive the "Distinguished Service Ruby" from Epsilon Sigma Phi, honorary fraternity of the U.S. Agricultural Extension Service.

McKimmon was one of the founders of the American Home Economics Association and one of its past presidents.

In 1976, the Jane S. McKimmon Center for Continuing Education opened its doors on the N.C. State University campus.

In 2009, Mrs. McKimmon was installed into the Raleigh Hall of Fame.

In 2010, the Jane McKimmon Society was established to recognize outstanding donors within the Foundations Office at N.C. State University.

Dr. Jane Simpson McKimmon

**Assistant Director, North Carolina Agricultural Extension Service,
State Leader of Home Demonstration and
Author, *When We're Green, We Grow***

saluting our grandmother's pioneering spirit and legacy
on behalf of the families of North Carolina as

Charles McKimmon Winston Family
James Horner Winston Family
Jane Winston Witherspoon Family
Rev. Charles McKimmon Family
William Simpson McKimmon Family

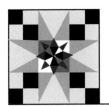

1910–1920
A QUIET REVOLUTION BEGINS

In 1911, a quiet revolution took place in North Carolina: a revolution that improved the lives of families and strengthened communities. It was the home demonstration program for rural women and girls.

Two earlier events may have helped nudge the innovative program into existence. One was the Farmers Institute. The other: farm girls who envied the corn clubs their brothers belonged to and wanted to know why they weren't given similar opportunities.

There had been early efforts to bring research information to farmers and farm boys that would help improve crop yields. Starting in 1902, farmers were invited to attend institutes that were offered in different counties throughout the state.

Four years later institute planners included sessions for the farmers' wives. The women gathered together to hear programs on health hints, home sanitation, household conveniences, child training, the home garden, best methods of cooking, and the country woman and her relations to the home and community.

Three home demonstration members getting ready for a workshop on bread making.

Farmers and farmers wives attend an institute on the campus of NC State.

Jane S. McKimmon was North Carolina's first state home demonstration leader.

Institute meetings were held in school houses, Sunday school rooms, halls of the Woodmen of the World or Masonic lodges, and sometimes, out-of-doors.

Not knowing where a meeting would be held meant the institute group, composed of agriculturists from State College and the State Department of Agriculture, and two women lecturers, had to plan carefully and be prepared for the unexpected.

About the same time, an effort was made to prepare the next generation for rural life. Farm boys were encouraged to join corn clubs. As club members, the lads planted an acre of corn using scientific methods ~ often doubling, tripling or even quadrupling the yields their fathers had obtained. The boys sold their crops, putting money in their pockets.

It is small wonder that their sisters asked why they were not given a similar opportunity. They needed clothes, books for school, and they wanted to live in a comfortable home.

Seaman A. Knapp, founder and director of Farmers' Co-operative Demonstration Work in America, agreed.

"If much can be done for boys to interest and instruct them in their life work, more can be done for girls," he noted. "Teach them how to mend and sew and cook; how to doctor; how to dress a wound, and how to adorn a simple house and make it appear like a palace."

Dr. Knapp, in his office in the Department of Agriculture in Washington, D.C., discussed the possibility of a project for farm girls with his assistant O. B. Martin, who was in charge of boys' corn clubs. Together they concluded that growing a garden and canning vegetables might furnish a farm girl with an outlet for her energies. There was also a strong possibility she could market her products, both fresh and canned.

They agreed to start the girls with a tenth of an acre of tomatoes, which were not difficult to cultivate and which could be used to teach the young women how to can the surplus for winter use or for market.

A pilot effort in South Carolina, Martin's home state, was moderately successful. Six southern states ~ Virginia, Mississippi, Tennessee, North Carolina, Alabama, and Georgia decided to follow the South Carolina experiment with girls' tomato clubs of their own.

North Carolina took advantage of the federal General Education Board's grant of $300 a year; money that could be used to employ a woman as state home demonstration agent. She would be in charge of girls' club work.

I.O. Schaub helped pioneer Extension work in North Carolina.

The beginning of home demonstration work in North Carolina was auspicious, for the initial effort to start girls' club work was under the guidance of I.O. Schaub, the state corn club leader.

Schaub visited several counties, consulting with superintendents of schools, as he tried to find a suitable demonstration center for a girls' tomato club. Two communities in Guilford County, Jamestown and Pleasant Garden, were selected. The results were somewhat satisfactory but finding a market for the fresh tomatoes proved difficult and some of the canned foods showed signs of spoilage.

Even so, the General Education Board again made $300 available for the employment of a woman state home demonstration agent. Jane S. McKimmon of Raleigh was offered the North Carolina post and began work on November 1, 1911. Space was found for the new leader and her files in the State Agriculture Building.

Home demonstration members get tomatoes ready for canning.

Home demonstration women check to see if tomatoes are ready for canning.

Mrs. McKimmon was a graduate of Peace Institute in Raleigh, a junior college for girls. She later received her bachelor's and master's degrees at the State College of Agriculture and Mechanic Arts. In addition to her new post, overseeing girls' club work, she continued to serve as a lecturer and director of woman's programs for the Farmer's Institute.

McKimmon believed her work with the Institute served her well as she undertook her job as state home demonstration agent. Thanks to her travel as an Institute lecturer, she was already well acquainted with rural families and the challenges they faced, from Morganton in the west to Roanoke Island in the east.

A bumper crop of produce means canning the surplus for winter meals.

As a beginning step, McKimmon went to the annual meeting of the county superintendents of education to explain the girls' tomato club program. Fourteen of the superintendents were interested enough to talk to their county boards about the matter. Each of the 14 counties agreed to match a $75 grant and employ a local agent for two months during the 1912 growing and canning season.

Pioneer counties were Alamance, Catawba, Edgecombe, Gates, Granville, Guilford, Hertford, Madison, Mecklenburg, Moore, Pitt, Wake, Wayne and Wilkes.

The first 14 home agents were well educated, with a practical knowledge of homemaking. They were familiar with farm life and its challenges. Each woman also was held in high esteem in her local area. Agents ranged in age from 23 to 40-plus.

The home agents organized farm girls into tomato clubs. Club members, who could not be older than 20 or younger than 10, were expected to do all the planting, cultivating, staking and gathering of the fruit. They were allowed to have the plowing, harrowing, and heavy work done for them.

The tomato canning season began about the first of July, but the girls were able to pick berries and beans before that time and became quite expert in the art of canning before beginning on their money crop.

For instruction, the agent gathered the girls at an appointed place, set up a canner and began work. Occasionally a hospitable farm woman had room in her kitchen to host the canners. More often canning was taught out-of-doors, often in a school yard or on the courthouse green.

The girls were divided into squads – sterilizers, peelers, packers, cappers, and those doing the actual cooking and tending to the fires. These positions changed frequently so that each girl learned every part of the process.

The first year 416 girls canned 79,000 jars of food.

The number of counties organized was kept at 14 for the first two years so agents and leaders might get their work well in hand before expansion. But from November 1913, to November 1914, the number of counties with agents jumped from 14 to 32. Enrollment reached 1,500 and the girls reported canning 209,686 half gallon tin cans of tomatoes and 49,405 glass jars of tomatoes, string beans, peaches, berries, and other edible produce.

Surplus canned foods were offered for sale. Cornell and Columbia Universities in New York purchased some of the items for use in winter meals.

Girls canning, products on display at New York Exposition. (Courtesy of The North Carolina State Achives.)

A community canning lesson, 1913, Alamance County. (Courtesy of The North Carolina State Achives.)

Many girls found sales outlets closer to home. The Moore County clubs sold everything they produced to county grocers. Alamance and Anson clubs filled orders for colleges and institutions, putting their products in gallon cans.

Two much needed assistants were brought into the state office to help county agents as new counties were added. Margaret Scott, who had done successful work as a home demonstration agent in Alamance County, joined the state staff in 1913 to work with canning programs and agent training.

Minnie Jamison, head of the Department of Home Economics, North Carolina College for Women in Greensboro, rendered an essential service as she traveled over the state visiting and assisting home agents with foods and nutrition problems and helping them learn demonstration techniques. She joined the state staff in 1915.

In the early years, neither office furnishings nor money for supplies was put into the budget for the state staff or the agents overseeing club work. The success of the organization depended on their commitment to the task and creativity.

As demand for services continued, it was necessary for the home agent to have dependable assistance through the canning season, and county commissioners were asked to appropriate a small amount for sub-agents. Boards generally appropriated $25 each for three months work. Seventy-five sub-agents began work in 1914. Practically all of them lived on farms and understood the difficulties a country woman experienced.

Reaching women in faraway counties took creativity on Mrs. McKimmon's part. She continued to be a member of the boxcar brigade, joining agricultural experts traveling on an "agricultural" train. The train was composed of baggage cars for preparing demonstration materials, day coaches in which to hold meetings, and dining and sleeping cars for the staff. The train ran on a special schedule, making a number of stops each day. This allowed Mrs. McKimmon to meet with women interested in starting a homemakers club.

Transportation was a challenge for local agents as well. They often traveled by horse and buggy, picking up homemakers along the way to take them to the meeting place. Some agents chose an older, gentler horse, rather than a frisky stallion, for their transport. Unfortunately, one agent's horse died before she got it paid for.

In one mountain county, the agent rode into the coves and hollows to visit families with her canner tied to the saddle. If the pathways were too challenging for her horse, the agent caught a ride in a car with the mailman.

In each county, the mothers worked side by side with their daughters as they grew and canned their tomatoes, and soon the women were asking the demonstration agents for assistance with problems connected to the home.

At the top of their wish list –learning how to make better biscuits and bread.

The first home demonstration clubs were organized in 1913. The state home economics staff also offered to teach and talk about their women's and girls' programs to students at the county institutes for rural teachers. Thirteen counties took advantage of the offer, thereby insuring teacher-agent cooperation in community work.

County teachers acted as leaders in both girls' and women's clubs and were indispensable in helping with such things as improved bread making. Teachers attended the home agents' demonstrations, learned how to make biscuits or bread, and became dependable judges in baking contests.

Breadmaking.

Extension pioneers often traveled by train to reach farm families across the state.

In every county with organized home demonstration clubs, bread contests had a popular following. Village merchants loaned their shop windows for the county display. Often scores of biscuits would be showcased as community competed against community for biscuit bragging rights. Country women became better acquainted as they compared baking tips and planned meetings where they could get together socially.

By the end of 1915, home demonstration clubs were organized in 31 counties with a state membership of 2,500. The farm women who joined were hungry: a) for the new experience of learning to do things through seeing them done; b) for the opportunity of coming together in interesting work; c) for the chance to produce an income which would furnish them with things they had so long desired; and d) for an outlet through which they could express themselves and get recognition from others for what they had done.

Using the demonstration method, the agent was able to teach all women including the uneducated woman, the high school graduate, and the college graduate. Agents worked with them all: the wives of big and small farmers, tenants and sharecroppers, country school teachers and storekeepers, all of whom came together to form home demonstration clubs with no thought to class distinction.

One labor saving device that peaked the interest of the rural women and their families was the fireless cooker. Someone discovered that if you confine heat in a small space, the cooking process would continue for hours. To most people it was unbelievable that a hot stone placed in an insulated container would cook a tough old rooster or hen until it was tender.

The proof was in the eating and for many the fireless cooker meant a hot dinner was being cooked while the homemaker helped in the fields or did other family chores.

Working together makes canning tomatoes a social event.

8

The fireless cooker was popular with rural families in the early 1900s.

One home agent who planned to give a fireless cooker demonstration ran into problems when her buggy broke down, preventing her from reaching her demonstration site. As people stopped to help her, she served an impromptu meal from the back of her buggy. The men who lent a hand to help the agent were impressed with the quality of the meal and several went home and built fireless cookers for their wives.

The fireless cooker was a lardstand surrounded by sawdust and placed in a wooden box. Two soapstones were heated to a high temperature. One was put in the bottom of the stand. The pot of food to be cooked was placed on top of it. The pan was covered and the other soapstone was placed on top and left for several hours. The result: a tender chicken or cut of meat.

Home Demonstration Agent Estelle Smith meets with county homemakers.

Three other unrelated incidents helped bring home demonstration into its own, garnering support for the program across the state.

First: in 1913, the North Carolina State Fair in Raleigh invited Mrs. McKimmon and her agents to show the results of home demonstration work.

Space was provided in the machinery building. Located next to the plowshares and pruning hooks, the home demonstration display featured pyramids of home canned fruits and vegetables. The exhibit attracted so much attention, it was moved into the center of the agricultural building the next year.

A bumper crop of produce means canning the surplus for winter meals.

North Carolina State Library,
Raleigh

N. C.
Doc.

PREMIUM LIST

FIFTY-SEVENTH GREAT

STATE FAIR

OF

NORTH CAROLINA

RALEIGH, OCTOBER 15-20, 1917

NEW BUILDING FOR WOMAN'S WORK

BETTER BABIES CONTEST

UNDER CHARGE WOMAN'S CLUB, RALEIGH

IN NEW WOMAN'S BUILDING

R. O. EVERETT, President
DURHAM, N. C.

POGUE, Secretary
LEIGH, N. C.

C. B. DENSON, Treasurer
RALEIGH, N. C.

A14
3:1917
c.2

Fair Book Cover 1917. (Courtesy of The North Carolina State Achives.)

Again it proved so popular, that in 1917 home demonstration was given its own building, 50 by 150 feet with a dressing room. Having a building for its exclusive use meant permanent improvements could be made in the display area. There was also enough space around and down the center for agents to stage demonstrations that let fair go-ers see what rural women were doing to improve family life.

The second: World War 1. America's entry into World War 1 in 1917 led to a call to arms and mobilization of those left on the farm to labor and produce.

When the government realized the part food production and conservation would play, it turned to the already organized forces of farm men and women. The Extension Service of the Department of Agriculture quickly became part of the nation's war machinery. Nationwide, Extension received more than four million dollars for the development and enlargement of its programs.

In North Carolina, calls from every direction came to the Division of Home Demonstration Work. In six months, the number of organized counties jumped from 44 to 60; all with trained home agents. In 1918, the number increased to 72 counties, with 72 white agents and 19 Black emergency agents.

Sixty-four of the counties employed agents 12 months of the year and in 47 counties agents had use of an automobile and a little money for travel expenses. Cities called for help so insistently that money was set aside for the employment of agents in Asheville, Winston-Salem, Charlotte, Durham, Raleigh, Wilmington and New Bern. The seven city agents were under the supervision of the state home demonstration agent and usually had office space with the chamber of commerce, where close cooperation was encouraged with Food Administration officials, women's clubs, churches and other organizations.

Residents in other cities in the state got help from their county agent and her assistants.

In addition to home food production, conservation and marketing, agents worked within a program that rationed wheat flour, fats, sugar, and red meats. They developed new recipes, making the changes in diet a little more palatable.

NC homemakers heed the call to assist during WWI. (Courtesy of The North Carolina State Achives.)

11

Mrs. Lillian Capehart, first home demonstration agent in Granville County.

People learned to use honey, sorghum and molasses in lieu of sugar, cut back their serving sizes of meat, and use corn meal rather than wheat flour.

Community canneries captured the public's imagination. Families would bring their produce to the community cannery where it would be checked for quality. How many filled cans of food a family got depended on how much usable produce they brought in.

In 1917, one hundred and thirty-two canneries were operating in towns, rural communities and mill villages, helping women put up 357,688 cans of food.

Many of these canneries were managed or run by home demonstration club women. The output of these canneries was only a fraction of the 8,978,262 containers filled by North Carolina's volunteer home canners on the farm that year.

State institutions also became interested in canning. In 1917 the superintendent of the State Hospital for the Insane, asked the Home Demonstration Division for help in building a cannery to cut food costs and add variety to the diet. The hospital continued the canning program for many years.

Third: The great influenza epidemic of 1918. When the epidemic hit, Extension home demonstration workers were asked to drop plans and do what they could to organize help for influenza sufferers. The agents were not trained nurses, but practically all had had some courses in home nursing.

Home demonstration women in farm communities were organized into nursing squads and volunteers made and distributed food to the sick. Procedures were outlined for practical nurses; and recipes and methods of preparing soup in quantities were provided to the volunteer cooks.

Very ill patients were taken to emergency hospitals in the towns, and home agents and their clubwomen helped organize and man these places of refuge.

Agents reported 75 kitchens established, each serving an average of 105 persons daily over a period of two to four weeks. In Buncombe County alone, Extension club members and their husbands helped set up a soup kitchen that dispensed 300 gallons of soup a day.

In Columbus County, the courtroom was converted to a hospital. The area was cleaned, cots obtained, and volunteers recruited. The agent and club women played

Community cannery, Proximity Cotton Mills, Greensboro. In this building fruits and vegetables raised by the inhabitants of the mill villages are canned and dried with the expert assistance and supervision of the Welfare Department maintained by the mills.

a major role in the transition from courtroom to place of refuge.

The white agent in Nash County organized a soup kitchen exclusively for Blacks, as well as one for whites. Black emergency nurses reported organizing others to help nurse and feed the sick and gratefully acknowledged getting recipes and strong support from white agents.

Charitable, fraternal and business institutions called upon Extension for aid and agents and club members tried to help, working long hours in the effort.

By the start of the next decade, home demonstration staff, agents and leaders had the respect of, and a commitment from, many families and communities across the state.

News and Observer newspaper in Raleigh, fall of 1918.

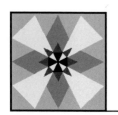

1920–1930

Improving Lives and Strengthening Communities

Due to her close association with farm families, the home demonstration agent had grown into a consultant homemaker for the county. She was a familiar sight as she manipulated the state highways and unimproved country roads. Sometimes she was a courier, bringing supplies from town, and sometimes she was the emergency nurse. But most often she was counselor and friend when financial conditions were hard and family adjustments not easy to make.

Home agents usually met kindness from fellow travelers when they had problems on the road.

A Hertford County agent's car became mired in the mud and no help was available until a man in a convict's suit appeared. "Can I help you, Miss Swindell?" he asked.

"How did you know me?" she wondered.

"Well ma'am, I know you are the same lady who talked to us down at the prison camp last year, and one

Agents in training to can tomatoes and green beans. The canner is the popular Flowers model manufactured in Hickory, North Carolina.

North Carolina home demonstration agent shows safe methods of home food preservation to a group of women.

of your food lists is tacked up there in our kitchen right now. Since your talk, we think our superintendent has given us better things to eat, and all of us appreciate it."

The grateful convict helped the agent get her car out of the mud and back on the road.

The sheriff of Moore County was much concerned about the home agent there as she drove over those lonely sand roads.

"Miss Gracie," he said. "Come into my office and let me swear you in as a deputy. I'll give you a gun and you'll be a lot safer, and I'll feel a lot happier about you."

Miss Gracie did allow herself to be sworn in and accepted the gun, but fortunately she never had to use it.

Agents in some counties faced unique situations. When Dare County appointed its Home Demonstration Agent, Alice Mary Carter, in 1929, she had to use a ferry or boat to get from her office in Manteo to some of her Extension clubs on the Outer Banks.

The environment and road conditions were a hazard. Many times Miss Carter's car would get stuck

in the deep sand or the motor would get drowned by high water, leaving her to be rescued by the U.S. Coast Guard.

Regardless of the conditions they faced, agents across the state continued to work with the farm family on the production and canning of foods at home.

To supplement family income, many women and their daughters sold surplus commodities, sometimes clearing $200 to $300 a year.

They began to wonder if an organized once-a-week market, conveniently situated in a town, and offering a variety of farm produce plus cakes and other home-baked products, might not be a business risk worth taking.

The first trial sales days were in 1921 in Anson and Pasquotank counties. Anson's market was located on the courthouse green and Pasquotank's was in a vacant lot near the center of town.

Both markets did business on Saturday mornings, drawing an interested and growing group of town housewives. Their success was enough to encourage other counties to try a similar venture.

North Carolina rural women sold approximately $300,000 worth of surplus produce at the curb markets established in various centers by home agents. The above picture shows the activity at a market immediately after its opening at eight o'clock Saturday morning.

In 1924, curb markets were organized to serve farm families in Nash, Anson, Cumberland, Robeson, Mecklenberg, Wake, Pasquotank, Vance, Durham, Guilford, and Richmond counties. Women sellers from New Hanover, Brunswick, and Pender counties operated the Cape Fear Home Demonstration Market at Wilmington.

At first women took just what they could find on the farm; and when they discovered that vegetables, poultry, butter, eggs, hams, sausage, and flowers all sold well, they began to increase production of these things. As a place for marketing, the curb served well in good weather, but the rain and cold drove sellers to cover, in spite of increasing patronage. In Cumberland and many other counties, county commissioners turned over the basement of the Courthouse to serve as a market, and tobacco men loaned their warehouses to home demonstration club members on Saturdays.

The city of Wilmington, which served sellers from a three-county area, offered its auditorium and had the firemen and local cleaning crew give the building a thorough overhauling before opening it up to the marketers.

The savvy women soon learned good marketing techniques. They found that clean vegetables sold much faster than dirty ones; that items that were placed on a tray or in an attractive manner sold better than those in a haphazard display; that eggs all the same color and size sold faster than a mix of eggs; and that chickens should look like they'd be tender and good to eat, rather than scruffy. Every home demonstration market

Home Demonstration Curb Market, 1929, Tarboro.

Home Demonstration Agent Rosalind Redfearn giving a bread-making demonstration to a group of girls and boys on the lawn of Anson County Courthouse, in 1920.

had its own procedure, but regulations varied only slightly from one to the next. Among the regulations:

- The market was to be organized and operated mainly for and by farm women who sell farm products and home-cooked food, and sellers were not permitted to buy and resell.
- The marketplace must be kept clean and sanitary and a "Home Sanitation Card" issued by the county board of health should be displayed at each booth stating that sanitary conditions in the home from which the products come are approved and members of the family are free from communicable diseases.
- All prepared food displayed must be covered for protection, and sellers must wear clean washable smocks or dresses covering the street clothes.
- Prices must be posted where all may see, and may not be changed by the sellers.
- Sellers are not permitted to solicit from buyers who are not within the bounds of their allotted market space.

Women often used the proceeds from their sales to make improvements and add comfort to their homes. "Marketing for me," one woman told State Leader Jane McKimmon, "is just turning my surplus vegetables, chickens, butter, and eggs into things we always wanted for our home and children. The ten or fifteen dollars I carry away from the curb market every Saturday makes all the difference in the world between what we now have in our home and what we had before. We are not only more comfortable, but we have a few pretty things along with it."

The curb market was more than a place of trade. It was a social gathering place with town and country mingling. The buyers and sellers talked politics, church and books, and shared tips on babies and housekeeping.

The Anson County Extension agent and home demonstration women took the curb market idea to a new level when they figured out a way to sell surplus

Mrs. Rosalind Redfearn, home demonstration agent in Anson County, began to teach her home demonstration club members the value of a good grade and pack in selling poultry and other products by parcel post and express shipments. This became one of the main sources of income for the women of that county.

A home demonstration agent shows the kinds of things that can be made from grapes at the 1922 State Fair.

poultry. After having a tour at N.C. State College and noticing the poultry used in meals came from Maryland, the Anson County women contracted with N.C. State to sell dressed chickens to the steward of the school. Soon afterwards, they added a "fancy grocery" in Raleigh, found additional buyers, and had a thriving business. The agent and leaders taught the poultry growers the proper way to kill and dress fowl. The training sessions were called "hen parties" and the people enjoyed them immensely. They also cultivated a dressed turkey market and eventually had a contract from Swift and Company for 1,132 birds.

Talking to homemakers about the health of their families continued to be a top priority for Extension home demonstration agents. Milk was lacking in most diets, even rural ones. Consumption was about one-half cup of milk per person per day.

Before the dairyman would buy more cows, the people needed to be educated on the value of milk in the diet and increase consumption. The Division of Home Demonstration Work, therefore joined forces

Promotional advertisement for lunch, from U.S. Department of Agriculture.

with the Dairy Division and the Department of Health, to plan a statewide milk campaign. One- or two-day milk schools were held, first in nine large towns in the state and later in county schools. So it was to city

"Cook with milk!!! A quart a day per child." Home demonstration by Mrs. Jonathan Danson, Duplin County. (Possibly photographed by G. W. Ackerman, United States Department of Agriculture, Extension Service)

Two generations enjoy the taste and benefits of milk.

school children that the story of what milk could do for the body was presented first. Agents also worked to inform adults in clubs, places of business, factories, mills, and laundries about the health benefits of milk. Milk consumption doubled, increasing up to one cup of milk per person per day.

The youngest members of the family also received attention from the Extension Service and the Public Health Service. Mothers and babies conferences were

Women holding their babies at a mother-baby conference sponsored by the King Hiram Home Demonstration Club in Greene County with assistance from the D. A. R. and the United States Public Health Service.

Little Eck Sims was examined in Brevard during Baby Welfare Week in 1923. About 53 babies were examined and mothers advised.

Mrs. Joe Kelly, president, presides at the Watha Home Demonstration Club meeting in 1925.

held around the state. Babies were given check-ups and mothers were given advice about keeping them healthy. Feeding the family, taking care of its health, and adding to the income all continued to be an important part of the homemaker's role in the family, but also important was the satisfaction she got from learning to select patterns, make new outfits, and remodel old ones. By using these new skills, she changed not only her appearance but her attitude toward life.

Rural women used fabrics that were readily available. They made dresses and suits from feed and fertilizer bags. They tailored suits for themselves from their husbands' old suits. One farmer laughingly admitted he was afraid to take his clothes off at night for fear his wife would use the fabric to make something for their children or herself.

Another farm woman said she passed the clothesline where her husband was drying fertilizer bags-the white kind. She got the idea that a spring suit could be made from them. So with five bags, 19 cents for accessories, and five cents for thread, she made a fine looking suit – one she happily wore on special occasions.

During the same period, homemakers across North Carolina made thousands of hats to complete the outfits they were tailoring. In the twenties, Alamance County women converted the county courtroom into a millinery workshop for rural families and a week was given over to hat making. Women came in from town and country and carried 425 hats home with them in various stages of completion.

State Fair hat demonstration.

Ricks Hall, 1920.

As clothing work advanced in the counties, home agents, assisted by leaders, held two- to five-day dressmaking and home millinery schools. The schools were followed by regular monthly clothing demonstrations at which proportion, line and design of the figure, color, the foundation pattern, and making a dress form were emphasized. One little boy thanked the home agent for teaching his sister to make a dress form to her measurements. "For," said he, "when she used

Clarendon Home Demonstration Club members of Columbus County in the southeastern district, holding their dress forms.

to go away to school, mother made me stand still while she fitted all Martha's clothes on me."

One Scotland County homemaker disliked her figure so much she burned her dress form.

In 1925, a specialist was employed by the North Carolina Extension Service to teach clothing and house improvement. Two years later, a second specialist was hired and the tasks were divided: one person worked with clothing, the other with housing and house furnishings.

Rural families were also encouraged to improve the looks of the outside of their houses and community buildings.

Changes were taking place at the state level as well. In 1926, the entire Agricultural Extension Service moved from the State Department of Agriculture to the campus of North Carolina State College and the School of Agriculture and Engineering. The state Home Demonstration offices found a home in Ricks Hall. Extension and other state agencies continued their close relationships.

In fiscal year 1925-26 the state prison system called on Extension for canning assistance. They wanted to grow and conserve enough vegetables to feed prison inmates summer and winter.

Caledonia Prison Farm in Halifax County and a second one at Camp Polk near Raleigh were selected from the 10 prison camps then in the state for canning demonstrations. Prisoners in both camps showed enough interest to produce promising results, even with their meager canning equipment.

Craven County Home Demonstration Agent Cornelia Simpson admires the upholstery skills of one of her club members.

Little River Home Demonstration Club members work to improve the school grounds, November 19, 1923.

In 1923, a homemaker in Brevard mill village makes a bright and cheery spot in the mill town by painting her house and planting flowers.

Dorothea Cowgill recruited women for the Sandhills Exchange.

The Anson County Curb Market is busy on a Saturday morning.

September 4, 1925, Farm Women's Short Course N.C. State College, Raleigh.

Edgar Shearon, a teacher and excellent canner, who did a good business with what he canned on his own farm, was hired to head up the effort.

As more and more rural women joined home demonstration clubs and showed a strong desire to improve family life and their own education levels, an idea came to the forefront. How about offering farm women the chance to come to North Carolina State College for their own week-long short course? Many of these women had already attended Farmers Institutes in their home counties, so they would be familiar with the types of program offered in a short course.

The short course was first offered in 1925 and 55 women signed up, including 13 women from Halifax County, who arrived in a school truck driven by a club woman's husband.

The 55 women lived in college dorm rooms, laughed and chatted like teenagers, and went to classes taught by Extension specialists and agents. Many went back to their home communities and shared what they learned with other club members and neighbors.

The successful "Country Woman's College" was the forerunner of Farm and Home Week, University Days

for Homemakers and University Days on Wheels.

The 1920s brought another important step for the Extension Service.

After the emergency appropriations of 1918 and 1919 were dropped, many temporary Extension workers were laid off, including the Black agents and leaders who did good work in the two summers in which they served.

In 27 counties with large Black populations, the part-time Black leaders volunteered to work without pay if the white agents would help them continue the work they had already begun with Black farm families. Without exception this was done, in the belief that when counties and the state recognized how important the Black agents were to rural families, they would appropriate monies for their employment.

The strategy paid off in July 1921, when enough money was turned over to the Home Demonstration division to employ six Black agents full time.

It was not easy to get educated, experienced Blacks to give up their posts as rural supervisors or teachers and serve as Extension agents, but in 1922 Sarah Williams, a teacher, agreed to take the Beaufort County post.

Anson, Wayne, Wake, Columbus and Johnston were the next counties to add Black home demonstration agents to their staffs.

The new Wayne County Agent, Emma McDougald, noted "The church, other clubs, and the school are about all that bring Black people together in the county, and all of these organizations have been very kind in their attitude toward me and my work."

McDougald added, "The first thing a family and I usually talked over was what they had to eat – did they raise the food themselves? Then I'd demonstrate good ways of preparing food; next, it was how to make the home more comfortable." By the end of her first year at work, McDougald had 14 woman's clubs with 235 members and two girls' clubs with 20 members.

The impact made by the six agents was so successful that in 1925, Dazelle Lowe was appointed to the state staff as district home agent to supervise Black programs. She had previously served as agent in Davidson and Wake counties.

Other noticeable changes took place in the decade: one in the structure of home demonstration programs and the other in the recognition of the State Home Demonstration Agent, Jane McKimmon.

Dazelle Foster Lowe was the first Black woman to hold a state agent position. (Photo by Bill Ray, a Journal and Sentinel photo)

Short Course, 1927.

Home demonstration club women in Rowan County.

A sewing demonstration at a club meeting in Durham County.

Students enjoy milk and hot soup for lunch, thanks to home demonstration club volunteers.

In the '20s, more and more country women joined the Extension home demonstration program. The county home demonstration agent needed help in meeting the needs of these women. She often trained leaders who would take information back to their communities.

All home demonstration clubs in a county joined together to form the Federation of Home Demonstration Clubs. The Executive Board of the Federation, called the County Council, was composed of three officers from each club and county projects chairman. The County Council was the supporting body behind the home agent and served in an advisory role. In 1924, Jane McKimmon was named assistant Extension director as well as State Home Demonstration Agent.

In 1927, home demonstration club members across the state established the Jane. S. McKimmon Loan Fund to honor Mrs. McKimmon and to help rural girls get a college education in home economics. Many of the young recipients worked for the Extension Service after graduation.

1930–1940
MAKING THE MOST OF WHAT YOU HAVE

The start of the 1930s found North Carolina families facing the full impact of the "Great Depression."

Extension administrators, specialists, agents, and leaders worked hard to help farm families cope with hard times and the "use what you have" doctrine was preached everywhere.

To meet the problems of low family income and inadequate or poorly balanced diets, the Home Demonstration division stressed year-round gardens: one planted in spring, the other in the fall. A fall and winter garden contest helped sell the idea. The first year 457 women entered the competition.

Extension workers encouraged farm families to can, preserve, or pickle fruits and vegetables for winter use. Most farm families had chickens, pigs and a cow or two, so home canning of meat products was also emphasized.

In just one year, 31,683 families conserved 4,318,811 quarts of fruits, vegetables, and meat. A canning contest sponsored by Ball Brothers Company helped add zest to the canning season. Winners received cash prizes of $5 or $10.

A display of fruits and vegetables canned by people on relief under the guidance of home demonstration club women, Durham County, 1933.

Black families at a canning center in the foothills. (Courtesy of The North Carolina State Achives.)

A woman, holding money in her hand, makes a notation in a ledger.

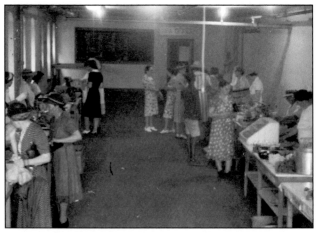

Women look for goods at the Granville Home Demonstration Curb Market.

Cutting okra at the community cannery.

Home demonstration agents gave canning demonstrations in 56 counties and trained leaders to help their neighbors use safe canning methods. In Gaston County, the county commissioners helped each of the 18 local home demonstration clubs buy a pressure canner. The canners were used by all club members.

An additional 67 people across the state came to Extension asking for advice in operating a commercial cannery.

Black families responded well to the idea of gardening and conserving food. One Robeson County homemaker displayed some of her jars of canned food at the courthouse in Lumberton telling her audience she always had a dollar or two in her pocket, thanks to the sales of her turnip greens, collards, onions, and canned goods in the winter and her tomatoes, corn, butterbeans, and other vegetables in the summer.

Pamlico County home demonstration club members made an effort to help neighbors. Almost 40,000 quarts

Mrs. Fred Christian of Stokes County peels potatoes in a model kitchen in 1939.

of fruits and vegetables were canned for families who were on relief. Home demonstration club women contributed to a "community chest" by making bed linens, night clothes, and other garments, or collecting articles needed in a sick room. Contents of the chest were loaned to any member of the community when needed. All that was asked was that cloth items be returned properly laundered.

As the depression widened and deepened in intensity, there was need for clothing and fuel as well as food in the rural areas. The Governor created a state Office of Relief and it was not hard to get home demonstration club members to get help to needy families. The state effort later merged with the Federal Administration of Relief. It was then possible to pay a small per diem for the work the farm leaders were doing.

Three women work together to prepare food for neighbors in need.

Mrs. Apple does the laundry in a well-lighted basement in 1939.

Woman pouring water in a wash tub, preparing to do laundry.

Women posing in storefront window to advertise drinking milk in the school room, on a picnic, and at a party.

The women in rural communities were called "visiting homemakers", and that is exactly what they were. Often no travel expense was provided, but that didn't stop them. The women walked, drove their own buggies or cars, or pressed a farm wagon into service when the distance was more than they could cover on foot.

Visiting homemakers would get a list of farm people in their own neighborhoods who had sought relief. They would visit the family, and once they gained the confidence of the housewife, they would talk with her about what the family had on hand, what could be done with it, and what must be supplied from the outside.

Sometimes needs were so great it was simply a matter of satisfying hunger and supplying food and clothing. Often, it meant bringing a broom and mop to the house and helping the family reach some semblance of comfort and cleanliness. Then visiting homemakers

A woman teaching the method of canning meat to a class of other women.

33

would show families how to make cleaning supplies at home and work with them to learn good housekeeping skills. Assistance was given to 8,427 families.

At the end of the 1920s and beginning of 1930s North Carolina families were suffering from a pellagra epidemic. The State Department of Health enlisted Extension agents and visiting homemakers to help stem the disease. When they found a family with pellagra they sent those with serious conditions to a doctor and they helped other family members recognize that the disease was caused by poor diet.

Extension personnel from 47 counties sent 486 North Carolinians with pellagra symptoms to the doctor and gave nutrition information and help to an additional 1,050 people.

As families became more at ease with the visiting homemaker, she could encourage them to spend their government supplements wisely, especially where food and clothing were concerned. Every farm family "on the dole" was also required to attend a canning demonstration in the neighborhood and to plant a family garden.

Most farm families on relief needed not only economic aid, but also the opportunity to socialize and work with their neighbors. The visiting homemakers helped families understand that much could be done when neighbors worked together.

As they learned about malnutrition and its causes from their agent, teachers, and leaders, the women understood that the limited diet served in their homes caused the undernourishment of their children. Many Tar Heel children suffered from rickets (lack of vitamin D) and scurvy (lack of vitamin C) and pellagra (lack of one of the B vitamins.) Education information emphasized the importance of milk and hot food in the diet. In many communities, mothers took turns preparing hot chocolate and hot soups that could be served in the schools.

Rural schools across the state adopted the "milk and soup" plan and 51 counties reported 554 rural schools serving a hot dish daily to 75,852 children in 1931, thanks to Extension home demonstration's efforts.

Home agents trained willing local leaders to prepare nutritious hot dishes with just a school room heater and a large kettle.

The Blalock family at the Wilson Home Demonstration Curb Market. Son, Carlton, seen behind the table, later became director of the NC Agricultural Extension Service.

Mrs. Blalock checking the prices on the black board at the curb market.

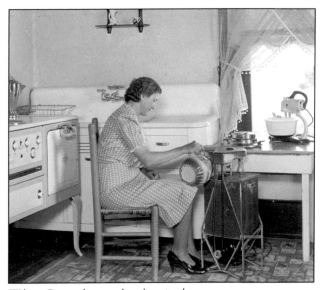

Wilson County homemaker churning butter.

Agents also encouraged parents to work together during the growing season to make large quantities of a canned soup mixture that could be used for school meals the next winter. This was the forerunner of the school hot lunch program.

In a related area, home demonstration club members and their families often found it necessary to supplement farm income through the sale of home products. More curb markets were established, providing a sales outlet for surplus farm products, jellies, jams, cakes, and other specialty items.

Currituck Curb Market.

Rocky Mount Home Demonstration Curb Market building erected in 1936 by the Works Progress Administration, a federal government program. Money donated by home demonstration clubs in Nash and Edgecombe counties, and by curb-market sellers paid for the materials.

The Extension agriculture agent seals canned goods for club women at a community cannery.

Curtain-making demonstration attracts Extension club members.

Carteret County founded its curb market in 1931 with 42 women selling home grown or homemade items under the trees. By 1942, the ladies had raised enough money to construct a building on land provided by the county. Eighty years later, the market is still in operation.

Granville County women displayed baked goods, produce and jellies in wheelbarrows in a local tobacco warehouse until they had enough business to merit an indoor space in the Extension office building.

Wake County's curb market was held in the basement of Memorial Auditorium in downtown Raleigh.

Beginning in 1936, the club women of Dare and Currituck counties got together and established a curb market at Nags Head. They sold fresh vegetables, eggs, and dairy products to the people who owned or rented summer cottages.

One market day, Hilda Mathias took a coconut marshmallow crème cake to sell. It happened to be the day President Franklin Delano Roosevelt was in the area to attend Paul Green's outdoor drama, "The Lost Colony." Someone brought the Mathias cake and gave it to the President.

In 1936, there were 36 home demonstration curb markets in the state, providing farm families with $262,841.99 of added income. Home demonstration club members sold an additional $26,245.49 worth of farm products to institutions, hotels, and merchants.

Several years later, members of the Black home demonstration clubs in Beaufort County decided to buy some land for a curb market. They got the site for $1,700. The group then went to the county commissioners for help in building the facility. Later, the clubs turned the deed over to Beaufort County with the understanding that the building would remain in use as a home demonstration curb market and as office space for the Black home and farm agents. If at any time the building or land became undesirable for such use, it would be returned to the home demonstration clubs.

Some counties encouraged "Barter Days" where rural women could trade their baked and canned goods, butter, eggs, fresh vegetables, ham, sausage, dressed fowl, and flowers for other things their families needed. These transactions allowed rural families to upgrade their quality of life.

To further stretch their limited dollars, home demonstration club members honed their sewing skills, often remodeling used garments. Women proudly wore their husbands' old suits tailored into a lady's suit or overcoat and made children's clothing from adult garments, pattered or decorated feed sacks, or other available fabrics.

Dress reviews held at the local level allowed farm women to model and proudly show off the garments they had made. At a fashion show during the 1933 Dress Revue at Farm and Home Week, Mrs. Mary Lamb of Sampson County modeled a dress she made using a 20-year-old lace curtain; Mrs. J.P. Owen of Duplin County fashioned the suit she was wearing from her husband's discarded suit; Mrs. L.J. Sloan of Lee County wore a dress and suit she made from fertilizer sacks, and Sarah Boswell of Currituck County was stylish in an organdie evening dress and cape that cost $3.90.

In 1936 home demonstration women who participated in clothing workshops saved their families a grand total of $102,674.09 on clothing costs. Often they could add to the family income by sewing for neighbors.

In one year, almost 1,400 homemakers supplemented their income by a grand total of $37,282.27 by taking in sewing, and 113 women sold $1,602.40 worth of clothing at curb markets.

Homemakers were also given tips on clothing care, including dry cleaning, spot and stain removal, and dyeing fabrics. The lessons were greeted with great enthusiasm – especially the one on dry cleaning. Some women set up "cleaning bees" in their neighborhoods. Several women would get together and buy five gallons of cleaning solvent. Clothes that needed dry cleaning were carried to the bee and a good, clean time was had by all.

Instruction in foundation or dress patterns is given to home demonstration club members on the porch of a house, 1930s.

Ladies from Richmond County making hats.

One agent noted, "the homemakers would greet her at church with smiling faces, wearing dresses that were spic and span, but smelling of gasoline."

North Carolina also had many farm families whose forbearers were experts in handicrafts. The craft know-how spread from family to family over generations, and in the '30s many women found they could turn these skills into additional income for their families.

There were broom makers, basket makers and those who made quilts, spreads, and other beautiful and saleable things. Craftswomen made do with what they had. Pine needles, white oak splits, willow, and honeysuckle furnished material for baskets. Scraps from knitting mills, yarn, or strips of cloth were used for crocheted or knitted rugs.

Mrs. Ben Nicholson of John's Creek, learned to make corn shuck hats. She made a hat each day in her spare time, in spite of the fact that each hat required

Shucking corn for food and crafts.

The home demonstration agent talks about child care skills with attentive young women.

15 yards of braided shuck, which she had to plait. She selected the shucks carefully, cut the inner ones into strips, and carefully braided them. Then she would block the hat into the shape desired by the buyer.

Mrs. Nicholson also used corn shucks to make belts, boutonnieres, and character dolls. Her enterprise was so successful she established a mail order business.

Other rural families found additional enterprising ways of providing family income. In 1937 Union County Agent Mrs. Pratt McSwain, noticed that 75 percent of the farm families she worked with fell into the lowest one-third of North Carolina families in terms of income. Many families rented their homes and moved frequently.

The agent worked with numerous families who currently sold whiskey to make ends meet. She helped to change this by teaching the women there were other options for making a farm profitable.

As farm families started to recover from the Great Depression, women were encouraged to brighten their homes. Agents reminded them to do all they could now to make their home cheerful and not to wait for the economy to get better "as five years is a long time in the life of a child, so make your homes prettier right now." Women found themselves dyeing burlap sacks,

fringing them to make draperies and hooking rugs to give the home a woman's touch.

Chair caning was a popular part of the house furnishings program, and in 1939 Extension farm women saved $90,396.75 by selecting quality materials and learning to do their own repairs.

Home demonstration women often improved the outside of their houses by beautifying their home grounds and places in the community. It's possible

Copper work made by Louise Weaver, a home demonstration woman from Franklin County. Using copper from old stills, she made a platter, card tray, and ashtrays.

40

these efforts helped relieve tension and made troublesome times a bit more bearable.

By 1937, more and more counties realized the value home demonstration agents and their trained leaders made to help rural families improve their lives. By then, 76 of 100 counties had full-time home agents, up from 56 in 1930.

Transportation continued to be a problem. In Polk County, for example, only one club woman had a telephone and only six club women could drive a car. Therefore, home demonstration work in Polk, and many other counties, was carried on in small groups in schools and in members' homes. Even so, Extension homemakers learned to cook nutritious meals, and improve their homes and their family wardrobes.

In spite of the huge obstacles facing the family, women in the neighborhoods gathered together to help solve some of the problems facing the community.

Currituck County families were upset at finding moldy bread in their stores. In 1931, a group of Extension homemakers went to visit General Baking Company in Norfolk Virginia and requested better bread. They were successful. Another county, Stanly,

sponsored a rat-killing competition between clubs.

Rural reading programs were fostered. Traveling libraries were provided and clubs established numerous community libraries. School libraries also merited attention. One Rutherford county club, the Gilkey Club, made improving the school library its community project for 1939.

The White Hall Club in Cabarrus County started a library project in 1934 and early in 1935 agreed to give its books to the county federation, provided the federation would sponsor a county library. This the federation gladly did, and the library proved popular. Cabarrus County has the distinction of having the first library in North Carolina started by home demonstration women.

In Polk County, home demonstration club members and their county council were the chief workers behind the formation of the Polk County Library and Bookmobile. One club, the Lanier Club of Tryon, started an office library with several hundred books that any county resident could borrow. When the Polk County Library Association was later formed, these books were donated to it.

Three women inspecting loaves of bread at a competition.

Home demonstration club women work diligently at a sewing workshop.

Reading was important to Pender County homemakers. The home demonstration agent working in the county in 1931 and 1932 encouraged senior 4-H'ers to begin collecting books and placing them in a room above the drug store in Atkinson. During 1935 and 1936 a WPA project leader enlisted the help of home demonstration club women, 4-H'ers, community leaders, and county government in planning and establishing a county library.

Ruth Current, state home demonstration agent, with the cooperation of Marjorie Beal from the State Library, conducted a successful reading program for women who belonged to home demonstration clubs. A list of 100 books was compiled by Miss Beal, approved by Miss Current, and given to the women, who were asked to select and read three books during the year.

When a woman could report reading at least three books and was prepared to give her club members a short synopsis of what she had read, she was awarded a reader's certificate. By the end of the decade, 1,493 women had earned a certificate.

During the 1930s, farm families were concerned that teachers had taken extreme cuts in salary. Home demonstration club members resolved to offer support and cooperation to teachers by providing desirable homes in their communities at reasonable rates.

The building of meeting houses was also on the agenda. In Lee County, the Dignus Club, one of 19 home demonstration clubs in the county, held their regular meetings in a log cabin clubhouse. The house was built by club women and their husbands, using a cash outlay of $350. The building was often used for other community events.

Many other counties picked up the library and club house banners and vast improvements were made in the next decade. Club members continued to make improvements at the local level as well. Currituck women even cleaned and refinished the benches in the county courtroom.

To help train Extension agents and leaders to carry out their important roles, the state staff was expanded to four full-time and three assistant specialists. They worked with foods and nutrition, clothing, home management, housing and house furnishings, and food conservation and marketing.

North Carolina had a change of leadership during the decade. In 1937, Ruth Current was appointed head of Extension home demonstration programs at the state level. Jane McKimmon kept the title of Assistant Director of Extension.

On the national level, rural women from across the country met in Washington, DC in June 1936 and helped form the National Home Demonstration Council (NHDC).

The purpose of the NHDC was to further strengthen, develop, coordinate, and extend adult

Caning chairs.

education in home economics though the Agricultural Extension Service of USDA and Land-Grant colleges.

North Carolina was one of 10 states to become a charter member.

1940–1950
THE CHALLENGES OF CHANGE

The 1940s was truly a decade of challenges. At the start, North Carolina rural families were coping with economic difficulties. Pearl Harbor and America's entry into World War II brought additional challenges. By 1946 the war was over and families and communities dealt with the realities of a very changed world. The Extension administrators, specialists, agents, and leaders did all they could to help families face each new situation as it came along.

The decade began as the previous one had ended: with North Carolina families coping with "the Great Depression." Of the federal aid programs established to help ease the pain, two had great significance for rural residents.

Cutting logs for the St. Mary's Community Building in Wilson County.

Husbands of the Wilson County club members mill the lumber.

Starting construction on the St. Mary's Community Building.

The State Planning Board, acting with the Works Progress Administration (WPA), approved the building of small community centers in rural areas. The farming community reacted with a rush of requests and the WPA responded. It recruited skilled carpenters and unskilled workers from the community, and furnished an agreed-upon amount of materials that the community could not supply on its own.

The Farm Engineering Division of N.C. State College drew simple, but artistic plans for the 36-by-20 or 50-by-30 square foot clubhouses. The design had an assembly room and kitchen at one end and a dressing room on the other. In many cases, thanks to the input from Extension home demonstration club members, a storage area or pantry was added to the plan.

Farmers cut and furnished logs for the building and gathered field rocks for chimneys and mantels. Then

St. Mary's Community Building begins to take shape.

the whole community helped clean the site and helped raise the building from the ground up.

When construction was finished, the home demonstration club women decorated and furnished their new neighborhood meeting place.

Of the 269 small, comfortable, and attractive home demonstration club houses located in 73 counties, 139 were built new; the remaining 130 were old buildings that had been remodeled.

The second government project to benefit rural families was one in which the surplus cotton of the South was released from storage and offered to low-income families, so they could make mattresses.

The Agricultural Adjustment Administration (AAA), the Extension Service, and the Surplus Commodity

Cotton layers being prepared for mattress-making.

Administration (SCA), with the co-operation of county commissioners, developed workable plans, and the project was turned over to the Division of Extension Home Demonstration programs in each state.

Farm families with no more than $400 gross income from farm or farm labor in 1939 qualified for the program.

In North Carolina, training schools were held to prepare farm and home agents and men and women volunteer leaders in at least 90 counties to supervise the mattress centers.

In counties where the Black population was large, there were special centers for the many Black families who applied for mattresses. Where the Black

Families made 221,377 mattresses in 18 months.

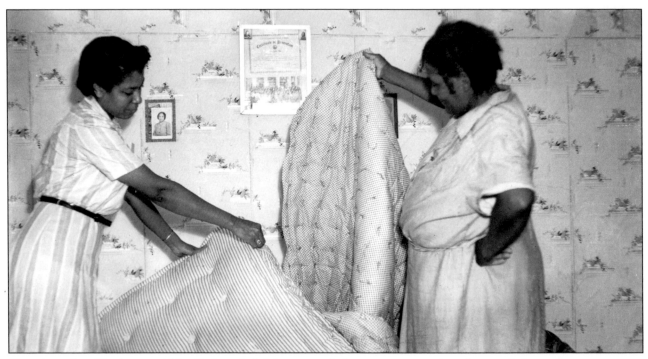

Home Agent Rosa Winchester and Mrs. Ida Sowe, Bethel Community, look over a mattress, and comforter made during the cotton mattress program.

Couple fluffing the cotton for a mattress.

Couple sewing the ticking to cover their cotton mattress.

The finished cotton mattress going home with a couple.

population was smaller, they were taken care of in the same centers as white families.

Together agents and leaders reached over 125,000 low-income farm families with such easy-to-follow directions that the families were able to make 221,377 mattresses for their own use in a little more than 18 months.

In Surry County, Grace Brown was called on to help local residents make 4,092 mattresses between August of 1940 and September of 1941. "She spent more hours each day making mattresses than she did sleeping on one!" observed a woman's editor for the *Winston-Salem Journal*.

In addition to mattresses, the need for warm coverings was so apparent that the joint Agricultural Committee agreed the surplus cotton could be used for comforters, too. In 1941, some 54,335 warm covers were made and used in the homes of needy North Carolina farm families.

Canning continued to be important, both at home and at institutions. In Moore County, the agent worked with prisoners at Troy Prison Camp to teach them how to can the produce grown in gardens at the prison. One year they had such an over abundant crop of beets, the prisoners "were sick" of canning them.

Farm families preserved 7,750,000 containers of fruits, vegetables, meats, jams, and jellies in 1940. The foodstuffs had a value of $1,141,513. Home demonstration club women also used their skills to refinish, repair, and remodel furniture, saving their families $65,736.

Woman adds one more jar to her pantry.

Ironing without electricity.

Freezer locker plants became popular. Extension home demonstration agents trained homemakers to package food so it would retain color and flavor after it was frozen. They also encouraged the women to make good use of the compact storage space.

Having running water in the home was a goal of many rural families. Home demonstration agents and specialists worked closely with Howard Ellis of the N.C. College of Agricultural Engineering to make this a reality for 1,374 farm families in 1940.

Ellis demonstrated types of water systems and the home demonstration agent would give information on the convenient location of water in the home.

Families were pleased with the results. The G. B. Carlton family of Wilkes County, noted "The best part is we always have plenty of hot water now. And the water never freezes like it did with our old water system."

Electricity was also coming to rural areas. In 1940 there were 27,078 miles of line in the state. Rural families were so eager to hasten the coming of current that all along stretches of approved lines they were either doing their own wiring or getting a willing workman to do it.

Extension agents noticed some homemakers were attaching an electric iron, lights, and the refrigerator to one inadequate drop cord. No wonder many families were unhappy with the performance of electric devices and somewhat leery of burning the house down.

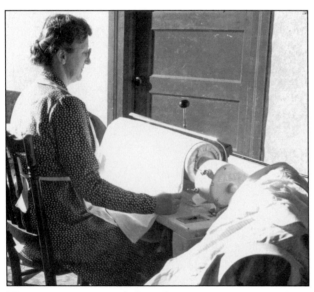

Woman operating a mangle (ironer).

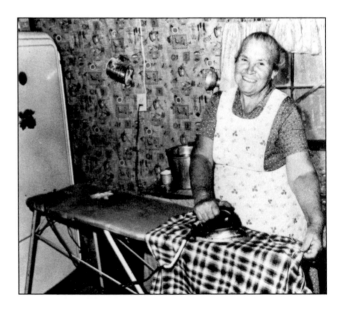

Nash County family gets a new water system designed by Extension engineers.

Electric stove being delivered to a happy homemaker.

Extension specialists and farm and home demonstration agents tried to keep families free from risk by offering schools on safe and convenient wiring; adequate lighting; and the selection, care, and repair of electrical equipment.

The success of the schools was immediate and in a three-year span 406 schools were held, with a total attendance of 21,740 people.

Food lockers were popular in mid 1940s.

Woman washing clothes with electric wringer washing machine.

Producing foods for better meals at home.

Checking out the poultry flock.

HD curb markets continued to be popular in war years.

Admiring a Victory Garden.

As the war clouds thickened, and especially after Pearl Harbor, rural families in North Carolina faced a shift in priorities. Change began with a) the mobilization of resources in support of World War II and b) a shifting of population due to the rapid expansion of industrial production.

More homemakers went to work in fields and factories. Lessons on reducing home labor, such as shortcuts in cooking, sewing, cleaning, and laundry were much appreciated. "Eat it up, Wear it out, Make it do or Do without," was the motto in many North Carolina homes.

Extension home demonstration members learned to repair appliances and to reupholster worn furniture. They continued to preserve food, make soap and mattresses, and they turned used cotton feed and flour sacks into clothing, sheets, table cloths, pillowcases, and curtains.

During the war years, home demonstration club members rolled bandages and knitted sweaters and socks for service men. Their home vegetable gardens became "Victory Gardens" and the preserved fruits and vegetables supplemented winter meals.

Members sewed for the Red Cross, purchased war bonds and stamps, donated to blood banks, and sponsored drives to collect scrap rubber, scrap metal, and waste cooking fat. The cooking fat received a high priority because the glycerin in it could be used to make gunpowder.

A letter dated January 21, 1944, written to home demonstration agents and the salvage committee chairman in each home demonstration club, spelled out the need. Estelle Smith, assistant to the state home demonstration agent, wrote "Our government is so dreadfully in need of glycerin that North Carolina's monthly quota of fats from dwellings has been raised from 115,000 pounds per month to 413,334 pounds per month.

Victory Garden promotion.

Woman spraying her garden to prevent pests.

With Victory Gardens popular, Extension agents test pressure canners for safety before canning season begins.

Ruth Current, state home demonstration agent, with Estelle T. Smith, assistant leader.

"A half cup of fat per week from every housewife (in the nation) would produce the glycerin needed to make 13,000,000 pounds of gunpowder. One tablespoon of fat saved each day would supply enough synthetic resin to produce enough paint to coat 25,000 medium tanks."

The state Home Demonstration office also produced a one-page leaflet called "It's Your Scrap, Sister" to alert women to the cause. In addition to fat, the leaflet encouraged families to save metals, tin cans, paper, silk and nylon hosiery, and rags.

A summary from Granville County shows how Extension home demonstration members supported the war effort. By making and remaking the family's clothes and repairing household articles, Granville County farm women saved money and bought War Bonds. In 1944, they purchased $41,000 worth of bonds. Other wartime activities included 1,167 hours spent in the Red Cross bandage room, 36 sweaters knitted and 85 other garments constructed for the Red Cross, and 575 pounds of waste fat collected and sold. An additional 2,000 pounds of scrap metal and 1,500 pounds of waste paper were saved, collected, and shipped.

Farm and Home in National Defense brochure.

Members of the Benvenue Home Demonstration Club in Nash County assisted with the bond and scrap drives, spent 6,000 hours knitting for soldiers and their families, sent over 100 "care packages" to soldiers in camps and hospitals, furnished a sun room at Fort Bragg, sent over 80 dozen cookies to soldiers, and made surgical dressings.

Homemakers in Moore County wanted to make the men who were at military training bases in their area feel at home. They made refreshments and sponsored

IT'S YOUR SCRAP SISTER!

Maybe you're wishing you were a WAVE, WAAC OR SPAR . . . .

Maybe you've got an idea you'd like to be a Nurse . . . .

Maybe you'd even settle for a welder's torch . . . .

Maybe you get a little restless sometimes, wondering if you shouldn't be doing a little more about this war than just looking after the kids, worrying about three square meals a day . . . .

Sister, you've got a job right at home, You've got to GET IN THE SCRAP! . . . . .

This is a hard, dirty, unromantic chore -- but nobody else can do this in your home . . . .

You and your 40 million civilian sisters represent the hardest-fighting woman-power in the country. The Army, Navy, the Nurses, the factories depend upon YOU. If you don't make it your business to get in ALL the scrap, War factories will close down for lack of vital materials. SCRAP IS THE BACKBONE OF A FIGHTING WAR! MAKE SALVAGE A HABIT IN YOUR HOME!

Here's what America is calling upon you to Salvage:

METALS: A systematic search will yield vast quantities of scrap metals which are lying around American homes and backyards, cellars and attics. BRING IN THAT SCRAP! Those old metal beds, doorknobs, electric fans and heaters, burned-out light bulbs, old coal stoves, obsolete copper engraving plates.

COOKING
 FATS: One to two billion pounds of waste fats vanish out of kitchens every year. Save those drippings from roasts and chops, poultry, bacon grease. After all the food value has been obtained, take them to your nearest meat dealer. Waste Fats are needed for making explosives, also essential medicinal supplies.

TIN CANS: ALL tin cans needed excepting conical shaped cans, evaporated milk, paint, varnish or oil containers. Prepare according to instructions of local Salvage Committee. It is hoped that collections will soon be arranged for every town throughout the country. At present, keep on salvaging tin cans whether you have a collection or not.

SILK AND
NYLON
HOSIERY: WANTED! All worn and discarded silk and nylon stockings. Wash them and take to nearest retail store where collection centers are set up. Essential in production of powder bags and other important war materials.

RAGS: Cotton, woolen, rayon, silk -- all needed for making wipers for machinery.

2 180

War effort It's Your Scrap, Sister.

Scrap metal collection in Nash County.

socials, giving soldiers a chance to meet the local residents. Johnston County homemakers entertained servicemen at USO centers as did many other Extension groups.

Nash County home demonstration women operated the Soldier's Feeding Station at the Union depot in Rocky Mount for two weeks at Christmas time. All soldiers passing through the state were served free coffee, chicken, ham, and other delicacies. The women's kindness attracted the attention of the national press and radio corps.

In 1944, the North Carolina Federation of Nurses, members of the Woman's Clubs of North Carolina, and home demonstration club members across the state raised $4,000,000 to renovate and launch the hospital ship, Larkspur. They got the money by selling War Bonds.

Homemakers in Wilson County may have held the record for War Bond sales. They sold $160,000 worth in just one week.

World War II also focused attention on improving the family's ability to cope with many of its own medical and nursing problems. To prepare, many

Larkspur.

Club members talk about how rationing affects them.

Home nursing class.

homemakers took training in first aid and home nursing.

Rationing of sugar, meat, butter, and coffee kept home demonstration agents busy teaching homemakers to plan and serve nutritionally balanced meals with the food on hand. Because sugar was rationed, jams and jellies couldn't be made. A new way of food preservation – dehydration – was taught and encouraged.

There was also a drive to enrich bread and flour as an economical way to improve American diets without interfering with deeply ingrained food habits. To inform North Carolina homemakers about the importance of enriched flour and bread, home demonstration agents gave 415 talks, wrote 26 news releases, and gave 8 radio programs on the subject.

Families gather around radio to hear news.

There were crises to deal with at the local as well as the international level. During the war years, several families often lived together under one roof, resulting in overcrowding and family tensions. An Extension family life specialist, hired in 1945, provided lessons and materials suggesting ways to keep harmony and peace in the home.

Home demonstration club members in Catawba County financially aided a polio hospital set up in Hickory during the epidemic of 1944. They also worked in community cancer drives and helped with the first Red Cross bloodmobile collections in their area.

There was continued interest in well-balanced meals for school children. Many club members took on the job of providing at least one hot food for rural school children's lunches. Clubs donated milk to supplement food brought from home. In some communities, women took turns preparing hot foods, such as soup or a casserole at home, and delivering them to the school at noon.

A display associated with the enrichment of flour program. Enrichment of flour, legislation passed in early '40s.

Canneries regained popularity during World War II.

Curb market, 1947.

Durham County Curb Market.

A and T College in Greensboro, June 27, 1940. An exhibit of home demonstration work assembled to be sent to the Negro Exposition in Chicago. Mrs. Dazelle Lowe, district home agent, inspects the exhibit before shipping.

Volunteers, Red Cross volunteers, Nash County canteen group.

When a national school lunch program was proposed, homemakers supported the idea and later campaigned for their schools to participate. They also provided cooking equipment, tea towels, hot pads, and other supplies.

From 1942 to 1946, Extension reading lists were revised to reflect the times. Among the categories were "Books to Interpret the World Crisis", "Books to Interpret Home Crisis", and "Victory by Vitamins."

In 1945, there were 1,637 home demonstration clubs in North Carolina with a membership of 40,594 women.

Following World War II, there was a program co-sponsored by county agents and county and district health officers to improve the health and sanitary conditions of North Carolina families. One of their successes: 3,000 sanitary privies were built in 1947.

In Jackson County's Cashiers area, home demonstration women saw a need for a community health center and began seeking donations to start construction of a building. In 1945, the Cashiers Community Health Center opened its doors. Preventive medicine was the focus of the clinic, with immunizations, dental care, eye examinations, prenatal

Club women watch a sewing demonstration.

Entertaining at the Durham County Curb Market, 1947.

Woman mending clothes by the fireplace.

Woman at wood cooking stove.

care, well-baby clinics, home nursing skill, and child care being included. The building was constructed by husbands of club women with materials donated by the community.

There was an acute housing shortage after the War. Housing, engineering, and landscaping specialists at N.C. State worked together to provide plans for houses that would be more livable and more attractive. In one year, Extension workers aided rural families in the construction of 4,887 new houses, the remodeling of 6,609 older houses and the improvement of 13,772 yards.

Although the War was over, North Carolina home demonstration club members did not forget their duties as patriotic citizens.

Home demonstration women reached out to help those in war-shattered countries. They gave the Red Cross thousands of children's garments that were sent to war-torn areas in a program known as "Hands Across the Sea." Jones County home demonstration women reported making 140 garments for the Red Cross. Clothing was made from feed sacks and one member noted her "bag dress" cost 40 cents.

Starting in 1948, members of home demonstration clubs in Rowan County sewed garments that they donated to the county welfare department, along with money for a shoe fund. From 1948 to 1980, the women made 20,547 garments and contributed $4,998 towards new shoes for the needy.

Homemakers in Catawba County also bought cases of corn and beans to send to war-savaged Europe in 1946 when the people there were suffering from starvation.

Post World War II, some home demonstration groups began to sponsor foreign students who were enrolled in the colleges of home economics and agriculture. There was also great interest in the United Nations, which was seen as an organization to prevent future world wars. Many club women took advantage of tours to United Nations Headquarters. Others made UN flags to present to schools, libraries, and churches.

On the home front, electric lines continued to bring power and light to more and more rural areas. Farm families improved water systems, again making homes more convenient.

Home freezers became popular, supplementing food lockers, so agents taught proper freezing techniques. The need was reinforced when an agent in Caswell County went to help a lady and found corn-on-the-cob still in the husk frozen in the freezer. The homemaker had heard the quicker you could get corn from the garden to the freezer, the better the quality.

Mrs. Carrie Wilson, home agent, Alamance County, gives a demonstration on the care of milk utensils.

She's ready for the stew pot, girls!

Home demonstration club women model pleated skirts they made.

First and second North Carolina State Home Demonstration agents, Jane S. McKimmon (right) and Ruth Current (left), posing with an unidentified woman in New York for the radio dramatization of McKimmon's life story on NBC's Cavalcade of America. Man behind Jane McKimmon is her nephew Jim. (Jay Seymour Studios).

The Extension Service hired a specialist in frozen foods to help with training and "how to" materials.

Kitchen planning and remodeling also received emphasis, as did better storage space.

New homes continued to be built and old homes remodeled in North Carolina's rural areas. In Granville County in 1948, tips on better storage, good arrangements of kitchen cabinets, refinishing and re-upholstering furniture, and selection of floor coverings by Home Agent Virginia Wilson aided in the effort. In one year alone, her accomplishments included: 69 kitchens rearranged for convenience; 96 homes with improved walls and floors; 14 homes now had screens added to windows and porches; seven families with better records of expenditures; and five who made yard

improvement plans.

Rural families also re-focused on their communities. Great emphasis was placed on the landscaping and beautification of church and school grounds.

North Carolina's first State Home Demonstration Agent, Jane McKimmon continued to receive recognitions for her important contributions to the betterment of Tar Heel rural families.

The success of her efforts was showcased during the radio documentation of *When We're Green We Grow* ~ a story about her life and career. The broadcast was on *Cavalcade of America*, a popular NBC program.

Mrs. McKimmon was also honored when a portrait of her was unveiled and given to North Carolina State College on August 27, 1947.

Mountain town with electric lines.

North Carolina State College alumna and Home Demonstration pioneer Jane S. McKimmon (right) in New York for the radio dramatization of her life story "When We're Green We Grow" on NBC's Cavalcade of America, posing with her successor, State Home Demonstration Agent Ruth Current (left), and Academy Award winning actress Jane Darwell. (Jay Seymour Studios).

A final look at the '40s.

Selling peas at the curb market.

Rural Electrification Authority changed rural life.

Clothing specialist teaching class to help women "make do".

Pleasant Hills Home Demonstration Club, Edgecombe County, shows what can be made from feedsacks.

Sewing machine representative shows off new gadgets.

Refurbishing old hats was popular in the 1940s.

Chavis Heights residents get together for canning session. (Courtesy of The North Carolina State Archives)

Chair caning workshop adds life to 'old' chairs.

		Veg.	Poultry	Eggs	Butter	Meat	Cake	Bread	Flowers	Fruits & Berries	Canned Products	Handwork	Order	Total
April	7	.50	65.10	4 90	2 70	60	17 30		.45					91 55
	14	.20	86.13	4 55	3 15		18 80		.22		1.25			114 30
	21		85.81	6 10	1 35		17 47							110 7
	28	1.00	103.40	7 00	1 35	1 23	22 00		.85					136 8
Total		1.70	340.44	22 55	8 55	1 83	75 57		1 62		1.25			453 4
May	5	2.40	105.50	10 55	3 15	1 00	24 50		3.05					150 1
	12	4.00	106.20	6 90	2 03	4 10	22 50			8.49				154 2
	19	7.62	95.35	8 44	3 15	1 50	19 33		1.00	14.94		2,357.88		151 23
	26	11.46	72.89	5 46	2 70	2 62	23 50							118 83
Total		25.48	379.94	31 35	11 03	9 22	89 83		4.05	23.43		2,357.		574 3
June	2	22.14	65.35	7 71	4 79		22 10	96	65	1.95				125 6
	9	17.10	51.72	11 02	5 40	1 14	19 50		45					106 3
	16	18.82	87.70	10 32	4 05		12 25		1.00					134 14
	23	11.60	129.84	12 64	4 95	80	17 50		1.00	1.90				180 2
	30	7.29	89.81	6 63	5 35		16 00		1.00				2 60	128 68
Total		76.95	424.42	48 32	24 54	1 94	87 35	96	4.10	3.85			2 60	675 03
July	7	12.81	119.87	9 62	4 90	1 80	10 00		2.00	4.27				163 2
	14	18.24	122.75	11 35	5 40	10 00	10 00		3.18					180 9
	21	13.86	85.05	11 95	3 90	3 00	12 00		2.00					131 76

Curb market ledger makes it possible to keep track of sales.

Agent assists with the location of a new window.

Installation of closet.

Home Agent Lois Rainwater taping radio program to reach home audience.

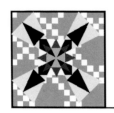

1950–1960
A WELCOME RESPITE

Following the Great Depression and World War II, the 1950s were a welcome respite for North Carolina families, rural and urban.

For many, living conditions improved. Electricity, running water, and bathroom facilities in the home added comfort, convenience, and sanitation to many a household.

Improved income encouraged many families to upgrade their current living space or build a new house. Extension engineering specialists at N.C. State designed house plans to meet those requests. Most houses had three bedrooms, living room, modern and convenient U-shaped kitchens, and indoor bathrooms. Extension agents worked with families to choose the right plan and make modifications, if needed.

Twenty-four families in the state participated in special demonstrations using Extension house plans and advice from specialists. They agreed, in advance, to hold "open houses" for their friends and neighbors and share with them the delight of their new homes.

One Black family built an 8-room brick veneer house at a cost of $6,490 by using timber from their land and

Nash County woman is pleased with her new kitchen.

family labor. The house would have cost twice as much if they had bought all the materials and hired the labor to build it.

So many families took advantage of this service that agents could ride down county roads pointing out houses built from Extension house plans 89, 90, 94 or one of the other designs.

Home demonstration women add new life to worn chairs during workshop in Vance County.

70

Extension Home Demonstration members give heirlooms a face lift.

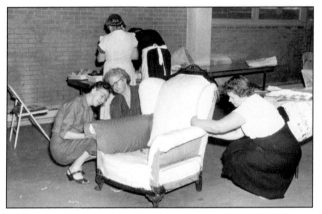

Wake reupholstery workshop in progress.

The finished product is beautiful.

Genevieve Greenlee, A&T specialist, conducts a reupholstery workshop.

Eleanor Roosevelt attended the third annual Conference on World Affairs, February 4, 1953, where the theme was "The United Nations: Our Best Instrument for World Understanding." Over 100 home demonstration club women, agents, and leaders from all over the state came to the University of North Carolina at Chapel Hill campus to participate in the conference and hear Mrs. Roosevelt speak.

Families wanted furnishings that would blend in with their remodeled or new houses. Extension agents and leaders offered workshops in curtain and drapery making, furniture refinishing, re-upholstering, and chair and stool caning. The Make-Your-Own Mattress program continued to garner attention into this decade.

Black home demonstration club women in Vance County were honored in 1958 for having the best refinishing project in the state. Their finished pieces were displayed at N.C. State College. Photos of some of the furniture appeared in the Extension publication *New Furniture from Old*. A national magazine, *Extension Service Review*, spread the story of the women's success across the country.

Families were also interested in making accessories for the home and they made good use of local resources. Copper was a desired material for accessories. In 1955, women from the home demonstration clubs in McDowell County were able to persuade the county sheriff to give them some of the copper stills he and his deputies had confiscated.

Mother-and-daughter fashion show contestants, Farm and Home Week, Raleigh. 1955.

72

Governor W. Kerr Scott addresses Extension club women at Farm and Home Week.

"Modernizing Old Picture Frames," at Farm and Home Week.

"You and Your Clothes" demonstration at Farm and Home Week. Woman on left is Mrs. Jane Scott, teacher, Simplicity Pattern Company, New York City.

Mitchell Kirkland of the American Red Cross answers questions from club women at 1957 Farm and Home Week.

Copper was expensive. No matter how much the home demonstration members wanted to decorate their homes with lovely copper vases, flower containers, fruit bowls and similar accessories, their budgets wouldn't permit it.

Home demonstration women practice how to walk and stand in the charm school held during the 1959 Farm and Home Week.

Then someone thought about the copper stills the sheriff's department had stored in the courthouse. The women used their powers of persuasion, and yes, got some of the stills to make home accessories.

Little did Sheriff Robinson think when he captured a copper still from a bootlegger's hideout, that some day it would be transformed into vessels of beauty and usefulness. But he had not reckoned with the resourcefulness of a woman's mind.

Using home-produced art to beautify the house was emphasized at the 1953 Farm and Home Week. Classes were offered in stenciling, silk screening, metal work, dried burrs and seed pod wreaths, weaving, wood carving, decorating wooden plates, cord weaving, and nature printing. The work sessions were taught by skilled craftswomen from Western North Carolina.

Classes at the 1953 Farm and Home Week reflected other changes taking place in family life. Although canning was still an important way to preserve food for winter use, more and more families had home freezers. They wanted to know how to prepare food so it would maintain color and flavor during freezing. Classes were also offered in family life, home management, charm and poise, and music. Extension specialists and agents taught some of the sessions, but representatives from E.I. DuPont de Nemours, Continental Can, and other large corporations were on hand as well. From 1950 through 1959 about 1,500 women attended Farm and Home Week each year.

Interest in home sewing seemed to double. Forty of the 100 counties had dress revues that allowed home demonstration women to show off their sewing skills. One home demonstration agent conducted the first radio sewing class ever held in the state. The class was designed to reach shut-ins and women who were not members of home demonstration clubs.

In 1953 a clothing specialist was hired to work with the Black home demonstration clubs. Also at the state level, the housing and house furnishings and home management departments were divided. A specialist was in charge of each department.

Homemakers turned their attention to beautification and cleanup projects at home and in their communities. Many roadside parks, road markers, and community signs were the results of club efforts.

Rowan County homemakers helped establish a memorial park honoring men who served in World War II and Cumberland County home demonstration club members sponsored a monument and memorial park to honor those who made the supreme sacrifice for our country's freedom.

Tour of North Carolina Museum of Art.

During this same period, North Carolina built 52 community club houses and remodeled nine more. The club house in Catawba County is a good example.

Familiar Foods in Fancy Fashion, by Ann Russell, American Institute of Baking, Chicago, Illinois; Miss Russell and club women - 1957 Farm and Home Week.

Home demonstration club women show off their sewing skills.

A rendering of a structure with the caption "Home Demonstration Building Fund," along with a map of North Carolina depicting how much money was raised in each region of the state.

Two home demonstration women check the results of their mail box project.

In 1953, a committee of Catawba County home demonstration members was appointed to contact stock holders of the unused potato house located on the grounds of Sherrills Ford School to see if it could be purchased for a club house. Most of the stock holders donated their shares; others sold them for half price. In 1954 the members received a deed to the property.

They built cabinets in the kitchen, installed bathrooms, and painted the building. Each club member donated a chair, dishes, silver, or other needed items.

For many years, home demonstration club women realized the need of having their own building on the North Carolina State College campus. In March 1951, the project was launched with pledges of $150 to start a building fund.

Committees were appointed to set up a plan for the building, investigate possible locations, and come up with means of funding. A leaflet "Our Vision 195_?" was prepared and distributed to the counties.

Women cleaning up roadside.

In 1952, the Home Demonstration State Council voted that each club member in the State should contribute $1 to the building fund. In 1955 the motion was carried that a goal of an additional 50 cents per member be set for 1956, 1957, and 1958. That would make a total of $2.50 per member.

Home demonstration club women clean up their community.

At an executive board meeting in 1956 it was decided that each county and district appoint a chairman to promote interest in the building and keep club members informed of the plan. This effort eventually resulted in the building of the Jane S. McKimmon Continuing Education Center on the North Carolina State University campus.

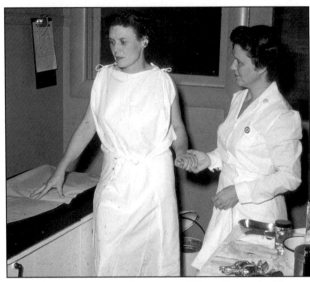

Home demonstration members assist at Wayne County health center.

In 1952, the HD club women of the county pledged $4,000 to help build Stokes-Reynolds Hospital. They wrote a cookbook and after selling 5,000 copies, they had $4,000 for the hospital. Here, club members admire the new stove purchased when they furnished the kitchen at the hospital.

Publications from the North Carolina Agricultural Extension Service are readily available.

Johnston County, 1952, people standing in line at a mobile health screening unit.

Health issues continued to receive emphasis from Extension home demonstration agents and club members. An effort was made to encourage women to get annual physicals.

Every county in the state was reached by the tuberculosis X-ray mobile unit. Home demonstration club members assisted with the publicity and often did a house-to-house canvas of their neighborhoods, letting friends know about the screening and why it was important. They also drove neighbors who had no other way to get to the X-ray mobile.

Home demonstration club members also assisted at cancer detection clinics. Again they informed neighbors of the importance of screening and offered transportation to the clinics.

Club members in every county worked in cooperation with the Red Cross Bloodmobile. They acted as hostesses, serving coffee and doughnuts, donated blood, and furnished transportation for donors. Extension home demonstration agents across the state cooperated with health departments and clinics. For example: Ashe County Extension club members were instrumental in helping to start a health center. That center evolved into the Ashe County

Health Department. Hoke County women bought a hospital bed and wheel chair for their local health facility.

Mrs. Emma Lanier, an Edgecombe County home demonstration club woman, was instrumental in establishing the Health Clinic in West Edgecombe community. Mrs. Lanier works in the clinic.

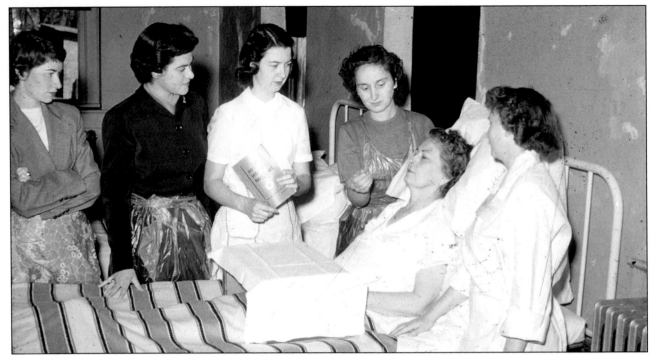

Home nursing course in home demonstration meeting in Cabarrus County.

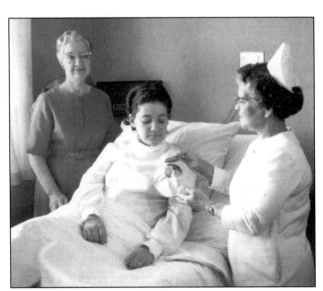

Three women participating in the baby bib project.

Stokes County home demonstration club members donated $4,000 to Stokes-Reynolds hospital to buy an industrial stove for the hospital kitchen. They raised the money from cookbook sales of their club member's recipes.

In 1953, one hundred fifty members of Stokes County home demonstration clubs received home nursing certificates. Members became involved in polio vaccine drives, bloodmobiles, and the TB X-ray mobile unit project.

Watauga County Health Department called on home demonstration members to help furnish and make linens for the new Health Building. The women made one dozen muslin sheets for examination tables, two dozen seersucker examination capes for children, one dozen muslin examination capes for adults, and two dozen towels.

Warren County homemakers furnished two rooms at a cost of $500 each when the Warren General Hospital opened in 1951. They also furnished

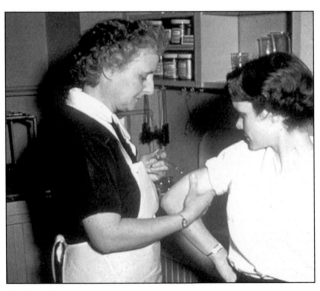

Ouch!

shrubbery for the hospital grounds and volunteered to mend linens and make gowns and aprons for the hospital.

Johnston County home demonstration club members sponsored a county cancer screening program starting in 1958. New Hanover homemakers who had attended first-aid classes conducted by the Red Cross, "adopted" the county home patients and gave bedside care every day.

In the fall of 1952, Mrs. C. Fred Reeves, a home demonstration club member, initiated a volunteer project with the local Veterans Administration hospital in Salisbury. Rowan County homemakers provided flowers for the chapel at least 24 Sundays a year and gave monthly birthday parties for patients.

As a preventive health measure, home demonstration agents and club members paid attention to sanitation issues, including flies and raw sewage, both carriers of disease.

Safety concerns came to the forefront as well. Extension agents and leaders were interested in safer highways, seat-belt legislation, and getting drunk drivers off the roads.

Those white lines on the edge of the highway that make driving so much safer?

They are there due to legislation spearheaded by home demonstration club members in Columbus County. One of their leaders was on the board of the North Carolina Safety Council and was able to voice the concerns of her sister club members until action was taken.

Rural families expressed the desire for recreation programs in their communities. So, the North Carolina

HD and Farm Bureau picnics help communities get together.

Recreation Commission and the North Carolina Agricultural Extension Service worked together to develop leadership in rural recreation. Lonnie Powell, specialist in recreation with the State Commission, held training schools for Extension agents and leaders in 20 counties.

The reading program, started in 1938, was going strong 20 years later.

In 1954, for example, Madison County homemakers set aside money from a *Progressive Farmer Award* to start a library fund.

Extension reading program is still popular.

Picnic fun for all.

Ruth Current, State Home Demonstration Leader, with foreign visitors. Portrait is of Mrs. Jane S. McKimmon.

One of their strong leaders, Mrs. Dorothy Shupe worked hard to persuade county commissioners to support the effort, even after she found that $3,000 would be needed to start a building fund. County officials said they could not include the money in the budget for that year. They did agree to set money aside the following year, provided the women could raise the $3,000 needed for the start-up.

County officials had no idea how serious the home demonstration women were. The women combed the county until they raised $3,344. The library started modestly in a used mobile home, but it was a beautiful sight to Madison County women.

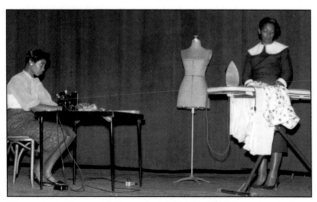

Two women demonstrating tasks on a stage 1959.

Bookmobile.

Orange County Home Demonstration Chorus making recording for WPTF, May 12, 1952.

Dr. Arnold E. Hoffman, music supervisor with the State Department of Public Instruction, with his assistants, has conducted 15 training schools for home demonstration club music leaders, reaching 2,200 for leadership in this project.

Music training school in Nash County finds men and women holding hymnals and singing in pews.

In the same vein, Polk County homemakers wanted to get a bookmobile in the county. They contacted the State Library for information and were told they might do well to organize a countywide meeting of all civic organizations, with a state library staff member as speaker.

When they learned a library for basing the bookmobile was essential, the home demonstration women decided to go all they way. They spoke at PTA meetings and civic clubs and borrowed a bookmobile from Henderson County, which they took to all the schools.

They also mimeographed information which they distributed across the county. A special tax election was held and funding for the library passed. The positive vote was in good part due to the efforts of the home demonstration women.

At the end of the 1950s, the North Carolina Rural Library Program was a network of libraries on wheels. Home demonstration agents and club members helped raise the funds needed to buy the bookmobiles. In fact, North Carolina had more bookmobiles serving rural areas than any other state. There were 105 bookmobiles serving 94 of the state's 100 counties.

Extension home demonstration also fostered the improvement of music programs in rural areas. Ruth Current, state home agent, initiated the program with the help of the State Education Supervisor of Public School Music, Dr. Arnold Hoffman, and six consultants.

Catawba music workshop, 1954.

The music program took hold in the counties in 1951 and was organized at the local level around rural church choirs and interested groups and individuals. A director and a pianist were chosen for each county. The "county chorus" met for weekly rehearsals, usually eight months a year.

The choruses sang at home demonstration club events from the local to the national level. They also sang at civic clubs, local special events, and on radio and television.

Extension and the public music staff offered a similar school to train rural church choirs. The first was held in Durham County. It was so successful, similar programs were requested across the state.

In 1958, Dr. W. Kenneth Cuyler of Durham gave the initial money to fund scholarships for the music training schools. Named in honor of Mrs. Cuyler, 12 scholarships were made available to rural music leaders to attend a home demonstration music workshop at Catawba College. The number and corresponding value of these scholarships grew steadily, eventually

reaching 32 awards. The scholarship and general music fund were completely financed by contributions from home demonstration club members and donations from interested people throughout the state, including Dr. Cuyler.

Home demonstration representatives and Latin American men and women in front of a training center built with funds donated by the Associated County Women of the World.

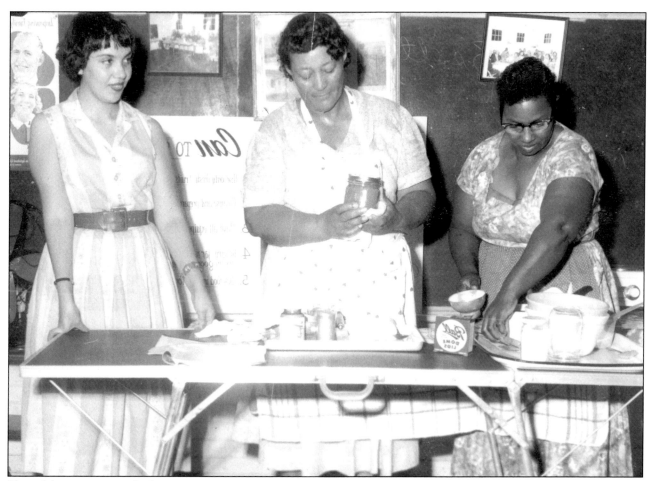

Three club women giving a leader program.

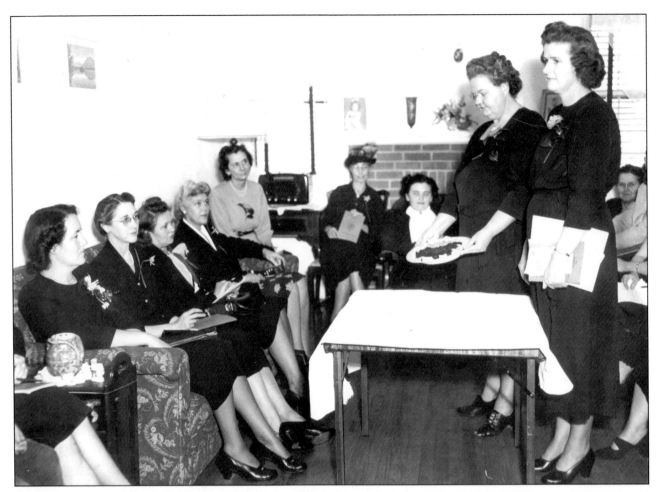

HD club leader meeting.

Dr. Frank Porter Graham addresses home demonstration women touring United Nations headquarters in New York.

North Carolina had the honor of hosting the National Home Demonstration Council (NHDC) annual conference in Raleigh in 1952. NHDC had representatives from Extension home demonstration clubs across the nation.

North Carolina's homemakers have been strong supporters of NHDC's international efforts. They supported UNICEF, the International Peace Garden on the US-Canadian border, and projects, such as Pennies for Friendship and Letter Friends. Money from Pennies for Friendship was used to support international programs.

Letter Friends allowed Tar Heel homemakers to get acquainted with rural women in other parts of the world by exchanging letters about family and community. In 1958, there were 163 Letter Friends among the club women and 57 friendship parcels were shipped overseas.

Club women also adopted a 10-year-old Korean girl war orphan, sent money to Ceylon for equipment for a village Home Demonstration Training Center, and sent money to Pakistan for books and other items needed for a home economics library.

Following the 16th annual National Home Demonstration Council meeting in Raleigh, October 25-29, 1952, the Country Women's Council sponsored an international tea to raise money for the Pennies for Friendship fund. Mrs. Everett Spangler of Nebraska, chairman, and collectors Nubuko Kawano, Japan, and Ziggie Smits, Mrs. David Yandle, and Sara Jo Anne Wireman, all of Raleigh.

Women carry international flags into the National Home Demonstration Council meeting held in Raleigh in 1952.

In a seven-year period, 588 home demonstration club members went on a tour to the United Nations Headquarters. They had briefings about the Security Council, General Assembly, and numerous international committees including UNICEF, the World Health Organization, and International Refugees.

During visits to the United Nations, the Extension home demonstration women had the chance to meet distinguished Americans including former first lady Eleanor Roosevelt, and diplomat Frank Porter Graham, a North Carolina native.

When they returned home, the Extension women gave talks, wrote news articles, and did radio programs about the UN. They sponsored poster contests for school children, encouraged schools to serve a foreign dish at lunch, and encouraged a study of the countries that make up the UN.

Club members had high praise for the UN tours. As one homemaker put it, "The only downside of the trip was that the bunions on my feet hurt."

United Nations seminar group, 1953.

Mrs. Pate, Dr. Frank Porter Graham, and Eleanor Roosevelt at United Nations, 1953.

Members of the Associated Country Women of the World visit North Carolina and meet with home demonstration agents Ruth Current and Verna Stanton and Agricultural Extension Director David S. Weaver.

Eleanor Roosevelt was no stranger to North Carolina. She often accepted speaking invitations including one to appear at a conference of North Carolina Extension home demonstration club members in October, 1959. She spoke about the refugee crisis around the world and what North Carolinians might do to help.

There were a couple of other important events in the decade:

In 1955, a contract was signed with the Bureau of Indian Affairs and the North Carolina State University for a local Extension office to be located on the Cherokee Reservation.

Homemaker clubs had been a part of the Reservation for many years, after sewing clubs had been established through the schools. In 1955, the sewing clubs became part of the Extension home demonstration program.

About the same time, the Village of Yesteryear became an important part of the North Carolina State Fair. The first year, home agents and home demonstration members from Western North Carolina conducted a craft fair in the Village. Men and women brought their crafts and worked throughout the week. Crafts included wood carving, weaving, wrought iron work, and lace making.

Mary Cornwell, home demonstration agent in Haywood County, supervised the popular fair attraction for many years.

Progressive Farmer cover-making UN flags.

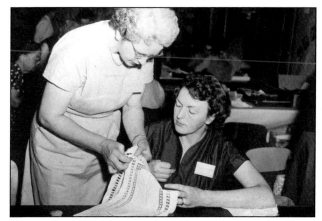

Two women working together on a crafts project.

A final look at the '50s.

Homemaker gets homemade cakes ready for curb market.

Durham County Curb Market-woman selling melons.

Nita Orr, foods specialist, freezing vegetables.

HD agent looks at canned goods in a family larder.

Display of canned fruits and vegetables needed to supply a family of five during nonproductive months, Moore County, October 1956.

Uses of Old Shirts

Display demonstrating clothing made from old shirts.

Lady making presentation to a group.

County dress revue.

Savings bond poster shows money home demonstration members saved by using Extension tips.

Tobacco referendum, home demonstration women assist with voting, Warren County.

Iola Pritchard, food specialist, canning green beans.

Home demonstration club women enjoy a sewing demonstration.

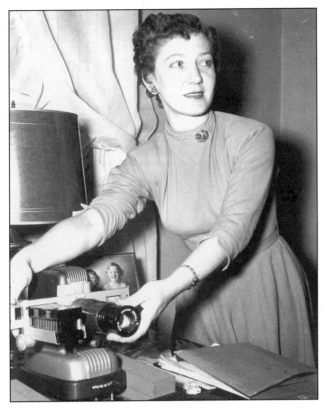

Slides help to get information across.

Donation to Red Cross.

Village of Yesteryear began at the State Fair in the 1950s.

A fun way to share Extension know-how.

New Hanover float at the Azalea Festival.

Float in parade, Conservation & Preservation of Food.

Home demonstration club members share what they learned with others.

1960–1970
A DECADE OF SOCIAL CHANGES

The 1960s could be described as a decade of change for the North Carolina Agricultural Extension Service.

One of the greatest changes was social. The Extension Service racially integrated its staff, offices, organizations, and programs.

Name changes followed integration. Extension agents received a title change from home demonstration agents to Extension home economics agents. The home demonstration clubs and councils became the Extension Homemakers Clubs and Councils. The traditional Farm and Home Week was renamed Extension Homemakers Week.

Name changes extended to the national level where the National Home Demonstration Council became the National Extension Homemakers Council.

Demand for Extension information also changed. Urban homemakers found out their country cousins had a pipeline to research-based information and they wanted to have the same services. By the 1960s Extension's homemakers members were 50 percent rural and 50 percent urban.

Extension home economics agent looks at blueprints with a couple planning to build a new house.

Extension staffers were well aware families had changed. No longer were most families composed of husband, wife, and two-and-a half children. There were singles, single parent households, blended families, two- or three-generation families, "empty nesters" and seniors. Extension wanted to serve all these family units, as well as traditional families, and program changes reflected this.

Beginning Families publication is popular with young married.

Home economics agent talks to mothers about child development.

Orange County Extension Home Economist Bonnie Davis leads a discussion of home finances.

Brides were on Extension's radar screen. The family life specialists prepared a packet of information about the significance of the marriage ceremony, marriage adjustment, in-laws, and money matters.

The information was available at register-of-deeds offices. Mailing lists were developed by reading newspaper announcements of marriages and from word-of-mouth, especially from relatives or friends of a bride-to-be.

Those who cared for young children received special attention from Extension agents and leaders. Young mothers had access to child care information as did day care, nursery school, kindergarten, and church school workers. Again, the information was prepared by Extension family life specialists and distributed by Extension agents and leaders.

More mothers of young children were joining the workforce, creating a need for child care services. Extension home economics agents helped individuals and groups with plans and resources for opening child care centers.

The agent in Cleveland County, who had advocated such a center for several years, happily reported that the Light Oak Community leased 10 acres in the community rent-free, so such a center could be built.

The senior citizen population in North Carolina was growing fast. Not only was attention to health and diet prolonging the lives of sons and daughters of the state – but North Carolina was gaining attention as a retirement mecca for people from other states.

Weaving is a popular craft.

Foods and nutrition specialist leading agent training class with poster showing a cartoon man in a cauldron and with text "How to cook a husband ~ the choice is yours".

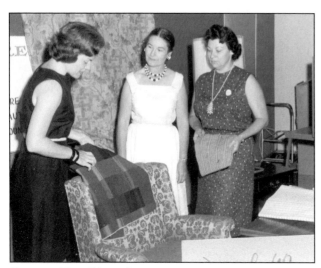

Consumer Tips: Fabric selection.

How to shop for furniture, how to spend food dollars wisely, how to shop for children's toys, how to buy insurance, and wise use of credit were just some of the topics.

To help reach busy families with consumer information, agents, specialists, and leaders hosted special interest and "lunch and learn" sessions. They did programs and gave out information in shopping centers, and used radio, television, newspapers, newsletters, and pamphlets to reach Extension and non-Extension families.

Extension hired a specialist in aging to develop programs and train agents in how to help meet the needs of senior citizens. Attention was given to retirement living choices, changes in nutritional needs, and living comfortably on a reduced income.

The consumer also received special attention. A statewide program *Calling Consumers* was launched by Extension and these programs emphasized the buying, rather than the production, of household necessities.

Consumer Tips: Buying Furniture.

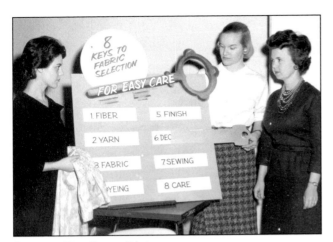

Consumer Tips: Buying Fabrics.

Proper nutrition and its importance to health was emphasized for young and old, families of moderate means, and low-income families.

Those receiving donated foods or participating in the food stamp program received help from Extension home economists and Extension homemakers club members.

Consumer Marketing Specialist Ruby Uzzle.

Home economics agent shows new fabrics and fabric finishes on camera in WUNC-TV studio, 1967.

Two women demonstrating how to prepare cornmeal mix.

The women gave food demonstrations at distribution sites using donated foods in the dishes they prepared. Of course, they offered samples of those dishes and most agreed the foods were mighty tasty. Welfare recipients were the audience most often reached at the food sites, and eight counties alone reported working with 3,087 families.

Demonstrations were popular with this group. When the program was evaluated, between 80 and 90 percent of the homemakers said they were preparing new dishes for their families using donated foods.

Agents in counties with the food stamp program took recipients into grocery stores and talked about food buying, with emphasis on making wise economic and nutritional choices.

Since low-income families as a whole were unaccustomed to participating in organized groups, much work was done one-on-one or in small groups. Extension homemakers club members did much of the neighbor-to-neighbor contact.

In addition to providing improved nutrition to needy families, the donated foods program was a launching pad for cooperation among Extension, health, and welfare workers. It also demonstrated the value of well-

EFNEP aide makes a home visit.

trained non-professionals on both a voluntary and paid basis.

The Expanded Food and Nutrition Education Program (EFNEP), a federally funded program, was launched in several counties. Program aides were hired and trained to visit the homes of lower-income families

102

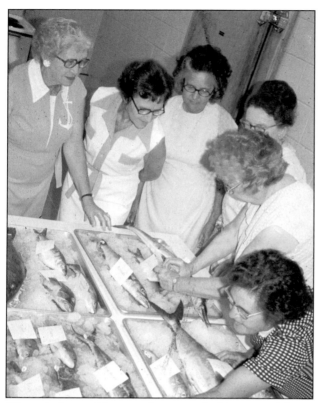
Women looking at fish on ice, during a seafood buying workshop.

to teach homemakers how to serve nutritious foods, while stretching the food dollar.

Special recipes were created that featured the donated ingredients from the surplus food program. Families were taught how to get the most value and nutrition from their food stamps and donated foods.

Once trust was established, the EFNEP aide could make suggestions on better sanitation in the home and outdoors and could keep an eye on the health of the family's children.

As families progressed in the program, EFNEP homemakers often got together for meetings and frequently formed a support group for each other. In the summer months many counties held camps for the children of EFNEP homemakers. The program continues today.

The housing program continued to gain momentum. Extension housing specialists continued to design house plans. One year they built a house with a plywood exterior as a state fair exhibit. The house, which cost about $6,000 to build, was paid for with money donated by the Eastern North Carolina Lumber Manufacturers Association.

Swain County Extension homemakers made housecoats for hospital patients.

Extension house plans prove popular with many families.

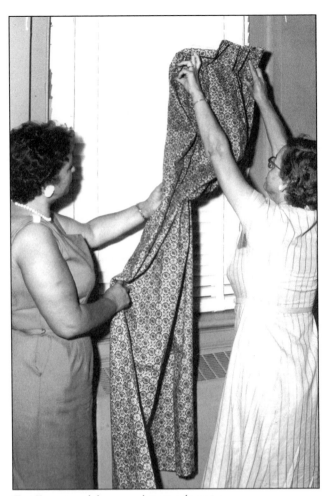

Woman and young girl enjoy updated kitchen.

Two Extension club women hanging draperies.

Demonstration House, Tyrrell County.

Demonstration House, Pender County.

Pender County family relaxes in their new home.

VANCE COUNTY

Demonstration Housing

EXTENSION
AGRICULTURAL ENGINEERING

Reupholstery workshop.

up to learn upholstering, mattress making, furniture refinishing, and curtain making. One neighbor was even inspired to clean her yard and plant a garden.

The county commissioners in Perquimans County not only gave Extension credit for helping improve housing conditions in the county; they gave it credit for improving the tax base.

The furniture, draperies, kitchen appliances, shrubbery, fencing, and materials for the driveway and sidewalk were donated as well.

The three-bedroom, wood frame house had 960 square feet of floor space, plus a carport and outside storage. It was planned for interior comfort, convenience, beauty, durability, and low maintenance. The ribbon cutting at the State Fair was covered by television, newspapers, and radio. Thousands of people walked through the house and asked the Extension staffers, who were hosts and hostesses, many questions.

Another very successful program was a demonstration house in the Kimberly Park area of Winston-Salem. An old six-room apartment was converted into a comfortable home setting to show what could be done with a lot of work and very little money.

Extension agents, program aides, and people who lived in the community bought and refinished second-hand furniture, made mattresses, bedspreads and curtains, and built storage areas for less than $500.

Neighborhood people saw what could be done with know-how and a limited budget. Many signed

Two HE agents discuss carpet selection.

Demonstration House, Orange County.

Before economic conditions improved, many houses in the county were dilapidated. They lacked running water, bathrooms, up-to-date wiring, or other modern conveniences.

To make people aware of modern housing, Extension had house tours of remodeled or new houses and gave housing workshops and seminars. They helped draw house plans and remodeling plans. As a result, houses were improved and so was the county tax base.

Demonstration House, an Orange County family shows off new home.

Better bedding programs gained renewed attention. In 1968, 58 counties held a total of 352 bedding workshops. This time mattresses were made with urethane foam, rather than surplus cotton.

In Caswell County, the county commissioners gave full support to the better bedding program. In fact, they advanced money as a loan to needy families, asking them to repay when "money was available."

One commissioner noted, "We are glad to give money to a program like that. Maybe everyone can't have a good house, but they can all have a comfortable, clean bed."

One Harnett County man said he enjoyed going to the Extension office to help make his mattress and he would not sell it for $100 unless he could have another one.

More than 2,096 foam mattresses were made in one year. A Richmond county woman appreciated her new mattress. She had been sleeping on an old, spotted, stained mattress and she smilingly observed, "I am proud of my nice, clean, new mattress, because I did not want to get sick and die on that old, dirty mattress."

Not all mattresses went into the homes of the makers. The women of Howard Memorial Presbyterian Church in Tarboro bought materials and made four mattresses which they donated to Welfare Department clients.

Money matters always garnered attention. As family incomes improved, families started trading up on clothing, house furnishings and appliances, and other desired products. They made greater use of a new financial tool – the credit card. Home management specialists and county agents held special interest classes and used mass media to encourage families to use credit wisely.

Health programs continued to be an important part of Extension programming. Mental health and the handicapped received special attention.

In 1962, Haywood County was the first in the state for Extension club members to work with the County Mental Health Association. They also worked with alcohol education programs and with special projects in conjunction with the Haywood County Hospital.

Stokes County, in cooperation with the health department, offered a series of seven classes on *Eat to Control Your Weight*. Homemakers also began a volunteer service at Stokes-Reynolds Memorial Hospital.

Home economics agent entering Johnston County Health Center, 1967.

Looking at newest health care products.

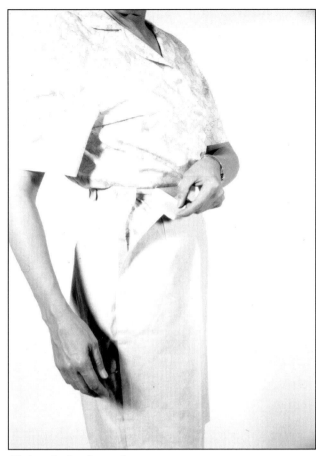

Clothing for handicapped.

Programs and help were also offered to the physically handicapped. Agents and leaders in McDowell County often worked with the deaf. Other counties worked to meet the needs of the blind or people confined to wheelchairs.

Agents offered suggestions on the restyling of garments so they would be easier for a person with arthritis or a similar handicap to put on and take off.

Jane Davidson of Forsyth County and Edith Hinshaw of Rowan designed gadgets to made it easier for handicapped homemakers to open jars, pick up objects from the floor, or do other household chores that are easy for the physically able, but difficult for the handicapped.

In the 1960s literacy continued to be an important issue for Extension and community leaders.

Extension volunteers were trained in district workshops throughout the state to learn the Frank and Robert Laubach method of teaching adults to read.

After the training, the volunteers with the assistance of their home agents, set up very small community classes in homes, in community buildings, and in churches where volunteers taught adults to read.

The most difficult part of the program was identifying non-readers. They had spent their lives keeping their secret.

A truck driver in a Moore County class came into the home agent's office and told her how pleased he was to be able to read. He said, "This is the first time I've been able to read the Bible."

Moore County club members served as tutors in elementary schools, high schools, the community college, and also, in prisons. One member tutored a blind girl who was enrolled in the community college.

The Moore EH Council helped the Rotarians provide every child in one grade in the county with a dictionary.

Extension homemakers, with an interest in international events, continued their study and interest in the United Nations. By the end of 1968, more than 1,300 had taken an Extension-sponsored trip to UN headquarters in New York City.

Safety also attracted attention and in 1961 the Extension clubs in Jackson County received an award

Reading is for everyone.

Child's play is important to child development.

state. Sales increased each year since the market opened in 1958 and by the mid-sixties total sales were at the $350,000 mark each year. Extension helped sellers with quality control, packaging, and marketing.

The first area Extension agent, Edna Bishop, was appointed to work in the state's northeast 10-county

Children learn about colors and shapes.

from the National Safety Council for their development of an effective traffic safety program. Vehicle safety checks and adult driver's training were two of the efforts recognized.

North Carolina became a vacation paradise for many. For years, North Carolina craftsman had been making quality items. Now it was time to set up more marketing opportunities for them.

Counties started working together within districts. There were 439 producers from ten counties working through the Trading Post in the northwest area of the

Children enjoy singing together.

What's New in Food class, 1963 Homemakers Program, North Carolina State College.

Homemakers Week.

Homemakers Week.

Homemakers Week.

Negro State Council meets in early 60s.

Speaker at Negro State Council meeting in the early 60s.

A&T Farmers and Homemakers Convention.

Quilting.

Albemarle area to help develop and market high quality crafts and foods for the tourist trade. The new position was based on a study of the local crafts industry, volume of tourist trade, and the needs of the people.

Workshops were held on pickle and preserves making. Forty people came to a watermelon rind pickle training session and 43 attended a workshop on fig preserves.

Three families in Currituck County made plans for jam kitchens in connection with their roadside stands. Extension helped them through the hurdles, which included conferences with a sanitarian, a representative of the Food and Drug Administration, food scientists, economists, chemists, and food conservation specialists.

Scotland County sewing class.

Crafts workshop.

The Albemarle Craftsman's Guild was organized in 1966 to lend prestige to top craftsmen. The Guild designed a label that members could use when selling their crafts. Guild membership and the use of the indentifying label indicated a certain standard in craftsmanship: a seal of approval.

The annual Albemarle Craftsman's Fair continues to promote the 10-county area and the production and sale of quality crafts. To participate in the fair, the craftsman's product must meet the approval of a Standards Committee.

Each year, more than 40 craftsmen welcome the chance to set up displays at the fair, which always draws more than 2,000 visitors. Small wonder the Albemarle Craftsman's Fair continues to have a high rating on the state Tourist Board's list of things to do.

Northeast district crafts workshop.

114

There were other notable happenings in the 1960s.

Eloise Cofer joined the state Extension staff in January 1963 as assistant Extension director for home economics programs, filling the leadership post previously held by Ruth Current.

Before her appointment in North Carolina, Dr. Cofer was a home economist at the Agricultural Research Station in Beltsville, Maryland.

In 1966, the President of the North Carolina Extension Homemakers Association, Billie Walker, presented Chancellor John T. Caldwell of North

Carolina Farmer Magazine cover about Albemarle Craftsman's Fair.

Woman from National Endowment for the Arts visits Albemarle Craftsman's Fair.

Albemarle Craftsman's Fair participants.

Dr. Cofer and staff in a meeting.

Carolina State University with a check for $100,000 as seed money for a Continuing Education Center on the campus. The check represented the "butter and egg money" of the Extension homemakers of North Carolina.

As another honor, in 1964 the National Extension Homemakers Council officers signed papers incorporating the National Council in the state of North Carolina.

That same year, a special 5-cent homemakers commemorative postage stamp was issued by the U.S postal service. The stamp, a tribute to Homemakers, was placed on sale at Honolulu, Hawaii, in conjunction

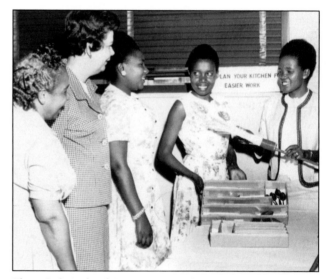

Eloise Cofer and and Genevieve Greenlee with Kenya agents at a kitchen demonstration event.

with the annual meeting of the National Extension Homemakers Council.

The stamp was issued to mark the 50th anniversary of the passage of the Smith-Lever Act, legislation that opened the way to improved home life throughout America by providing Home Economics experts to advise women on better ways to feed, clothe, and care for their families.

Homemakers stamp.

116

Extension Homemakers State President presents check for $100,000 to NCSU Chancellor John T. Caldwell. The check is "Seed Money" for a continuing education center on the university campus.

Traditional skills are still important.

Mother and little girl...dress revue.

Hat making workshop.

Woman with a freezer full of home frozen food.

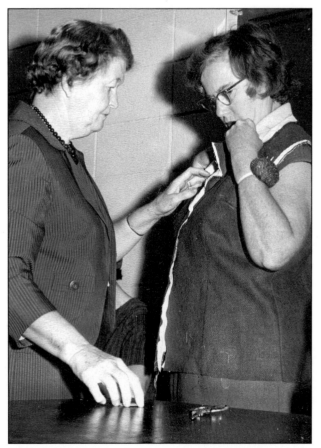

Scotland County sewing class.

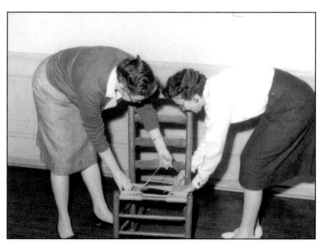

Chair weaving workshop.

Agents Research Tour, Washington, DC.

Home Economics agents are effective whether teaching indoors or out.

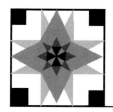

1970–1980
CELEBRATING THE PAST AND PRESENT

The dynamics of North Carolina families continued to change in the 70s, but the commitment of Extension to help families improve their lives and their communities remained the same.

Traditional programs had their place. But new programs needed to be emphasized as well. For example, in addition to canning, freezing, and nutrition, foods leaders stressed getting good value for the money spent in the grocery store. Nutrition labeling materials were developed at the state level and Extension agents used the materials to stress the value of reading labels in relation to wise buying.

Weight control classes and other modified diet programs were developed, in part because of physician referrals and other requests. The programs were especially helpful to those with specific diet needs, including diabetics, or those with a food allergy.

Another innovative program was started in Carteret County. In April, 1973, the Carteret County Extension Homemakers formed an advisory council to work with the staff at the NCSU Seafood Laboratory in Morehead City. This committee assisted the laboratory staff in solving practical problems in the processing, preparing, and cooking of seafood.

This cooperative venture continues today on a one-day-a-month basis and has been the source of a tremendous exchange of knowledge and rapport between the staff and leaders.

The Expanded Food and Nutrition Program (EFNEP) continued to reach low-income families

Extension Food Specialist Marjorie Donnelly tapes a TV program.

throughout the decade. Homemakers in the program received visits from an EFNEP aide for 18 months. After that they graduated into group sessions or received services from Extension through other channels.

Day camps proved to be a popular and rewarding way to reach children of EFNEP families. In 1973, day camps were held in 85 counties, reaching 45,646 youth.

Clothing specialists, agents and leaders still did some sewing and tailoring workshops, but additional attention was given to money-saving tips. Two special interest programs, *Investment Wardrobe Planning* and *Second Edition*, encouraged families to spend their clothing dollars wisely and to take care of clothes so they would last longer.

Making simple alterations give garments more pizzazz and a well-fitted look. The home economics agent on the Cherokee Reservation worked with six senior citizens in correcting low necklines, adjusting shoulder length, and altering for a short waistline in front and lengthened waistline in back. Having clothes that fit properly made the seniors feel more comfortable and look more fashionable.

Physically handicapped people often found shopping for suitable clothing difficult. Extension specialists designed clothing for men, women, and children with certain handicaps. Fashion shows featuring these garments were held for those who worked with the

EFNEP aide helps homemaker can home-grown food.

United Cerebral Palsy Foundation and in rehabilitation services.

Mollye Briley, home economics agent in Robeson County, decided men should be included in the clothing program. She recruited the livestock agent to be her male model. Those at the "fashion show" saw it was possible for a man to make 16 different outfits with just three suits, three shirts, four ties, a vest, and two pairs of shoes.

Carteret County Extension Homemakers form advisory council to NCSU Seafood Lab.

EFNEP kids get together to learn and have fun.

EFNEP lad cultivates family garden.

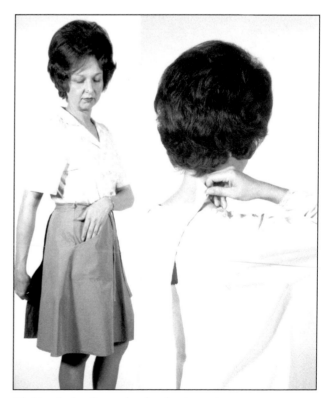

Clothing for handicapped makes dressing easier.

Housing continued to be an important part of the Extension program. With cost of land, building, and financing continuing to go up, families were concerned about getting the best housing for their money.

In 1978, the state office supplied over 4,000 house plans, several of them designed for limited budgets. Six new energy-saving house plans were added in the decade.

Workshops on do-it-yourself home improvements had a lot of people signing up. For good reason. In just one year, 16,225 families, using skills learned from Extension home repair workshops, saved $824,000.

House furnishings specialists, agents and leaders still offered upholstery and chair caning workshops, and drapery- and curtain-making classes. They also helped families select fabrics, furnishings, and floor coverings with an eye to quality and the best value for their dollar.

Attendance at skill training classes increased during the 70s. In 20 counties alone, 10,720 people came to workshops on refinishing, reupholstering, and chair caning. More men were attending Extension-taught

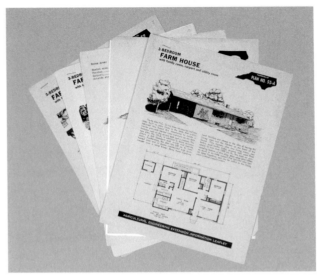

Using Extension house plans means top value for housing dollars.

workshops. These men were often retired and wanted to learn a skill that would give them satisfaction and provide additional income during their retirement years.

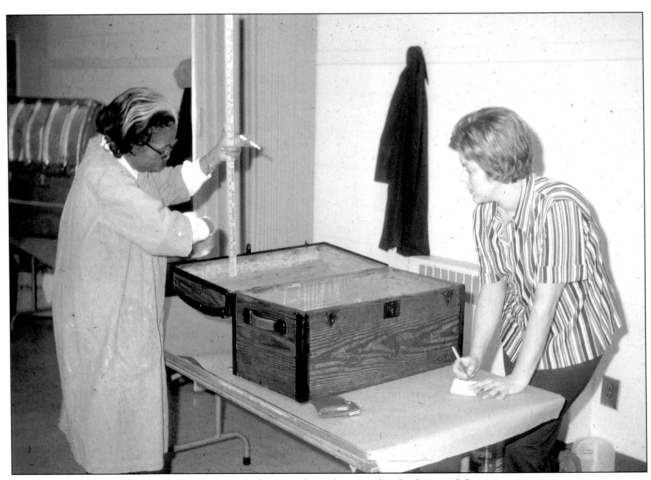

Helen Payne, home economics agent, measures for the lining as she teaches a trunk refinishing workshop.

124

Using skills learned at an Extension workshop lets homemaker give a bedroom a designers touch.

Juanita Lagg, Rowan County, shares information with a legislator.

In Transylvania County, 61 people came to learn refinishing. Their completed pieces had a market value of $3,400.

Iredell County Extension Homemakers worked together to furnish an "idea" house at a cost of about $400. Skills of refinishing furniture, making draperies and accessories spread throughout the county, as visitors saw results of the workshops and requested how-to-do-it information.

Family resource management specialists, agents and leaders helped families meet economic challenges by offering programs and workshops on budgeting, wise use of consumer credit, and estate planning.

Women who worked outside the home and didn't have time to go to meetings, could still get help with financial planning. A home study course in money management was available. In just two years time, 2,367 people used the do-it-yourself packet.

Do-It-Yourself home business area.

decisions about the most costly purchase most would ever make – their house.

Legal rights was a new programming area. A program called *Women and the Law*, helped women navigate Social Security benefits, estate planning and taxes. Two other programs, Family Insurance and Planning for Funerals captured the interest of both husbands and wives.

Two new money decision-making programs, using a programmable calculator, were developed by Extension specialists for use by Extension agents. They used the programs during individual counseling sessions with families. One program *Budget Analysis*, helped clients analyze income, spending, savings, and credit, and made suggestions for improvement. The second program, *Determining the Economic Costs and Benefits of Buying a House*, helped families make

Teletip had messages on financial planning.

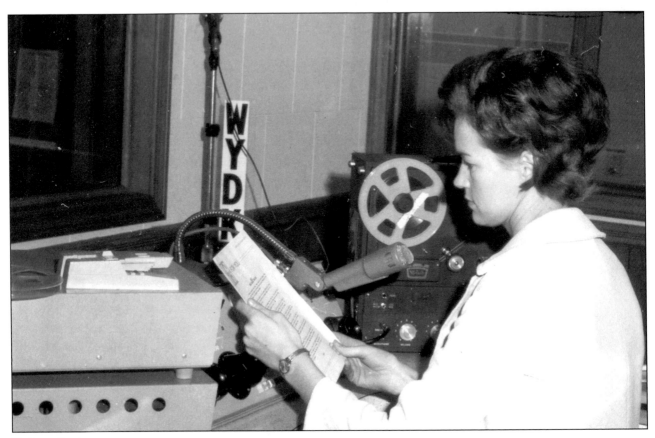
Taping radio show.

One agent used the information about insurance for a radio program. She got five calls from insurance salesmen, complimenting her on the comprehensive and educational value of the program. After she did another program on banking, three bankers called to compliment her on the accurate and helpful information she gave radio listeners.

Senior citizens were given special attention with classes on diet and nutrition needs, clothing that was stylish, but easy to put on and remove. They were shown how to get their homes ready for the retirement years – cabinets at the right height, halls and doorways wide enough for a wheel chair, grab bars in the bathroom shower and tub; brighter lighting, and similar adjustments.

Seniors also were given guidance in living within their smaller incomes. Having a will was stressed, so property would be passed on to their heirs as they wished.

Homemakers get help with nutrition needs.

Extension homemakers listen intently to their home agent.

consumerama '70
now ideas for today's consumers

March 11-15, 1970

Winston-Salem Convention Center

Show Hours 10:00 a.m. - 9:00 p.m.   Sunday 1:00 p.m.-5:00 p.m.

Sponsored by: Forsyth Extension Homemakers Association

Estate planning information proved beneficial to executors of estates as well. One man said what he learned from an Extension estate planning class four years earlier, saved $45,000 in taxes on his aunt's estate. The lawyer figured federal estate taxes to be $50,000. The man challenged the lawyer's figures, got his reference literature, and demanded that the lawyer refigure the taxes. The final amount due ~ $5,000.

On a regional level, agents and leaders in the Northwestern district worked together to sponsor Consumerama – a first-of-its-kind event in Winston-Salem. The 8-day show featured scores of exhibits and demonstrations by professionals in all fields of consumerism. Lectures by nationally known speakers were given daily. Thousands attended the first event in 1970 and Consumerama II in 1972.

Children also received attention from Extension agents and leaders.

In the mid-70s, Extension initiated the Lap Reading Program. Homemaker volunteers worked with Dr. Myrle Swicegood, of the state staff, in helping parents see the need for early childhood involvement to stimulate learning. The American Home Economics

Golden Nuggets booth at Consumerama event.

128

OPEN THE WORLD
BECOME A LAP READER

Ask an Extension Homemaker
North Carolina Agricultural Extension Service

Open the World Lap Reading poster.

the yard to look at plants and animals. In just one year, Extension Homemakers Club members logged 447,725 hours with their 1,920 young lap reader partners.

As part of the Lap Reading program, Sampson County donated hand-crafted dolls to local public libraries to use during story-telling sessions. Polk County Extension Homemakers assisted the Stony Knoll Day Care Center by making a lap quilt for each child. Mecklenburg County homemakers made 40 "learning cubes" for day care centers and kindergartens.

The six sides of the 15-inch "cube" were filled with learning opportunities: a belt to buckle; zippers to zip; snaps, buttons, sneaker eyelet and shoe string for lacings, and similar challenges. The "cubes," if purchased, would have cost at least $98 each.

Years later when Governor Jim Hunt initiated his program for getting preschoolers ready for school, his staff called the Agricultural Extension Service for permission to use materials developed for the Lap Reading program. The effort to stimulate young children to observe and learn continues today under different titles and improvements based on new findings.

Children with special needs received the attention of homemakers in Cabarrus County. They planned parties and special events for the children in the Cerebral Palsy class at Kimball Memorial Church in Kannapolis. In 1972, Stokes County Extension Homemakers helped sponsor a nutrition camp for mentally handicapped children.

Older children also received help from Extension Homemakers. For example, club members in Montgomery County furnished a room for Girl's Haven near Asheboro.

In 1975, Cabarrus County Extension Homemakers decided to "adopt" a ten-year-old Korean child, as the

Association (AHEA) provided a $1,500 grant for the development of leader training materials.

Parents and leaders were encouraged to read to children and interact with them, to look at pictures with them and ask questions, to take them on short trips and talk about their surroundings, or even out in

Lap Reading learning cubes.

Humanities seminar.

129

State gathering of Past Presidents of Home Demonstration and Extension Homemakers organizations.

county project for the year. Chung A Song brought Beethoven to life when she played from memory for 35 minutes at the Extension Homemakers annual achievement program. Club members found ways to help further Chung A in her music education. Bake sales, plant sales and craft sales helped raise over $200 to buy a stereo, which the girl needed so she could practice with training records.

Chung A Song became well known in the Charlotte area, appearing more than 20 times as soloist with the chamber orchestra of the Charlotte Symphony. Audiences were spellbound as they saw a mere child of 10 striking the keys. The Cabarrus Homemakers support of the young prodigy was awarded the "outstanding international project of the year" by the National Extension Homemakers Council.

With Extension programs in 100 counties and the Cherokee Reservation, it's understandable that interests and opportunities would be diverse.

A home economics club for deaf adults was organized in Burke County in 1973 and continued for 25 years.

The National Extension Homemakers Council magazine.

Sarah Nixon working on Tarheel Homemakers newsletter.

130

Cherry Hospital clothing closet, an Extension homemaker community project.

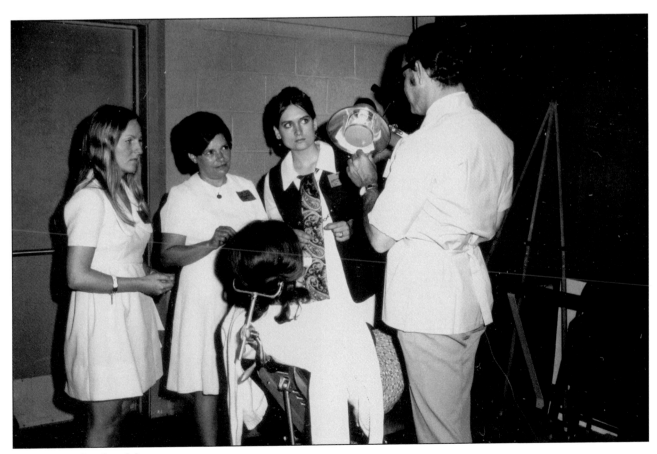

Surry County dental workshop.

Governor Bob Scott signs Proclamation for Extension Homemakers Week.

In 1976, retired teacher Catherine Safrit began an adult literacy program in Rowan County. Twenty years later, she won TV 9's coveted "nine who care" award.

Burke County Extension Homemakers started supporting projects at Options, Inc. in 1978. Options, Inc. is an emergency shelter for victims of domestic violence.

Myrtle McKnight Franks, a former Jones County home agent, continued her association with Extension homemakers clubs after her retirement. Providing garments to those in need was one of her special interests. After securing a donation of tricot fabric, she encouraged her sister club members to make undergarments for the women in the Coastal Woman's Shelter, which assists victims of domestic violence.

Health, safety, and citizenship continued to be of special concern to Extension home economics agents and club members.

Extension homemakers actively supported the drive for a Gates County medical center, which opened September 1979. They helped raise the initial $3,000 and then helped collect an additional $40,000.

A county-wide water system was introduced in Jones County. Homemakers were active in promoting the referendum that made this upgrade of the county water supply possible.

Neighborhood Watch.

Safety was of special concern to Extension home economics agents and club members in several North Carolina counties.

Extension Homemakers in Gaston County, under the leadership of Helen Bess, organized a Concerned Citizens for Justice (CJC) program. Since its birth in the 1970s the program spread to at least 35 other states, which now have Court Watcher programs. The movement served notice to those in the judicial system that ordinary citizens were interested in fair and equal justice for all.

This innovative program won the National Volunteer Award, the North Carolina Rural Safety Council Award, the National Extension Homemakers' Award for Outstanding County Project, and the National Citizenship Award for N.C. Extension Homemakers.

Scotland County Extension Homemakers assisted their local Sheriff's Department in launching the Neighborhood Watch Program, a national effort aimed at helping individuals and families prevent and reduce crime to their home and property. North Carolina Extension Homemakers helped promote the Neighborhood Watch Program across the state.

A different type of opportunity greeted homemakers in one western North Carolina county. In 1972, Buncombe County Homemakers presented a Christmas Ideas exhibit by decorating the Governor's western residence and opening it to the public. More than 1,000 people went through the house in one day,

Extension Homemakers visit General Assembly.

which was the largest number to attend a gathering there.

Far away communities received Extension Homemakers Club members' attention. While serving as International Chairman for the National Extension Homemakers Council (NEHC) Juanita Lagg of Rowan County, traveled to Guatemala on a fact-finding mission for a new project to undertake with International Understanding Funds.

In cooperation with the American Home Economics Association (AHEA) and the Ministry of Education in Guatemala, NEHC provided a salary for a full-time home economics worker in the village of San Pedro, Aympuc. They also gave funds for a three-room community center, where nutrition, sanitation and sewing lessons could be provided. This project continued until the political leadership in Guatemala changed hands.

Dr. Eloise Cofer and Juanita Lagg on a fact-finding mission in a Guatemalan village.

EH quilters in Alamance County.

Bi-Cenntenial Celebration encourages traditional crafts.

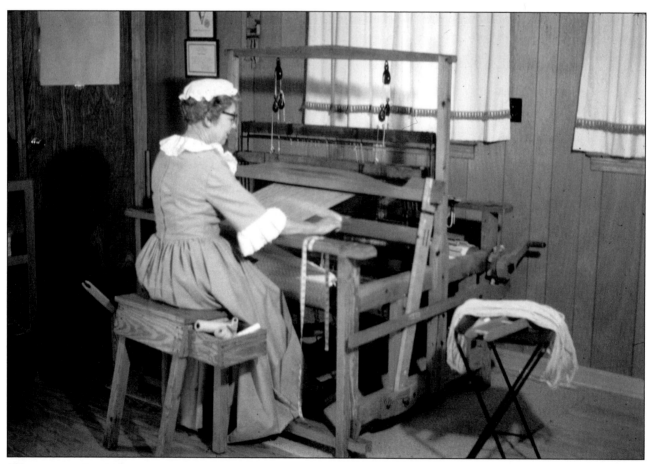

EH woman weaving at a loom.

In the 70s, there was one event that was an attention-grabber nationwide. The United States was getting ready for, and then celebrating, its 200th anniversary.

When the United States celebrated its bicentennial in 1976, Extension agents and leaders eagerly delved into the country's heritage. Many Extension Homemakers enjoyed learning traditional skills, such as quilting, weaving, and embroidery and they relished playing an important part in their community bicentennial events.

Forsyth County Extension Homemakers staged a two-day celebration at the Dixie Classic fairgounds. Dressed in costumes of pioneer days, club members demonstrated methods of baking bread, making kraut, turning ice cream, churning butter, pressing apple cider, curing hams, and everything in between. They explained root cellars and herb gardens, dried apples, and demonstrated tying tobacco, quilting, soap making, weaving, chair caning, and other crafts they had revived for the occasion.

In Polk County, Extension leaders taught quilting to senior citizens, girls groups, and other homemakers club members. The Extension Homemakers club members made a quilt and sold it. They used the profit to set up a hearing aid bank for testing hearing, reconditioning old hearing aids and fitting them for customers.

Many hand-crafted bicentennial quilts now proudly hang in Extension offices, county buildings, and mayor's offices.

EH Hand-crafted quilt.

Group of women attend a quilting activity.

Group of women attend a decorative painting workshop.

North Carolina residents also used the bi-centennial as an incentive to clean up and improve home grounds and communities. In Chowan County, club women worked to help establish a county-wide trash pick-up and water system. In Dare County, Hatteras club members designed, built, and put up street signs in their village.

In preparation for the bi-centennial celebration, Extension Homemakers in Ashe County planted dogwood trees and painted the picket fence and masonry on the Jefferson village green.

To celebrate the bi-centennial, Buncombe County Extension Homemakers chose to participate in the restoration of the Smith-McDowell House, which later became a Heritage Center for western North Carolina. Built in 1840, the Smith-McDowell house was one of the oldest homes in Asheville. Homemakers restored one room in the house.

Village of Yesteryear at State Fair.

Village of Yesteryear celebrates traditional crafts.

Permanent home for traditional crafts.

In 1975, homemakers clubs in Haywood County launched a $50,000 campaign to have a house that would serve as a permanent home for authentic heritage handicrafts of North Carolina and the Appalachian region. In 1978, as a result of dinners, bake sales, cookbook sales, flea markets, bazaars and individual contributions, the money was raised.

The bi-centennial found Extension homemakers in Craven County operating a "tea-tasting" shop and holding a craft show and sale in the Mohn house of the Tryon Palace complex. Over 3,000 visitors from 28 states and three foreign countries enjoyed the tea and benne seed cookies served by homemakers dressed in authentic colonial costumes during the two-day event.

Extension Homemakers were very involved in the bi-centennial celebration in Halifax County. They launched an 18th century craft house during the Halifax Week celebration. The craft house was so popular it became part of an annual event in which local craftsmen demonstrate and sell their handiwork.

EH 50th Anniversary celebration, 1970.

The bi-centennial was a reason to celebrate, but there was another important anniversary. In 1970, the North Carolina Extension Homemakers Association celebrated its 50th anniversary.

There were other notable events that marked the 70s.

The opening of the Jane S. McKimmon Continuing Education Center was a dream come true for Extension Home Economics club leaders, agents and state staff. The center opened its doors on the NC State University Campus October 18, 1976.

Six hundred people attended the first Family Living Seminar, *Living with Change*, sponsored by Extension, October 5-7, 1976. Dr. Edward Metzen, President, American Consumers Council, was the keynote speaker.

Extension Home Economics became a department at North Carolina State University and specialists could get academic rank.

The Extension Homemakers Association held a statewide conference on human abuse in 1976. More

EH 50th Anniversary celebration.

than 400 people received information on the problem, laws concerning abuse, resources, and what citizens could do.

Extension Homemakers were pleased to have Isabelle Fletcher from Kinston elected to the National

Extension Homemakers Council (NEHC) Board of Directors. The Lenoir County resident was the first North Carolinian to be elected to the national board. Juanita Hudson from Harnett County was appointed to a two-year term as NEHC national cultural arts chairman. Juanita Lagg of Rowan County was the national organization's chair for International for two years.

In 1972, North Carolina delegates to the NEHC national meeting in Baltimore, Maryland, spearheaded a *Nickels for National* campaign. A fund was set up to

Jane McKimmon's son at McKimmon Center dedication.

Jane McKimmon's son at McKimmon Center dedication.

accept nickels from members across the country and those nickels were used for leadership development. In 1987 the fund was renamed *Nickels for Leadership*.

Women advanced in leadership roles. Frances Voliva was the first woman named as County Extension Chairman. Betsy Meldau was the first woman appointed as a district chairman.

McKimmon Center becomes a reality in 1976.

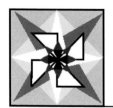

1980-1990
THREE BIG "E's" DEMAND ATTENTION FROM EXTENSION

Three big "E's" – economics, energy, and the environment – demanded the attention of Extension staffers and leaders during the 1980s.

In the early years of the decade, the inflation rate was hitting double digits and interest rates were running as high as 20 percent. The traditional areas of Extension – clothing, foods and nutrition, family resource management, and housing and house furnishings – offered practical information to families that could help them live within their means.

For example, most families could cut clothing bills by 10 percent a year, if they followed wise buying practices and found additional ways to extend the life of garments. Making clothes at home also meant substantial savings. Sewing workshops were held in 75 counties. Agents noticed many women had basic sewing skills, but needed help with construction details.

A recycling workshop in Cumberland County found women transforming mini-dresses into blouses and jackets, and revamping outdated, ill-fitting coats into attractive "new" styles.

Food often takes up a fair share of the family's budget. To help make ends meet, families were given

Family enjoys healthy meal and saves dollars using Extension tips.

tips on nutrition, food buying, preparation, and preservation.

North Carolina had a higher mortality rate than the national average for heart disease, stroke, and diabetes. Extension's *Eat Right for Life* program offered reliable research-based information about altering food choices to prevent illness and improve wellness.

Extension homemakers learn to use leadership skills for "greater good."

Inflation headlines.

Master Food Preserver shares tips with others.

In one innovative effort, 37 food leaders in Forsyth County's Extension homemakers clubs were trained to talk about good nutrition and the use of fruits and vegetables in the diet. Those leaders worked for three days in seven different stores, talking with more than 2,000 shoppers about wise food choices.

Also, Extension food and nutrition specialists kept an eye on the prices of a North Carolina "Market Basket" of selected foods. Every other week, consumers could get an update on best food buys from Extension just by making a telephone call.

Food preservation remained an important part of the Extension program. In 1980, the value of foods preserved at home reached the $7 million mark. Perhaps because of hard times, home drying of foods was also on the rise. In Beaufort County alone, programs on drying food attracted over 300 people.

Home management specialists and agents were ready with information on budgeting, shopping, and credit practices.

Home study courses on money control and home buying were popular with people who didn't have time to go to meetings or wished to keep their financial information private. For those who asked for assistance, counseling on money management was available.

When it came to improving shopping skills, families were encouraged to comparison shop, evaluate claims, know the difference between family "wants" and "needs", use coupons and refunds, and shop at discount and outlet stores. Almost 55,000 people gave Extension credit for helping them improve their shopping skills.

Young family shopping for household items.

Eat Right for Life computer program.

Home management agent training.

Inflation and high interest rates resulted in a farm crisis in the '80s, leaving many families on the edge of bankruptcy. Agriculture economists and home economics specialists with law degrees, prepared materials and held meetings on bankruptcy laws. Extension also initiated *Farmline*, where families could telephone for advice from the attorneys. Each call required 2 to 2-1/2 hours for intake, research, and follow up.

The attorneys also networked with the N.C. Bar Association, N.C. Farm Bureau, and the Land Loss

Master Food Preserver takes phone calls about home canning.

prevention project and trained other attorneys on bankruptcy law provisions for farm reorganization.

Hard times had some people thinking about taking their sewing, crafts, baking, or other skills and starting a home business. Extension lawyers prepared fact sheets on the legal aspects of owning your own business.

Farm crisis hits home

Sen. Jesse Helms got riled aplenty in late July when a colleague addressed Republican Majority Leader Bob Dole of Kansas as the "real chairman" of the Senate Agriculture Committee. Yet, considering all of the farm crises that have cropped up in the Reagan administration, it's a wonder that Helms isn't happy to give Dole all the credit.

Credit was something withdrawn temporarily this week from FCX Inc., the Carolina farmer-owned cooperative that filed for reorganization under federal bankruptcy

of the committee could "like it or lump it." Helms' bull-in-a-china-shop approach is why Dole had to take a major role in 1981 to get a farm bill passed.

Helms and some of his staff have spent a lot of time and energy trying to reshape the federal tobacco program, of course. He could hardly represent North Carolina and ignore tobacco's problems. But he's just struck a deal on tobacco with the Senate Finance Committee that's more favorable to cigarette manufacturers than to growers.

It's also clear that Helms has

Farm crisis headline.

142

Refinishing furniture can lead to small business opportunity.

More than 950 people attended a one-day seminar on small business ownership. Extension materials were also used in community college classes and by workers in the Small Business Program.

Also, Extension specialists and agents gave 248 programs on wise use of credit. More than 16,000 people found the information helpful.

Housing specialists and agents did numerous workshops emphasizing home repairs. In just one year, families used their Extension-learned skills to save $1,091,838 in home repair and care expenses.

An additional 22,008 families saved another $800,000 by becoming do-it-yourselfers in the house furnishings area – making draperies, caning chairs, or refinishing furniture.

Extension agents and leaders found many different ways to share their information with others.

They knew more and more women were working outside the home and had limited time for meetings outside the workplace. Extension agents and leaders often went to work places, presenting "lunch and learn" programs. Some women signed up to be "mail box" members of Extension Homemakers.

Agents worked closely with their local media, writing news articles, and often were in a radio station doing interviews or seen on a local television program doing interviews or special demonstrations.

In addition, Extension offered three economics-related radio services to commercial stations across the state. *The Economic Perspective* gave in-depth information on the causes and cures of inflation. *Money Matters* zeroed in on home management and consumer tips and *Just a Minute* offered 60-second messages, emphasizing consumer and energy tips.

EH member sells handmade baskets at craft fair sponsored by Extension.

Extension agent offers advice on buying furniture.

A newsletter was another fast way to get information to people.

Agents and leaders found that giving presentations or having exhibits in shopping areas helped them reach a lot of county residents.

In the 1980s, Extension Teletip was in constant use. Teletip, a dial access program launched in the late '70s, made information on more than 1,000 topics as close as the telephone. Topics included home economics subjects, such as nutrition and family finance, and homeowner topics, including gardening, lawn care, and getting rid of household pests.

The information for Teletip messages was prepared by subject matter specialists at N.C. State University and edited and voiced by editors in the Agricultural Communications Department. Messages were dubbed onto cassettes that could be inserted into a playback unit attached to a telephone line. Eight lines were needed to handle the calls.

Couple talks with Extension agent about money management.

A Teletip directory was prepared listing all the topics. In each county, the directory was distributed by agents and leaders. With directory-in-hand, the caller would dial a toll-free number, an operator would answer, and the information was sent over the phone line.

Teletip operators answered their one millionth telephone call on June 26, 1986.

"Master" programs in food preservation, money manager, and waste management made Extension agents' time more elastic, while ensuring that North Carolina residents had the information they needed when they sought it. Master volunteers received in-depth training in exchange for hours of volunteer service. Master volunteers could help with training and demonstrations, answer questions, and lend a helping hand where needed.

Credit cards.

The scarcity and increased costs of fuels had a severe impact on family life. The Synergy program, developed by N.C. State Extension specialists offered numerous ways that families could save energy dollars. Families were reminded that federal tax credits were available for using energy conserving materials in home remodeling or building, and that state tax credits were available for passive and active solar systems.

Clothing specialists and agents emphasized the thermal properties of certain fabrics and layering of clothes. They also noted that you lose 90 percent of body heat through the top of the head. Wearing a hat in winter would increase comfort. They also suggested laundering techniques that would help save water.

Extension Teletip operators Louise and Betty get their 1,000,000th call.

Alexander County Extension energy workshop attracts many.

Door stop saves energy dollars.

house, proving a solar house could look like a "regular house" both inside and out.

To complete their work, the specialists secured $12,000 worth of donated furnishings and designed window treatments that added beauty and energy efficiency to the house.

There was increased interest in energy-saving alternatives in house building, such as solar, earth-sheltered, and other less traditional methods of construction. In 1981, a passive solar research and demonstration house was built on the N.C. State University campus.

Extension home furnishings specialists decorated the inside to complement the traditional architecture of the

Caulk windows to stay warm, save money.

Solar House sun room.

Solar House living room.

Solar House exterior shows passive solar sunspace and solar panels on the roof.

Living area in the Solar House is warm and inviting.

Extension home furnishings specialists work in the Solar House.

The house allowed building professionals to update their knowledge of solar design from the research and training programs conducted at the center. Over 50,000 people toured the house each year through the '80s.

The Guilford County Solar Communities Program (GSCP) was an outreach of the North Carolina Cooperative Extension Service. Guilford Solar was made up of citizens with a wide range of interests relating to solar and other forms of renewable energy.

Formed in 1982, the Guilford County program is the longest running of its type in North Carolina. Over the years, the organization has conducted numerous workshops and in the early '90s sponsored the first green building conference in the state.

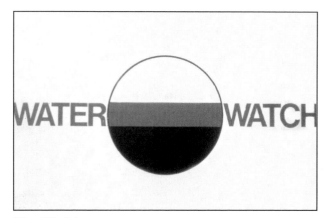

Water Watch logo.

Water conservation, installing a toilet dam.

Other Extension offerings had the environment in their sights. In 1981, Extension established a *Water Watch* program to help residents conserve water supplies.

The use of water saving devices, such as low-volume showerheads, faucet aerators, and toilet dams, was encouraged, as were smart laundering practices. By using suggestions offered in *Water Watch*, many families saved more than $100 a year.

In the mid '80s, more than 121,000 families reduced their energy and water use, saving $132,832 by installing auxiliary heating devices, water-saving gadgets, and selecting energy-saving window treatments.

Extension educated the public and trained professionals to deal with radon, a naturally occurring gas that poses a health risk if it accumulates in a building.

EH member who designed Scotland County flag.

Adding weatherstripping to windows equals warmth and money savings.

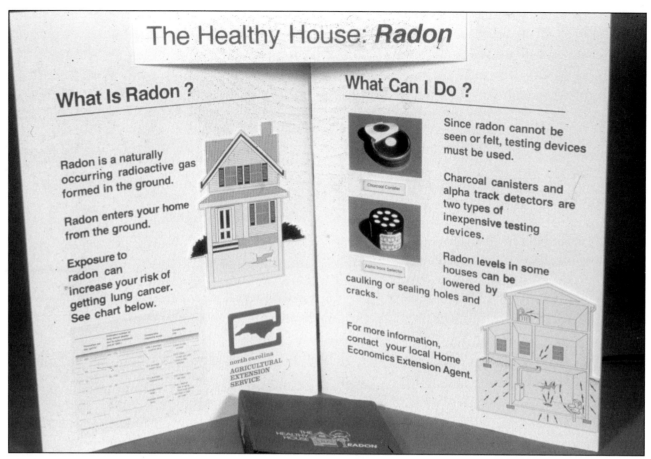

The Healthy House: *Radon*

What Is Radon?

Radon is a naturally occurring radioactive gas formed in the ground.

Radon enters your home from the ground.

Exposure to radon can increase your risk of getting lung cancer. See chart below.

north carolina
AGRICULTURAL
EXTENSION
SERVICE

What Can I Do?

Since radon cannot be seen or felt, testing devices must be used.

Charcoal Canister

Charcoal canisters and alpha track detectors are two types of inexpensive testing devices.

Alpha Track Detector

Radon levels in some houses can be lowered by caulking or sealing holes and cracks.

For more information, contact your local Home Economics Extension Agent.

Extension educated the public and trained professionals to indentify and deal with radon, a naturally occurring gas that poses a health risk if it accumulates inside a building.

More than 44,480 North Carolina households learned about radon health risks, tested their homes for radon, or adopted measures to reduce radon levels in their homes. More than 200 builders and county building inspectors received training on radon-resistant new construction.

Stanly County EH members helped get recycling started in this county.

Recycling caught on. At least one county, Lincoln, made sure people could find the recycling site. Homemakers club members bought a sign that directed residents to the right location.

A newly organized Extension homemakers club in Moore County voted to make the environment their special project. Among their efforts: adopt a highway

These Orange County EH members helped get this green box in their area.

Two Stanly County EH members educate shoppers about recycling.

Salk, clinical professor, pediatrics psychology, Cornell University Medical College.

In some counties, Extension agents and leaders were trained to help establish widowhood support groups in conjunction with churches or mental health organizations. By the end of 1982, almost 600 widowhood support groups were organized and 5,408 people were participating in the program.

to clean, and recycle glass, newspapers, and aluminum cans. They also sponsored a recycling poster contest for second and third graders.

Extension Family Living programs contributed substantially to the quality of life of North Carolina citizens.

Stepfamilies received special attention in 1981. A one-day conference on stepfamilies was so well received, the Extension staff decided to hold eight or nine similar regional conferences and invite the general public. One-parent families were the thrust of a family living seminar held the next year. Keynoter was Dr. Lee

Grandmother reading to child is fun for both.

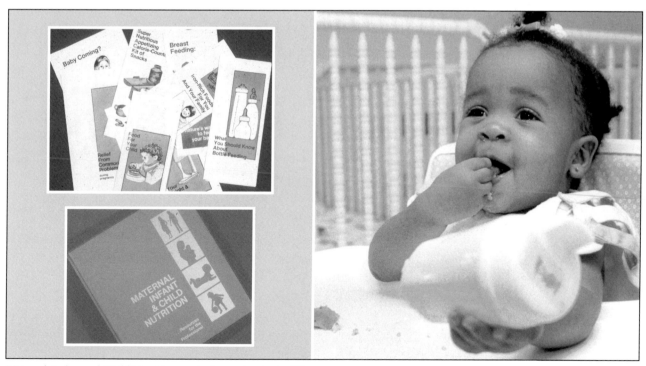

Maternal, Infant and Child Nutrition received attention in the '80s.

151

Agents and leaders in some counties became part of a support group for pregnant teens. Extension had an important role in encouraging teens to eat right, so they would be healthy mothers and have healthy babies.

Extension agents and leaders also focused on family violence and abuse – not so much as counselors, but as spokespersons who helped others understand how widespread the problem was and what could be done to help the victims of abuse.

Homemakers in Lee and several other counties made anatomically-correct dolls for use by school nurses, guidance counselors, and social services representatives. The dolls were used in suspected cases of child abuse, so young children or adults with limited English, could manipulate the dolls to show abuse and molestation.

At least five counties credit EH with initiating some of the first recycling programs through such activities as helping get recycling bins in county locations and at several schools, as well as speaking to different groups about recycling.

Efforts were made to gear Extension programs to focus on the interests and needs of homemakers and families.

Lincoln EH members purchased signs with WalMart grant directing people to recycling site.

EH member promotes proper installation of child safety seats.

Family starts using the computer for learning and fun.

Stay-at-home homemakers had diversified interests, depending on age. Women who had been Extension Homemakers for several years were often interested in bettering the community and getting an understanding of issues facing the state and nation.

Young homemakers were interested in these topics, too, but also might need help with food preservation, tailoring or sewing, family budgeting, and child rearing. Some county agents organized Young Extension Homemakers clubs to meet this needs. Others supported a Healthy Mothers, Healthy Babies program that directed attention to the health of new mothers and babies.

Concern for others in the community was channeled. In the 1980s, Wake County Extension homemakers joined in a collaborative program to teach basic life skills to foster care young people between the ages of 14 and 18. The youth learned about budgeting, credit, insurance, and banking.

Safety projects continued to receive attention from Extension.

Cumberland County Extension Homemakers worked with Emergency Services in the area to sell the new 911 flashlight. The flashlights assisted police, rescue squad, fire departments, and other emergency personnel in the event of a crisis. Proceeds from the sales went for scholarships.

Foods with Finesse seafood school.

Sampson County Extension Homemakers made "dummies" for the county rescue squads. They were used to demonstrate safety practices on various pieces of farm machinery.

Helping families to improve health continued to garner emphasis. Many counties organized health screening and health education events in conjunction with local health agencies. Workers in mobile trailer units used by 30 counties screened 4,851 people for high blood pressure and elevated cholesterol.

Motion for Life.

Legislative Day finds Extension Homemakers at General Assembly discussing family issues.

Gates County Extension agents and leaders held a health fair in 1989. Those attending the fair could have their blood pressure and cholesterol checked. The event also featured displays on nutrition and dental care.

Caldwell County Extension Homemakers adopted patients at Meadowbrook, a retirement center. They visited and made bibs and lap robes for the residents.

Other projects receiving attention from many counties included seat-belt safety and the organ donor program.

The arts captured the attention of Lee County Extension Homemakers. In 1982, they sponsored a cooking school at one of the high schools. Proceeds went to the restoration of Temple Theatre, a regional venue located in Sanford.

Many interests were international in scope. Cabarrus County Extension Homemakers hosted international students from Japan, Liberia, and Zambia. Columbus County Extension homemakers hosted a family from Nepal and a student from Venezuela, who was working on a master's degree at N.C. State.

Extension homemakers across the state supported and helped finance a clean drinking water project for

Juanita Hudson, at her business in Harnett County, gives credit to Extension for teaching her decorating and business skills.

1,100 Indians in Poza, Guatemala. Juanita Lagg of Rowan County spearheaded the effort.

In 1981, four British women spent a few days in Columbus and Brunswick counties, observing Extension work. They left impressed with the variety of homemaking projects available. The four were

Buncombe County EH members make heart-shaped pillows for patients at VA and other hospitals.

155

National Extension Homemakers Council meeting in Charlotte.

members of the Welsh Woman's Institute of London, an organization similar to Extension. The Institute is part of the Associated Country Women of the World (ACWW), the as is Extension Homemakers Association.

Leadership development and paying attention to legislation coming before the General Assembly and the Congress continued to receive attention from Extension agents and leaders.

In 1987, Extension co-sponsored the North Carolina Family Community Leadership Institute (FCL) in Raleigh. The institute, funded by the W.C. Kellogg Foundation and the North Carolina Extension Homemakers was designed to help women and families influence public policy. Extension Homemakers were also encouraged to run for public office, using their leadership for the greater good. The FCL program, eventually conducted at the district, county, and community level, had 5,073 graduates.

Earlier in the '80s, North Carolina Extension

Homemakers emphasized studying national and state legislation that would affect women. They were then asked to talk with their representatives in the U.S. Congress and North Carolina General Assembly to make their views known. This effort received a top award and recognition from the National Extension Homemakers Council.

Two other important events happened in the '80s.

In 1980, a change in leadership took place at the state level. Dr. Martha Johnson was name assistant Extension director, home economics. She followed Dr. Eloise Cofer who retired earlier. The Extension Family Living Seminar was changed to the Eloise S. Cofer Family Living Seminar to honor Dr. Cofer on her retirement.

North Carolina hosted the 52nd annual National Extension Homemakers Council (NEHC) national meeting, "Footprints for the Future...Building by Caring...Enriching by Sharing," in Charlotte, July 10-14, 1988. The event attracted 3,011 people from around the country.

1990-2000
NEW WAYS TO LEARN

The 90s marked a time of rapid growth in the area of technology. Despite the tight financial times in 1990, Extension invested in a new computer system. For the first time agents had a personal computer on their desks. Extension's investment in this technology would prove to be a key to working more efficiently to reach new audiences who would search for information at home.

The World Wide Web was "born" in 1992. Two years later, some 3 million Americans were online. By the end of the decade, an estimated 100 million people were surfing the web and communicating via e-mail. Extension was still a trusted source of information.

The 1990s also saw a shift to issues-based programming, as Extension home economics focused on solutions to health, environmental, and economic issues related to the health and well-being of the family. Names also changed. In 1995 Extension Home Economics became Family and Consumer Sciences (FCS). By the end of the decade, the North Carolina Agricultural Extension Service was NC Cooperative Extension, and Extension Homemakers were Extension and Community Association (ECA) members.

FCS specialists, agents, and Extension homemakers provided information needed by virtually every family in the state. Dietary guidance began before birth, helping to improve the birth weights and decrease infant mortality. Dietary and childrearing information was given so parents could raise healthy children who did well in school. FCS agents and EH club members

FCS agents welcomed computers when they were placed on each agent's desk in 1990s.

Counties worked together to sponsor day-long regional events that offered seniors information on healthy living. Aging With Gusto programs continued through the next decade. This photo was taken event in Pasquotank County.

worked with 4-H'ers, schoolchildren, and other groups of youth. Families got information on relationships, from recognizing and avoiding abusive relationships, to communicating effectively, and strengthening marriages.

Eldercare was a major focus in the 1990s, as specialists, agents, and club members worked to help families support older family members, friends, and neighbors who were less able to do their daily routines. They also reached out to a new audience, the influx of retirees who had decided to spend their senior years in North Carolina.

Aging with Gusto, an interdisciplinary program in FCS, was designed in 1995 by a team of 11 specialists to emphasize health and positive outcomes in later life. The program quickly became popular with counties, and many day-long multi-county *Aging With Gusto Extravaganzas* were held.

In 1999, the *Aging with Gusto* program won the US Committees National Award for Excellence in Aging Programs, one of 12 awards from 400 applications.

In 1990 a $150,397 grant from Glaxo for programming to help support caregivers was announced. The program still helped provide support materials and training for family members care for older adults at home. In 1987 specialists started seeking private funding, and by 1992, a total of $6 million had been secured by the Extension Home Economics Department at N.C. State.

Whatever the source of funding, Extension's mission had not changed. The educational program begun in 1911 to help North Carolina families and communities would continue to do so throughout the 1990s. Extension club members would continue to learn and serve, improving their homes, themselves, and their communities.

As the economy began to rebound in 1992, jobs drew people to North Carolina. The total population increased by a fifth and the number of employed increased by a quarter. The unemployment rate dropped from 6 percent in 1992 to 3.2 percent in 1999. Per-capita personal income rose by 19 percent in inflation-adjusted terms over the 1990s. Rising wages and incomes helped reduce the state's poverty rate from 15.7 percent in 1992 to 13.5 percent in 2000.

While new jobs were becoming available in many areas of the state, mills and other traditional manufacturing plants were shutting down. Extension FCS was there with programs to help the jobless manage with less income. They addressed the stress of having to find new jobs, often in new fields. Agents and specialists provided information on starting a variety of small businesses, as people struggled to find a way to survive when everyone from the plant was now unemployed and job openings were scarce. Extension was there with support groups and information on budgeting, interviewing, and dressing for success.

Extension and EH club members had many new opportunities to work with Hispanic and Latino families. Some 76,000 Hispanic and Latino people called North Carolina home in 1990. By 2000, that figure had climbed to 250,000 and the number was increasing at the rate of about 21 percent per year. In addition, more than 142,000 migrant farmworkers — most of them Hispanic — were coming to the state each growing season.

Extension and Extension Homemakers in Watauga County recognized loneliness and homesickness as critical issues for new residents. The newcomers tended to be isolated because of their lack of English-speaking skills and access to transportation. In collaboration with churches, the health community, and Appalachian State University, Extension helped expand church services, establish cultural events, start a soccer team, offer volunteer-run English as a Second Language classes, and begin an Extension homemakers club for Latinas.

Statewide, family resource management agents, specialists, and volunteers helped everyone with their

Children's activities were offered at the Hispanic Health Fair in Pitt County, making the event attractive to the whole family.

budgets. Specialists and agents talked about consumer rights and responsibilities. Credit cards and home equity loans made it a little too easy for consumers to "shop 'til you drop," and personal debt was on the rise.

An attorney on the Extension FCS faculty at N.C. State University provided information on the importance of wills, the living will, and health care power of attorney. Hospitals throughout the state valued these easy-to-understand publications and gave copies to patients as they entered the hospital.

Extension volunteers in Watauga County teach English as a Second Language classes. The effort began in the 1990s and continued throughout the 2000s.

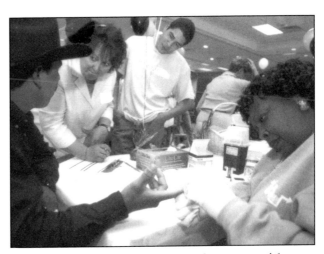

A man at the Hispanic Health Fair in Pitt County is tested for diabetes.

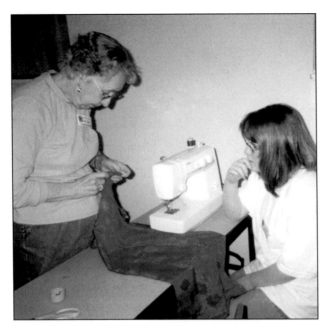

Buncombe County EH member teach sewing to a teen.

Extension's FCS specialist-attorney created a series of publications on the legal aspects of creating a small business. She also expanded the emphasis on estate planning. She never gave legal advice, but helped the public understand the legal ramifications of owning a business as a sole proprietor, in partnership, or as a corporation. She translated terms like "tenancy in the entirety" as she explained practical aspects of estate planning.

The FCS agent in Perquimans County was asked to teach employees at a local health facility about living wills and advanced directives. The 1999 program included the importance of family communication and decision-making. Facility administrators were so impressed by the agent's presentation that they asked her to do additional training in 2000. And 10 of the 51 employees attending the class contacted the agent for more information regarding other estate planning resources. Learning the "who, what, when, and how" of estate planning saves time and makes visits to a lawyer less stressful.

Clothing specialists helped people construct clothing, dress for success, and begin their own small businesses. The FCS agent in Forsyth County said that the office got regular requests for someone who could teach heritage crafts and sewing classes. In response, the Extension Sewing Club sponsored a Sewing and Needle Arts Expo in 1999. The Expo featured quilting classes, heirloom sewing, ribbon embroidery, knitting, crocheting, basic sewing, and alterations. Forty-eight people from Forsyth and adjoining counties attended, learning skills they could use to teach others and to enhance garments and home decor as well as income.

EH members in Cabarrus County contribute afghans to the national Warm Up America program.

HomePlate delivered nutrition information to families who wanted to receive it through the mail.

Extension homemakers in Halifax County started a *Hand Up Clothing Closet*, which provided men's dress clothing for inmates' use when appearing in court or attending the funeral of an immediate family member. The court specified that inmates appear in court in appropriate clothing, not prison uniforms. Before the closet was started, the Corrections Department paid for items used by inmates. With EH club members providing the clothing for the closet, fewer tax dollars were needed. The clothes were available to 1,550 men in correction units at Halifax, Tillery, Caledonia, or the Odom complexes.

The demand for reliable information on food, nutrition, and health-related programs continued to grow, particularly for optimal health, diabetes management, weight control, and prevention of major problems like cardiovascular disease and cancer. Between 1992 and 1995, some 441,673 citizens participated in nutrition, diet, and health programs, learning how to select and prepare foods to promote health and reduce the risk of chronic diseases.

One such program was *Noonliting*, an Extension program that stressed healthy food choices and physical activities. The program was offered across the state as many North Carolinians strived to achieve and maintain a healthy weight.

Lenoir County Extension offered the popular 15-week program quarterly in 1999. The 23 participants in the last class of the year lost 138 pounds and logged 3,626 minutes of physical activities. Ninety-seven percent said they had reduced their fat, sugar, and sodium intakes, and reported increased self-esteem.

An Orange County man took part in *Noonliting* classes for two years, losing 85 pounds, which brought his weight below 300 pounds. *Noonliting* success stories from Nash County include two participants being taken off cholesterol medication and another who used diet and exercise to lower his cholesterol level from 400 to 189.

Nash County also started a support group for *Noonliting* graduates, because participants found it was too easy to stop exercising and slip back into unhealthy eating patterns.

Reaching parents with nutrition information for their families was the focus of another nutrition program called *HomePlate*. In the planning stage, research was conducted to determine the best way to provide information for parents of young children. Parents were less interested in attending traditional face-to-face workshops and wanted a self-taught delivery strategy. Materials were then designed to encourage parents and children to work together in the kitchen to

Extension women in Henderson County put together a quilt
commemorating breast cancer survivors.

County Extension centers have notebooks that contain the information needed to respond quickly should a natural disaster occur.

prepare healthy meals. Recipes, kids' kitchen activities, and a video for the children were mailed to interested parents across the state.

Extension participated in the National Nutrition Screening Initiative, which revealed that 69 percent of elder North Carolinians were at moderate or high risk for nutrional deficiencies. The study was a collaborative effort with the NC Department of Environment, Health and Natural Resources, NC Department of Human Resources, and the American Association of Retired Persons.

At the opposite end of the age spectrum, programs on prenatal care, nutrition during teenage pregnancy, infant feeding, and parent education reached 20,759 people.

Between 1996 and 1999, some 214,102 people received nutrition and wellness information, either meeting face-to-face with an Extension agent or as a part of a class lead by an agent. Another 410,027 people got Extension's nutrition and wellness information indirectly, via newspaper articles, telephone calls, e-mail messages, publications, and newsletters.

Trained volunteer EH members helped extend the message. Over 2,330 volunteers provided 19,398 hours of service, donating $193,980 in service to the state. For example, a Vance County EH club member held a series of *NoonLiting* classes for other club members from 1990 through 1993.

In February 1999, FCS agents from seven counties held a kick-off event at Johnson C. Smith University highlighting Extension's *Give Your Heart a Healthy Beat!* (GYHHB). Some 440 people viewed exhibits and were screened for cholesterol and blood pressure levels, sickle cell anemia, bone density, and received mammograms to detect breast cancer. During the months to follow, each of the seven counties sponsored GYHHB sessions. In Mecklenburg, Friendship Missionary Baptist Church and Greater Providence Baptist Church held *Give Your Heart a Healthy Beat* classes, teaching 50 people to manage stress, eat healthy, lower blood pressure and cholesterol levels, and engage in more physical activity.

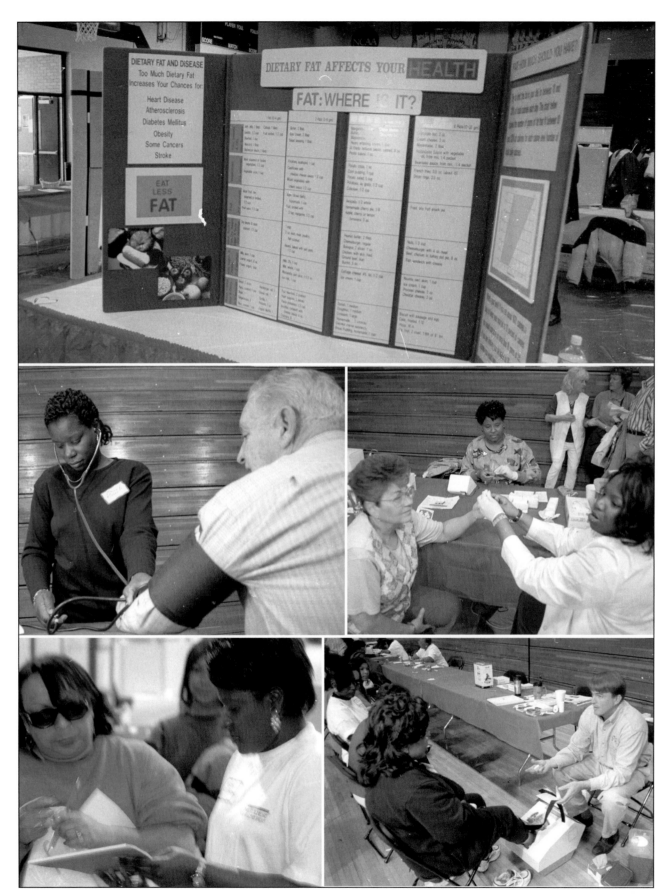

Hundreds attend a Give Your Heart a Healthy Beat health fair in Mecklenburg County. Participants had their blood pressure, bone density, and cholesterol measured. They also learned about managing stress, eating healthy, lowering blood pressure, and becoming physically active.

Since the organization's beginning, Extension has taught food safety and food quality, but Hurricane Fran in 1996 presented a special challenge. Residents needed to know how to handle possibly contaminated food and water following the extensive flooding. The same was true in 1999 with Floyd. In both cases FCS and Extension were prepared with information. Extension agents had been trained for disaster response and recovery and had notebooks with in-depth information so they could answer questions efficiently and effectively. Prepared radio scripts provided timely information to the public at large and publications were available as "print-on-demand" to get information was available to people even when electricity was not. Information and fact sheets were added to the Extension web site for anyone to use. Agents printed copies before the storms. Local television stations included Extension's information on their web sites, and newspapers printed stories using FCS information and referred people to the web. Eight states purchased the notebooks.

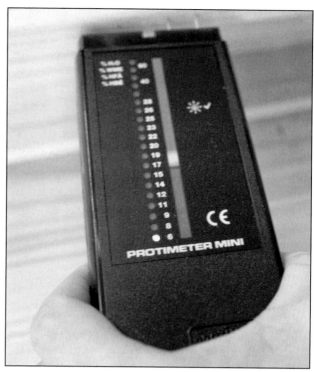

Moisture meter used to test the moisture in wood.

In 1999 when the floods from Hurricane Floyd devastated 33 counties in the eastern part of the state, FCS housing and furnishings specialists presented information on proper cleaning to prevent illness from reoccurring mold and mildew to area doctors in those areas as part of the ECU Medical School's teleconference program called *Grand Rounds*.

In Edgecombe County, about 900 homes were flooded. Extension provided 15 moisture meters so

After Hurricane Floyd hit, Extension stepped in to help people recover. This photo shows flooding in Edgecombe County, where the moisture meters were used extensively.

165

Lenoir County teen checks her weight and dairy to her diet with yogurt.

that residents could test levels in wood in their homes before rebuilding. The meters were in constant use for months, testing an estimated 500 homes and businesses. Wood needed to dry out before rebuilding. Moisture content in remaining studs, beams, and floors had to be 19 percent or less in order to prevent future moisture problems, indoor air quality concerns, and health problems.

Extension's Disaster: Readiness, Response, Recovery information remains online so it can be accessed at any time anywhere in the world.

Foodborne illness sickens millions of Americans each year, and more than 5,000 people die as a result of these illnesses. Daycare workers, congregate nutrition site food handlers, restaurant employees, and hospital, school and other institutional foodservice workers were taught safe food handling. Between 1996 and 1999, some 15,193 people were trained directly, and 67,036 received indirect counseling. Some 458 volunteers gave 1,800 hours of service worth $18,000 to the state.

The *Expanded Food and Nutrition Program* (EFNEP) continued to teach healthy eating on a limited budget, reaching 24,000 adults and 26,000 young people. Two major shifts occurred during the four-year period: groups of clients came to EFNEP through cooperating agencies. EFNEP also was reaching adult groups in shelters and correctional centers, and children in alternative school programs, after-school programs, foster homes, and Boys and Girls Clubs.

Lenoir County teens learn to eat healthy.

Sowing Seeds in the Mountains

COMMUNITY-BASED COALITIONS FOR CANCER PREVENTION AND CONTROL

NATIONAL INSTITUTES OF HEALTH
National Cancer Institute

The Southern Appalachia Leadership Initiative on Cancer (SALIC) was commemorated with this quilt.

Grants allowed EFNEP to grow in several new directions. With outside funding, Extension reached 4,300 WIC clients in nine counties. As a result, more mothers chose to breastfeed, and breastfed for a longer period of time.

Extension and WIC grant funds also supported development of *Hey, What's Cookin'*, a curriculum for pregnant teens. After field testing and evaluation, the curriculum was introduced to all EFNEP staff in 1994. By mid 1995, more than 1,000 pregnant teens were

enrolled, bringing EFNEP's four-year total to more than 3,000 pregnant teenagers.

To reach a wide variety of people in a very urban county, the Guilford FCS agent prepared tasty, low-fat foods live at a local television station. The monthly show reached an audience of 61,000 people and was continued for 14 months in 1998 and 1999. In addition to sharing healthy dishes, the program helped position Extension as a credible source of nutrition, health, and food safety information. Extension was called upon by other television stations when they needed a source of consumer information, and requests for nutrition information increased from the general public.

Between 1992 and 1995, health and human safety programs helped 365,442 adults and young people prevent disease and injuries, and 349 communities had ongoing health promotion and disease and injury prevention programs. Extension taught over 10,000 farm workers and their families and the general public how to handle and launder pesticide-contaminated clothing so that the chemicals would not harm anyone. They also helped flood victims restore soiled clothing and textiles following the flooding after Hurricane Fran in 1996 and Floyd in 1999.

Agents continued to work on early childhood immunization in the *Rural Health Program*. Breast and cervical cancer prevention and control became a focus thanks to the National Cancer Institute-funded *Southern Appalachia Leadership Initiative on Cancer* (SALIC) project. The eight-year project, funded with a $4.6 million grant from the National Cancer Institute, was begun to see if rural women could be organized to work on their own behalf to control cancer in their communities. Forty community action groups addressed the problem, and the mammography rates for women 50 and older in four North Carolina project counties increased from 50 percent to 70 percent in the first four years of the project.

Black Churches United for Better Health program.

168

Buncombe County Angel dolls for kids moving into foster care.

In another wellness effort, an FCS specialist chaired the *Black Churches United for Better Health Intervention Task Force*. Resulting projects reached more than 3,700 members from 50 churches.

Black Churches United for Better Health was a joint effort by Extension, Duke University, UNC-Chapel Hill, and the North Carolina Department of Health and Human Services. The community-based research project promoted nutrition education to reduce the risk of cancer in African Americans. Fifty churches from 10 counties participated in the study. The program focused on eating five servings of fruits and vegetables every day, using the church as a channel.

During the 1990s, Extension programming and EH club work also targeted child care, parent education, family strengths, and aging. Between 1992 and 1995, staffs at NC State University and NC A & T State University provided information on effective parenting that reached 76,540 parents and 37,193 youth. More than 22,000 childcare workers adopted recommended practices for classroom management, scheduling and curriculum development.

Playing to Learn was begun in 1992 in Rockingham County by an Extension family education assistant who noticed the lack of activities available to young children

in public housing. That year, 32 children, ages 3 to 12, joined. By 1996, the program had expanded to six sites and was reaching more than 150 youngsters, thanks to community volunteers, who saw the value of the program. Extension trained them to lead the programs and to present age-appropriate learning activities for children.

In 1996 and 1997, members of Wayne County Extension Homemakers bought 70 videos for schools, day care centers, and churches to use to develop *Kids for Character*. The videos focused on developing the six pillars of character: trustworthiness, respect, sharing, responsibility, caring, and citizenship. Songs, skits, activities, and discussions reinforced the idea that character counts. In addition, 11 club members were trained and have used these videos in their communities with neighborhood groups. Statewide, Extension clubs provided videos to elementary schools as part of their *Building Stronger Families* focus, reaching 412,664 kids, teachers, and parents.

Literacy programs were held throughout the state, with Extension homemakers giving over 2 million hours in local, state, and global efforts between 1992 and 1995. For example, in 1993 Haywood County Extension Homemakers had a literacy project entitled

A Moore County EH club member volunteers at a correctional center as part of her club's commitment to increasing literacy in the county.

Buy a Book — Help A Child. Their project put 232 books into the hands of children in the county's four Head Start centers. Popular titles among the 3- to 5-year-olds were *101 Dalmations, Beauty and the Beast, Aladdin,* and *Fire Engines to the Rescue.* Each child's name was printed in the front of the book he selected.

In 1991, McDowell County Extension Homemakers began its literacy efforts at birth. They provided a book of Mother Goose nursery rhymes to each of the 350 children born at McDowell Hospital. Mom and Dad were not forgotten. They got Extension publications on parenting, child development, choosing day care, and building self-esteem.

In 1992, 200 club members gave 6,000 volunteer hours tutoring adults and children. They also donated 25,546 books to schools and libraries. The Cherokee Indian Extension Homemakers Council sponsored distribution of 10,000 books contributed by national public companies.

Extension homemakers in Johnston County joined with the Johnston County Public Library for a *Books Come In All Flavors* summer reading program offered throughout the county in 1993.

During the same year, Rowan County EH started its own lending library so that club members could exchange books. They also continued tutoring adults, reading with children, giving books to children, and collecting magazines for schools and nursing homes.

Club members throughout the state continued to raise money for scholarships that helped young people continue their education beyond high school. Over a two-year period, Extension clubs awarded $362,745 in scholarships and loans to worthy students.

Iredell County held a number of caregiver programs for family members and friends caring for a dependent older adult. A woman from a local church asked the FCS agent if she could help in involving church members in helping older members. The agent worked with a committee to match people needing help with those who were willing to help, and the agent gave a presentation on caregiving to 350 people in 1999.

Another request to an FCS agent in Rowan County led to the establishment in 1999 of The Caring and Sharing Support Group for widowed people. Group members took turns coordinating the meetings, and the agent and volunteers presented educational programs.

Time was set aside for fellowship, but the main purpose of the group was to help people deal with the feelings of emptiness, sadness, shock, and disbelief that come with the death of a loved one.

In 1996, Harnett County held its second State of the Child Conference at Campbell University. Extension networked with the Harnett Helpnet organization to plan and initiate the conference titled *Their Future is in Our Hands.*

Some 250 people discussed problems and issues facing children in the county. Attendees included Extension club members, civic group members, parents, religious leaders, educators, and elected officials. Successful programs were showcased. Elaine Marshall, honorary chair of Harnett Helpnet, was one of the speakers. The conference generated new ideas for community programs, fostered networking, and explored needs and potential resources for community action.

Knowing that great ideas often come from laypeople, the *North Carolina Family Community Leadership Program* trained 7,480 volunteers to resolve public issues. The program focused on public policy education and targeted women and families. Eighty-four donors contributed more than $186,365 to support the leadership programs throughout the state.

Community Voices, a leadership development program for limited-resource people, helped more than

EH survival kits for foster care children.

800 people develop the skills they needed to work to improve their rural communities and counties.

In just two years, more than 14,000 Extension homemakers completed Extension's *Family and Community Leadership Program.* Extension also started a *North Carolina Family and Community Leadership Scholars Graduate Program* to prepare participants for elected office or appointed "power brokers" positions within 10 years after completing the program. By the end of the decade, one participant had been elected to the NC House of Representatives, two became school board members, one became mayor, and others were members of local, county, and state boards.

Extension homemakers are a dedicated group of women who feel they gain while giving.

As Pine Valley club member JoAnne Jarret said in 1991, "The program has helped me to organize and maintain a home, rear our children, conduct community service, and communicate with others. I have had the opportunity to teach programs and share

Vance County Out for Lunch graduate shows off her skills.

Yvonne Mullen, FCS agent in Pasquotank County, helps ECA members make cooling neck wraps for soldiers and firefighters.

skills with others, and this has been a very rewarding and satisfying experience. Experiences in Extension Homemakers helped me prepare for a leadership role on the Wilmington City Planning Commission and for service in my church."

Extension and Scotland County club women sponsored leadership development seminars for minority women in 1991, 1993, and 1996. Approximately 115 women attended the 1996 seminar at St. Andrews Presbyterian College. Keynote speaker Rev. Shirley Hines, pastor of Zion Campbell A.M.E. Church, reminded her listeners, "Now women can do anything they want to. We, as women, cannot afford to go half stepping. Today's woman has to invest in herself and realize she can make a difference."

As a part of a statewide Economic Development for Women Project, seven FCS agents in Northeastern North Carolina partnered with Z. Smith-Reynolds Foundation to "help individuals develop to their full potential, both personally and professionally." With $7,750 in grant money, the agents designed a series of programs. Each month, participants helped organize and host meetings in a different county. They learned about resources outside their home county, and met wonderful contacts who shared ideas like how to be more organized, manage time, and deal with different or difficult people. Overall, they were learning how to become community leaders. They also listened to each other's hopes and dreams. Then they discussed how these dreams might be brought to fruition. Twenty-eight women completed this program.

At the last assembly, Yvonne Mullen from Pasquotank County said, "This program helped build my confidence." Following the workshop, she pursued her dream to finish college. She earned her bachelor's degree in 1997, a teaching certification in 1999, and her master's degree in 2002. When the position became available in 2003, she was hired as the Pasquotank County FCS agent. Her peers elected her president-elect of the NC Extension Association of Family & Consumer Sciences for 2011.

172

Lee County residents learn that healthy cooking can also be tasty in Out for Lunch class at the Extension Center.

Extension club women extended a helping hand to support projects around the world. Shown here, Ashe, and Orange County women contribute Operation Christmas Child boxes and pack them to go to a state conference.

Union County EH members pack Operation Christmas Child boxes into a car.

Thirty-two counties participated in the Economic Development for Women Project, reaching 1,628 limited-resource women. Ninety-eight found a job as a result of the training, and more than 25 percent said the program had increased their self-esteem and increased confidence.

Another Extension program called *Out for Lunch* helped women improve their lives and find work. One success story out of Chatham County involved a disabled woman who started a small sewing business. She was so pleased with the support and information she'd received in *Out for Lunch*, she volunteered with subsequent classes. She also started teaching sewing and craft classes to 4-H'ers.

The Catawba County EH received the Governor's Volunteer Award for its work in 1998 and 1999. "Their outstanding record becomes more significant in view of the fact that most of these Extension volunteers are in their '70s, '80s, and even '90s," said Glennie Daniels, Catawba County agent who nominated the group for the award. "Instead of being content to be served, they make a valuable contribution by actively seeking ways of improving quality of life for their neighbors in Catawba County, the state, the nation, and throughout the world."

Extension club members continued to reach out a helping hand to families in other nations throughout the 1990s. For example, club members donated more than $1,000 by simply setting aside their extra pennies. *Pennies for Friendship* supported a number of projects around the world. They also gave a similar amount of money to International Service Association for Health for projects in Haiti. The previous year, they sent money to establish a knitting cooperative at a women's jail in Bolivia.

Programs have helped limited-income families manage their time and money, work toward purchasing a car, a house, and control spending. For example, one agent taught budgeting, shopping, and decision-making to handicapped adults. Others have taught budgeting, parenting, and managing conflict skills to male and female inmates.

Operation Christmas Child boxes collected from all the county EH clubs are ready to be packed for transport.

Operation Christmas Child boxes packed in semi-truck at state conference ready for shipping.

In 1995, the U.S. Marine Corps contracted with family resource management specialists in North Carolina, California, and Georgia to create a program to reduce widespread financial problems among Marines. These problems were seriously affecting personal and family life, thereby reducing military readiness. The Extension team developed an extensive *Financial Fitness* curriculum and in 1996 presented it to FCS agents from counties with a USMC camp or air station and representatives from every USMC base. Over the next four years, FCS agents from Onslow and Craven counties and the project's NC State University family resource management specialist took part in 30 training sessions in North Carolina, preparing 540 military financial specialists to teach and counsel Marines.

Over the first four years in North Carolina, there was a 33 percent reduction in the number of bounced checks on base, a measurable impact and benefit of Extension curriculum and training.

The training materials were also adapted for use by the US Air Force, and training materials were shared with FCS agents in counties with Air Force, Army, and Coast Guard bases, helping Extension address the needs of its tens of thousands of military residents and their families.

Family resource management specialists and the Extension homemakers helped the State Attorney General's Consumer Protection Office identify fraud. Extension homemakers collected suspicious mail and kept logs of phone calls and door-to-door solicitations for one month. The 18,000 pieces of mail plus the logs were then analyzed by the Attorney General's Office, which was able to identify a number of firms and individuals engaged in fraudulent telemarketing, mail, and door-to-door practices.

Extension's home ownership program in Buncombe County showed potential buyers the obstacles they might experience and then told them how they could remove them. With Extension's educational assistance and the financial backing of Mountain Housing Opportunities Inc., limited-income families were able to buy homes.

"This is your problem. This is how you fix it. I love it. I've been giving Extension high praise ever since I started this program," said one mother who was able to purchase a home in 1992.

Extension has a solar-powered shed to power electric tools at the community gardens in Guilford County.

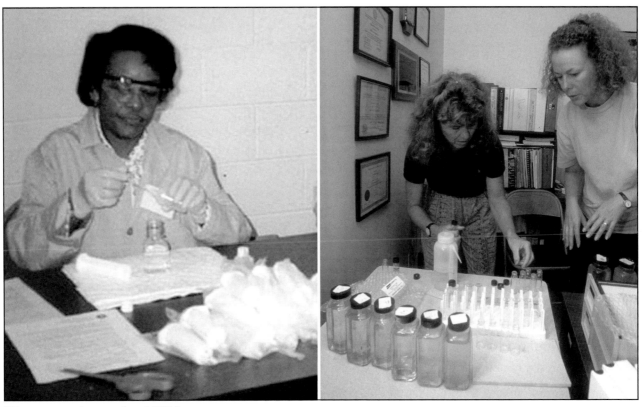

Water testing technicians from NCSU.

Extension club women in Ashe, Wayne, and Lee Counties are shown assisting as local residents bring water samples, while technicians from N.C. State University test water samples at Durham and Pamlico Extension centers.

Some 370,000 individuals or families used Extension services in budgeting and smart shopping between 1989 and 1992. By their own estimates, they reported savings of over $15.4 million.

Guilford County, with two of the state's largest cities, established as a solar community in 1990, becoming the second area so designated in the state. The Extension FCS agent took the lead in establishing a coalition with businesses and organizations to sponsor numerous conferences, workshops, seminars, tours, and training sessions to help educate both its citizens and professionals on the value of solar energy. A consumer training workshop on solar home building, an exhibit for builders and the public on solar

applications, and a solar resource center at the public library was established in 1999.

In 1990, Vance County was one of 20 counties testing well water for nitrates and chlorides, indicators of contamination from septic tank seepage and fertilizers. Extension Homemakers volunteered with the collections, and 379 wells were tested. Promoting water quality by assisting with water screening programs was a state project for club members.

Between 1992 and 1995, agents focused on residential water quality education and some held screening programs for lead and nitrates, which cause health problems. Ten percent of 1,230 homes screened for lead and three percent of 1,129 screened for nitrates

had elevated readings. Some homeowners had to install new wells. Those with elevated lead levels learned to flush pipes before consuming the water or had their plumbing updated or replaced.

In 1999, the Buncombe County FCS agent helped people adapt their home either for themselves or for another older adult. This allows a person to remain at home instead of moving into an alternative housing arrangement. One woman wanted to make changes so that her husband could return home from a nursing home. While modifications are not inexpensive, they do cost less than nursing home care, and they allow more people to age at home.

Making activity aprons, also called "fidget aprons," for Alzheimers patients was a state project of the Extension homemakers clubs. These aprons offer various repetitive actions, like zipping, tying, buttoning, or pulling a piece of Velcro, to keep fidgety hands busy. Different fabric textures provide a variety of tactile sensations as well. Thousands have been made by the club members since the project began. The aprons are donated to nursing homes and caregivers. A few examples are shown on the next page.

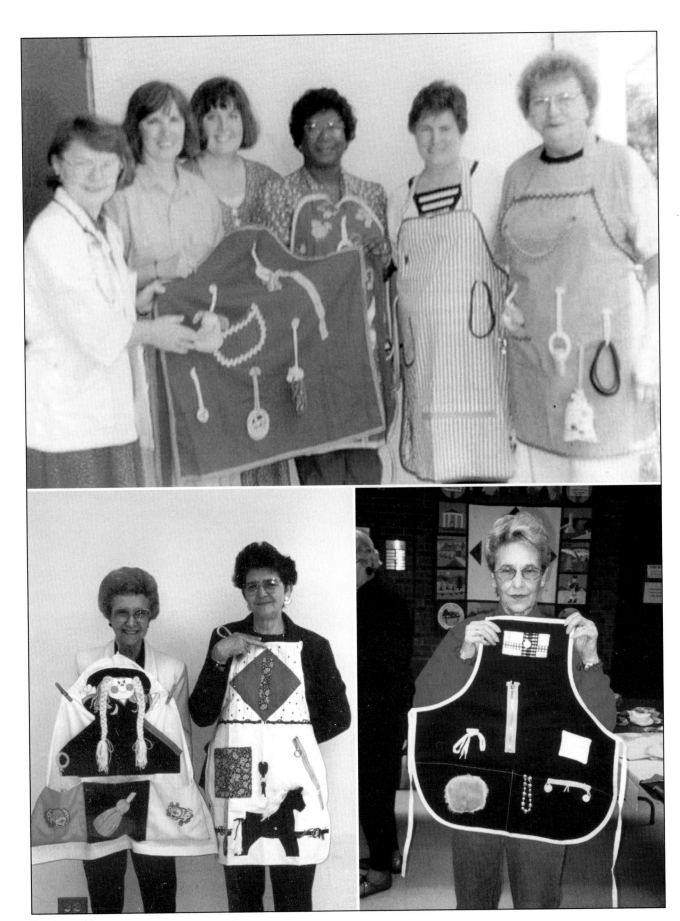

Displaying fidget aprons.

In 1999, at the National Association of Family and Community Education Conference in Kona, Hawaii, The North Carolina Extension Homemakers Council submitted a letter of intent to disaffiliate with the national association. At the State Council held in Raleigh that year, the name was changed to North Carolina Extension & Community Association, Inc. The mission of the ECA Association is to strengthen families through leadership development, volunteer work, and educational support, using research-based education from North Carolina State University and NC A&T State University.

Dr. Judy Mock was interim head of Family and Consumer Sciences at N.C. State University from 1991 to 1993, when Dr. Marilyn Corbin was appointed. Dr. Corbin left in 1998, and Dr. Mock again became interim head of the FCS department, serving until Dr. Sandy Zaslow was appointed in 1999.

By December 31, 1999, FCS agents, specialists, and ECA members had successfully met the challenges of another decade, and they were ready to face the new millennium.

Virginia Buffkin, Columbus ECA member, designed the ECA logo that is used today.

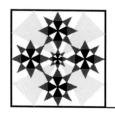

2000-2010
INTO THE NEW MILLENNIUM

More than two-thirds of North Carolina adults are overweight or obese, which increases their risk of type 2 diabetes, heart disease, and some forms of cancer. Approximately one-third of children in the state are overweight or obese as well, increasing their risk of health problems later in life.

Heart disease, stroke, and cancer continue to be leading causes of death. Eating healthy and staying active are critical in these and other major health issues facing North Carolinians.

FCS specialists, agents, and ECA club members all promote and teach healthy eating and physical activity to help people improve overall health and reduce the risk of chronic illnesses. Nutrition programs that address the needs of children and adults are conducted across the state. Programs are offered at worksites, faith communities, schools, shopping areas, and community events, such as the Southern Women's Show. Lessons are taught face-to-face and also delivered using technology, such as distance education, the Internet, and phone.

Extension led an interagency team to create *Families Eating Smart and Moving More*, a program designed to encourage families to eat healthy and be physically active.

"I never turned the stove on before attending *Families Eating Smart, Moving More*. Now I am cooking at least four meals a week at home," said one of the Murfreesboro Head Start parents who completed the Hertford County FCS agent's program. All of the parents reported learning new information on eating healthier and being active. Forty percent made at least one change, such as eating more meals at home, making healthy choices when eating out, moving more, and watching TV less often.

Using a computer program, people attending the Southern Women's Show analyze the nutritional value of menu selections from popular fast food restaurants.

182

An FCS specialist from NC State University teaches an Eat Smart, Move More lesson, an agent demonstrates healthy and delicious foods, and the public enjoys samples at the Southern Women's Show.

Eat Smart, Move More, Weigh Less (ESMMWL) is a weight management program delivered primarily in worksites or at Extension centers. This 15-week program does not prescribe a diet but teaches small steps to change lifestyle habits of eating and physical activity.

In the first two years of the program, more than 7,000 North Carolinians participated. Most reported losing weight, decreasing blood pressure, and reducing waist size. Participants also made better food choices and ate smaller portions.

In Avery County, 164 residents kept their 2008 New Year's resolution with Extension's *Eat Smart, Move More, Weigh Less*. At the end of 15 weeks, participants had lost 914 pounds in a safe, healthy manner.

Wayne County's *Fit and Fabulous* is another example of a program addressing the issues of

Participants in Wayne County's Fit and Fabulous Program work out twice a week.

Eat Smart, Move More, Weigh Less participants in Sampson County taste test a variety of smoothies while learning how to make

overweight and obesity. Each week, local experts taught nutrition, and twice a week a fitness instructor conducted exercise classes. The program, organized by Extension and the county health department, had a long waiting list in 2010.

Extension specialists, along with the Division of Public Health and Department of Public Instruction, developed standards regarding food available in schools. Legislation in 2005 used those standards to regulate the content of vending machines in schools. *North Carolina's Recommended Standards for Physical Activity in Schools* also was released in 2005.

To appeal to teenagers, *SyberShop ... digital solutions for healthy eating and being active* was

created by FCS specialists. The interactive CD-ROM can be used by an individual, in a classroom, or in a group. Teens learn about physical activity, healthy food choices, and visit a virtual food court to learn about the nutritional content of food from six fast food restaurants.

Some county agents also trained teachers to use it in their classrooms. By 2007, more than 600 middle school teachers had been trained, and agents and teachers had reached more than 80,000 youth. Several schools placed *SyberShop* on the school's server. *SyberShop* was also sold to 14 other states. Evaluations of *SyberShop* show the computer program actually increases learning and behavior change better than a traditional classroom lecture.

What's the difference between 10 pounds of fat and 10 pounds of muscle? Sampson County participants see for themselves.

Orange County families "get with the program," learning and living healthy.

Sampson County teens learn to select and prepare healthy foods.

*Women Living Healthy, Women Living Well ...
digital solutions for living your best life* addresses
nutrition and health concerns for women. The
interactive CD has reached over 10,000 North Carolina
women and is also used by 11 other states.

Cook Smart, Eat Smart to encourages people to
prepare and eat more meals at home. This hands-
on program was developed by a team of specialists
and agents. Agents and ECA club members teach
basic cooking skills using easy recipes and simple
ingredients. Results show that the program is getting
more families to eat at home and to rely less on
processed foods. The Dinah Gore Food, Nutrition,
and Fitness Endowment funded *Cook Smart, Eat
Smart.*

Color Me Healthy uses fun activities to teach 4- and
5-year-olds about physical activity and healthy eating. It
is used in family daycare homes, Head Start classrooms,
and childcare centers. More than 10,000 childcare
providers serving over 100,000 preschoolers have been
trained to use the program.

Color Me Healthy is currently being used across
the country by 49 states. Over 50,000 *Color Me
Healthy* kits are now in classrooms across the country.
Evaluations show that children are more willing to try
new fruits and vegetables and actually eat more fruits
and vegetables as a result of *Color Me Healthy*. The
program has received several state and national awards
and has been chosen as a practice-tested intervention by
the Centers for Disease Control.

Workable Wellness is a series of 12 lessons designed
to be presented at the workplace. Topics include
preparing quick meals, making the most of your time,
housekeeping shortcuts, seeking financial fitness,
practicing preventive health, parenting, balancing work
and family, and managing stress.

The Currituck County FCS agent used the
curriculum in several ways. She taught stress
management and time management lessons for groups
of nursing home employees, childcare workers and
Extension secretaries in her district. She held six
sessions at a local library for parents of preschoolers.
While parents were in class, their children participated
in Extension's *Read Me a Story* program.

*Children in classes in Wake and Guilford counties get excited about
vegetables, thanks to Color Me Healthy, an Extension program for
4- and 5-year-olds.*

The next generation is growing food in Greene, Clay, Hoke, Watauga, and Rutherford counties. When kids grow vegetables, they are more likely to want to eat vegetables!

Workable Wellness materials help people with a wide variety of wellness concerns.

Read Me a Story, begun in 2006, uses books with food themes to encourage youngsters to try new foods. The books are used in reading programs in libraries, childcare centers, churches, WIC clinics, and other sites where children accompany parents.

Many factory workers can't attend a wellness class at work because of tight production schedules. However, an Iredell County company invited Extension to be a part of its wellness fair. The company's wellness coordinator was concerned about the unhealthy choices many employees were making in the company cafeteria. Extension responded with an exhibit on food choices. The 400 employees who participated were surprised to learn the amount of fat, sugar, and salt in some foods. The wellness coordinator reported that employees considered better food choices following the wellness fair.

After a *Cooperative Lifestyle Intervention Program* in Guilford County, one-third of the 113 older adults met their weight loss goals, two-thirds reached their weekly walking goal, and about three-quarters improved their diets.

The Person County FCS agent teaches children about nutrition at a library.

An Extension ServSafe class in Montgomery County teaches foodservice workers how to handle, prepare, and store food safely.

In 2008, the Bertie County FCS agent challenged county teachers and staff to use *Step Up To Better Health*, an AARP walking program. Participants were given pedometers, a weekly newsletter, and a walking log. They hit the trails for 10 weeks. One teacher said, "Thank you for organizing this walking program. It gave me the motivation I needed not only to walk but to eat better. I lost 21 pounds but most importantly, I feel better."

Healthy choices also extend to cancer prevention and detection. Extension participated in the Southern Appalachian Leadership Initiative in the 1990s. When federal funding ended in 2000, the North Carolina communities involved formed The Blue Ridge Cancer Coalition Initiative to continue working against cancer.

With a grant from the NC Department of Health and Human Services, the group continued to provide cancer prevention and early detection education, and resources and support to cancer survivors and the community. In fiscal year 2002-03, the group reached almost 60,000 in Alleghany, Ashe, Surry, and Wilkes counties.

Foodborne illness is nearly 100 percent preventable if safe food handling practices are used. ServSafe, which has been used in the counties since 1997, teams Extension FCS agents with local health departments. The material used to train people working in the foodservice industry is available in Spanish, Chinese, and English. ServSafe is a national program developed by the food service industry.

FCS agents prepare nutritious and tasty dishes using local foods in Lincoln and Wilson counties.

Partners in Wellness encourages group interaction, skill building, taste testing, and other activities. Additionally, lyrics that teach nutrition were put to old tunes. Here, seniors in Alexander County sing about nutrition and learn about supplements.

Extension is known for its work on food safety. When one of Beaufort County's rural hospitals applied for accreditation, it received less than a satisfactory rating in the kitchen. The hospital asked Extension to teach a food safety course to the entire kitchen staff. After the staff put what they'd learned into action, the kitchen passed without a single demerit.

FCS agents are supporting Extension's *10% Campaign*, which encourages North Carolinians to commit 10 percent of their food dollars to support local food producers and food-related businesses. North Carolinians spend about $35 billion a year on food. Ten percent — just $1.05 per day — would make about $3.5 billion available in the local economy. It's an "easy sell" when FCS agents and club members help by preparing tasty foods and handing out recipes.

In just one year *Partners in Wellness*, which combats malnutrition among older adults living on limited incomes, reached 2,315 older adults in 47 North Carolina counties. Participants learned to make positive changes, such as eating two or more different kinds of vegetables and fruits per day, draining and rinsing canned foods to remove excess salt, reading food labels to find low-sodium and low-fat products, choosing lower fat dairy products, and drinking more water to prevent dehydration. The program has been shared with seven other states and the Centers for Disease Control has included it in its chronic disease prevention and health promotion database.

Participants received a "wellness checkbook" to write down medications and medical conditions and were told to carry it with them. An Alexander County

Participants are screened for health problems at the Senior Wellness Expo in Monroe.

woman had an emergency and was taken to the hospital. The staff there found the "checkbook" in her purse and they were able to treat her successfully because they had the proper information. The doctor said he wished all people had a wellness checkbook.

Aging With Gusto gives thousands of North Carolina seniors information that will help them maintain a healthy lifestyle. In addition to health, the day-long extravaganzas cover topics like finances, legal issues, caregiving, and housing choices.

At a recent *Aging with Gusto* conference hosted by Extension, participants from seven northeastern counties attented classes on Understanding Medicare, Cooking for 1 or 2, Computer Basics, and Who Gets Grandma's Yellow Pie Plate.

Extension and two other local agencies in Monroe began an annual Senior Wellness Expo in 2006. The Expo brings healthcare service providers and screeners together so seniors can get information in one place, at one time. On average, 400 seniors have attended each year. In 2009, some 75 vendors and screeners set up booths or provided cholesterol, blood sugar, blood pressure, dental, eye, and spinal checks. Pharmacy students answered questions on medications.

Dining With Diabetes is a series of classes with cooking demonstrations to help people with diabetes manage blood sugar levels effectively. One county,

Robeson, took the program to church, calling it *Project Divine.*

In Halifax County, the program was delivered to the Haliwa-Saponi Tribe. Each week, two class members served as guest chefs and prepared food samples.

In Stokes County, 25 people took the classes, and three months later, 66 percent had lowered their blood pressure, increased their fiber intake, and had better-controlled blood sugars.

Expanded Foods and Nutrition Education Program (EFNEP) continues to help limited-income families learn and improve skills and attitudes necessary to eat healthy while stretching their food dollars. Focusing on nutrition, the program reaches over 18,000 families and youth in the state each year.

"During a shopping trip, a smiling former graduate greeted me," said a Cleveland County EFNEP program assistant. "She proceeded to tell me that since graduating from EFNEP, she has been applying what she learned about planning, budgeting, comparison shopping, reading food labels, and using coupons, and that she and her family had not run out of food by the end of the month in two months. She also said that not having to worry about being able to feed her family meant less tension in her family life and her bouts with migraines had virtually disappeared. Then she asked if she might volunteer in the next class held in her community."

FCS and ECA support a number of festivals and events that bring dollars into communities. Lincoln County's Apple Festival draws between 40,000 and 60,000 people each year into Lincolnton. It was started by Extension Agent Melinda Houser.

192

Children in Cumberland, Currituck, and Davie counties learn to prepare healthy foods.

FCS agents, ECA volunteers, and local chefs work with Rutherford County children in the kitchen. The process begins with shopping for local fruits and vegetables at the farmer's market.

Programming in Family and Consumer Sciences has come full circle. Home gardens, buying locally, and food preservation are back in style. Today's home canners are women between 39 and 55. They can for many reasons, including the desire to save money, to control the amount of salt, sugar, and preservatives in their foods, to support local growers, and to avoid wasting the surplus from their own gardens.

In the past 10 years, one of Henderson County's major focuses during the summer months has been food preservation. Approximately 700 participants have taken part in food preservation workshops.

The Iredell County FCS agent had numerous requests to test dial gauges on pressure canners. Testing showed that half of the gauges were faulty and several lids had gaskets that needed to be replaced. The agent partnered with local hardware stores so lids could be repaired immediately. Faulty gauges can result in improperly processed food, which can lead to spoiled food or foodborne illness.

In 2010, the FCS agent position in Mecklenburg County was reinstated because of the renewed interest and requests for information on local foods and food preservation.

Demand for the basics of canning in *Food Preservation 101* in Macon County increased so much that multiple classes were taught. The FCS agent also held additional workshops for people who wanted more than the basics. The classes were offered in partnership with Extension in Jackson, Swain, and the Eastern Band of Cherokee.

The Chatham County FCS agent helped organize food preservation classes in Durham, Chatham, and Granville counties in 2010. Classes were so popular there was a waiting list.

Extension programming has also come full circle with its support of people selling produce and homemade foods. The Craven County FCS agent helped a woman get a $10,000 grant that allowed her to process and sell some of the produce from her father's farm. The grant helped pay for required kitchen upgrades and necessary equipment.

The Rockingham Community Kitchen began in 2006 as a collaborative project with Extension and other county agencies. Farmers and food entrepreneurs used the commercial kitchen to produce large quantities

Children in Grandparents Raising Grandchildren in Robeson County create their family shield.

of specialty products. By 2008, one of the farmer's sugared pecans and blackberry jam was in such demand that he was ready to build his own facility.

The recession, vanishing job security, and financial losses stressed North Carolina families during the 2000s.

Many grandparents were rearing grandchildren. *Broad River Grandparents Raising Grandchildren* in Shelby helps grandparents and other relatives get services, strengthen support systems, and promote family stability. While adults get information and emotional support, volunteer ECA members teach the children.

In Robeson County, Extension FCS partnered with another local agency and the City of Lumberton to begin a *Grandparents Raising Grandchildren Support Group*. In addition to sharing problems and support, each meeting had an educational component on topics affecting both the grandparent and the child.

Home canning is back in style as North Carolinians conserve food from home gardens. These photos are from recent classes in Robeson, Stanly, Union, and Lincoln counties.

The next generation of home canners in Holk and Lee counties.

Cleveland County ECA members work on a gardening project with children in the Broad River Grandparents Raising Grandchildren group.

Over 20 counties have active GRG programs that grandparents say provide much needed support and make their lives easier.

Caring for older adults and handicapped family members can also take a physical, emotional, and financial toll on caregivers. Extension's *Powerful Tools for Caregiving*, a six-session course on self-care and management for the caregivers began in 2000. Caregivers reported they felt less isolated and less stressed after taking the course

Powerful Tools is spread across the state now and is led by NC AARP, with Extension and the Area Agencies on Aging as the major partners. This cooperation avoids duplication and reaches more

people more efficiently. Some North Carolina FCS agents, who are Master Trainers, have provided training for other states in the southeast.

When the FCS agent in Iredell piloted the AARP's new *Prepare to Care* program for employed caregivers of older adults in 2008, she taught the class in front of a film crew. The Centers for Medicare/Medicaid and AARP wanted more than 1,900 Extension and other professionals across the United States to view her teaching. The program helps families develop a plan, which reduces stress and time away from work when caregiving actually begins.

Parenting and child development programs reached almost 60,000 North Carolinians in a five year period. Among those taking classes between 2003 and 2005 were childcare providers who were responsible for 113,244 children.

Parents as Teacher (PAT), a grant-funded program, teaches parents about early childhood development and improves parenting practices. The PAT *Born to Learn* model provides families with personal visits by certified parent educators; group meetings; developmental, health, hearing, and vision screenings; and links to community resources.

While numbers are impressive, the truest measure of a program's success is the difference it makes in an individual's life. In 2002, a Harnett County mother wrote about Extension's *Parents as Teachers* program. "PAT is a life-saver. We were provided with a wonderful in-home teacher named Kim Beaver. She's been a teacher, friend, playmate, a shoulder to cry on, and an angel. Thanks PAT."

At Blockfest, Harnett County families see how block play encourages math and science learning. The event, which is part of Parents As Teachers, was featured on North Carolina Now, the UNC-TV show.

Wayne County parents attend a PAT group meeting.

North Carolina requires staff development for licensed childcare facilities. Extension FCS agents throughout the state are providing the training childcare providers need.

Extension FCS agents in Currituck and surrounding counties, Smart Start, and local health departments held the 11th annual regional childcare conference in 2007. The day-long event trained 228 providers who cared for 3,852 children.

FCS agents from five southwest counties began the annual Foothills Regional Conference for Early Childhood Educators in 2006. The 2010 conference, *Celebrating Every Child's Ability*, had workshops ranging from autism to nutrition to children's need for physical activity.

Extension's *Building Quality Child Care Conference* at Martin Community College in Williamston in 2008 offered a day of learning to 112 childcare providers, owners, and operators from 10 counties. The focus was on creating safer learning environments with stimulating learning materials. The conference was co-sponsored by Smart Start.

People could see too many Warren County teens were going down the wrong path. Extension trained members of cooperating agencies and groups to use *Healthy Marriage Matters, A Relationship Smarts Program for Teens*. Within six months, HMM's co-ordinator reached more than 500 teens. They said the program taught them to decide rather than to slide into a relationship, the difference between healthy and unhealthy relationships, and the importance of friends, family, and setting goals in life.

Leaders in Harnett County relied on Extension FCS for a program to lower the teen pregnancy rate. Extension's FCS pregnancy prevention program was so successful that the agent was asked to share the program in 2007 at the American Public Health Association Conference in Washington, D.C. The program supported pregnant teens' efforts to keep prenatal appointments, stay in school or at work, and practice birth control to prevent a second pregnancy.

In 2006, the repeat pregnancy rate for program participants was zero, much lower than the previous repeat pregnancy rate of 32 percent. That decrease was enough to move the county's teen pregnancy rate from 46th in 2005 to 78th in 2006. All the 100 teens in the program made their prenatal appointments and all had healthy babies.

Graduates of the Healthy Marriage Matters class for teens celebrate.

ECA clubs across the state participated in *Making a Difference for Children in Foster Care* by donating books, suitcases, book bags, school supplies, toiletries, and clothing.

Some clubs have taken that a step further by "adopting" a foster child or teen as their own.

In Moore County, ECA club members provide food for *Back Pack Pals*, a program that sends food home on Fridays so that children do not go hungry over the weekend.

Lemon Springs ECA Club "adopted" Greenwood School. They read to students, helped with the health-o-rama, gathered and donated materials and supplies for individual classrooms, and even helped with landscaping at the school. A highly successful project was the sewing of hundreds of cloth backpacks. They fit on the backs of students' chairs for storing books and supplies. The club also "adopted" first-year teachers, helping them with supplies.

With the country at war, ECA club members reached out to military families. In 2003 and 2004, over 350,000 manufacturer's coupons were collected and shipped to military families here and abroad. Club

Cleveland County ECA club members prepare books for kids in foster care, and ECA club members in Person County pack school supplies.

Daycare workers can borrow educational materials from Extension's Child Care Resources and Referral Lending Library in Harnett County.

members baked cookies and sent them to troops in Iraq and Afghanistan.

A special gift presentation was held at the 2008 ECA State Council meeting in Fayetteville, when three truckloads of baked goods and gifts from ECA club members throughout the state were presented to members of HHC 3rd Brigade at Ft. Bragg.

Some Alleghany County ECA members put their knitting needles together to make helmet liners for more than 90 soldiers from the county who were serving in areas with cold climates. Staff Sgt. Brandon Brown of Wellsville was the first to write to thank them. "I work the midnight shift, securing the base perimeter and I am outside in the elements all night. I have already found them to be very useful," Brown wrote. "Thank you so much for all your support and your prayers." Brown was assigned to Kirkuk Air Force Base in northern Iraq.

As a member of the newly-formed Catawba County Breast Cancer Coalition in late 1990s, the FCS agent saw that the sewing expertise of ECA club members could be used to make comfort garments for county breast cancer patients who were already overwhelmed with expenses.

The agent took the idea, a T-shirt pattern, and some fabric to Doris York, an ECA member, who was an expert seamstress. Doris made a prototype garment. She revised the design after evaluation by cancer patients in a local hospital. She invited other ECA members to join her, and the Camisole Project group started.

Once a month, for the last 10 years, a group of dedicated ECA members made camisoles, which are

Some of the baked goods and snacks given by ECA clubs to the HHC 3rd Brigade at Fort Bragg in 2008.

ECA club members in Union and Moore counties teach creative summer enrichment programs for children.

given to breast cancer patients in the county. Attached to each garment is a handwritten note from the group. As the project progressed, Susie bags (small bags to contain drainage tubes while the patient showers) and tote bags were added. Another ECA group, the Piedmont Piecemakers, sew mastectomy pillows.

This small group of women makes more than 300 camisoles, pillows, and tote bags annually. News of the camisoles has spread and requests for information have come from Maine to Montana. Every month the Camisole Project group receives notes from grateful recipients. The group has received several awards, including the Governor's Leadership Award.

Ashe County continues to be one of the most economically deprived counties in the state with limited resources, high unemployment, and a lack of transportation. County human service agencies have been facing tight budgets. So trained ECA volunteers are helping to fill the gaps. In 2008, ECA volunteers helped with educational programs and provided resources for groups such as the domestic violence shelter, saving taxpayers over $45,000.

Senior citizens need help navigating the Medicare system and its options for healthcare. That is why the NC Department of Insurance developed the SHIIP program.

Extension FCS has been one of the strongest partners working with the NC Department of Insurance since the '80s when the SHIIP program began. Extension provides the local "office" where

ECA club members in Catawba County have made special camisoles, Susie bags, tote bags, and mastectomy pillows for breast cancer patients for 10 years.

ECA club members in many counties made mastectomy pillows, caps, and other items to help cancer patients. Shown here are women from Perquimans, Lenoir, and Wayne counties.

where ECA and other volunteers are trained and where they meet with clients. They can sit with clients to review the details about the various Medicare D options. SHIIP volunteers do not recommend a specific plan, but help clients see the differences.

The FCS agent in Gates County is the volunteer SHIIP coordinator. In one year she helped 140 Medicare beneficiaries with eligibility and enrollment services in Part D plans. With the information she provided, each client saved between $3,000 and $4,000. Her help has saved county residents between $429,000 and $572,000.

Between 2007 and 2010, six trained SHIIP volunteers in Surry County conducted over 1,200 individual counseling sessions with Medicare recipients. If each person saved $2,000, that is a savings of $2,400,000.

Two important issues emerged in the 2000s in the housing and environment arena. The first involved the safety of homes, and the second was energy efficiency.

Research has shown that indoor air can be more seriously polluted than outdoor air. Most people spend about 90 percent of their time inside.

Mold is a major contributor to indoor air pollution and a health hazard, especially for those with asthma or allergies. To help homeowners check and combat mold, Extension specialists developed a program that could detect and prevent excess moisture.

FCS agents work with residents in Gates and Perquimans counties, helping them compare Medicare prescription drug plans.

Over 5,400 people used moisture management measures in and around the home in a two-year period.

Poor indoor air quality can also be a problem in schools. Extension received an EPA grant to pilot an *Indoor Air Quality Tools for Schools* program. Nash County and Cherokee Qualla Boundary were selected for the initial phase.

Nash County had been greatly affected by floods from Hurricane Floyd, leaving 26 schools with air quality problems. Schools on the Cherokee Reservation and in the adjacent counties of Swain and Cherokee were also experiencing indoor air quality problems and asked to be included in the project.

School personnel attended 21 training sessions and 11 workshops on indoor quality.

The conditions in 15 Lincoln County schools resulted in the passage of a $46 million school bond for mold removal, and Beaufort County passed a $1.4 million school bond to replace two schools that had been closed due to mold problems.

The NC Department of Public Instruction School Support Division asked Extension to conduct four regional training sessions on indoor air quality, which reached 85 percent of the school districts in the state. The Department of Public Instruction also formed a commission to address air quality in schools.

The second major housing issue is energy costs. An *E-Conservation* program was begun in 2005. Consumer workshops focused on easy energy-efficient changes, like installing fluorescent light bulbs, bathroom aerators, nightlights, wall outlet gaskets,

Members of Tyrrell County's Teen ECA Club put together goody bags for homebound senior citizens.

A Madison County librarian shows off the water heater that was wrapped after an Extension program on saving energy.

weatherstripping, insulation, adjusting hot water temperature settings, and turning off lights.

Stanly County seniors looking for ways to conserve energy attended the FCS agent's quarterly *E-Conservation* meetings. They learned tips for keeping their homes warmer during the winter months while saving money.

The project also involved 42 extensive energy audits. Audit findings revealed, on average, nine recommendations for each homeowner. The blower door test indicated 55 percent of the homes as leaky, 17 percent as average, and only 14 percent as tight.

Extension also helped older residents stay safe at home. Programs identified hazards and offered practical modifications and assistive technology to allow people to maintain their independence.

Extension is always looking for new ways to reach audiences. The FCS housing specialist is part of a team with faculty at Kansas State University who developed an Internet learning tool called *The LiveAbility House*. By accessing the Internet, a family can discover a *LiveAbility House*. The house allows the user to add universal design features to lessen the burdens of care and improve independence.

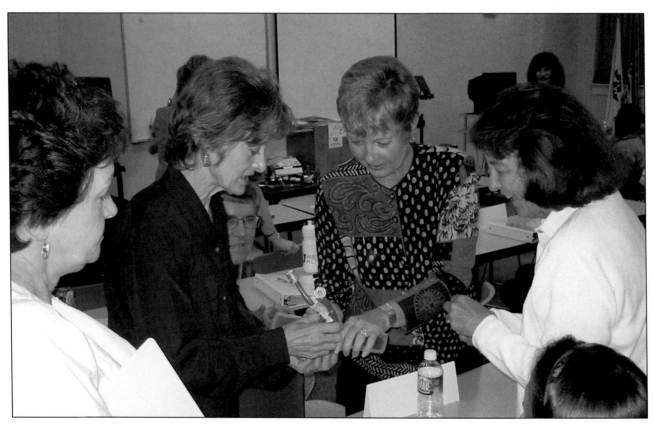

Buncombe County residents attend a Basic Home Maintenance course taught by the FCS agent.

In Craven County, ECA volunteers teach sewing and cooking, in Stanly County an ECA volunteer teaches home canning in a county without an FCS agent; and in Cabarrus County, ECA members teach at a fair.

ECA club members in Harnett and Johnston counties share hertiage skills, like quilting, with the younger generation.

State University
A&T State University
COOPERATIVE EXTENSION
Empowering People · Providing Solutions

eXtensi

The LiveAbility House
Last Updated: January 13, 2011

Table of Contents (Hide) (#)

What is Second Life®?

Second Life® is a free, Internet-based virtual world. Global users, called residents, interact with each other within the Second Life® environment in real time. Some residents simply visit places or events, while others may actually choose to create their own. Residents choose what and who to visit within Second Life®. Social activities such as dances and concerts, recreational pursuits such as skydiving and golfing, educational opportunities, such as attending lectures or attending classes, are just a few examples of things that Residents can do. Search functions help residents find events and items of interest.

Front of The LiveAbility House

http://www.extension.org/pages/The_LiveAbility_House

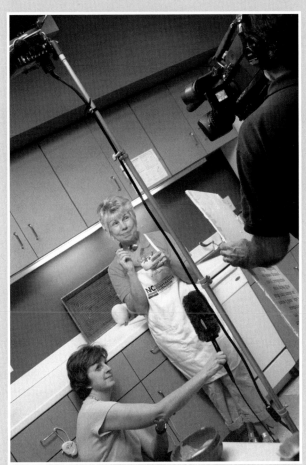
The Produce Lady films her show.

Computer-based programs like Extension's SyberShop make learning easy, as these Person County teens would attest.

Only six percent of the public had fast access broadband Internet in 2000; that figure skyrocketed to 75 percent by the end of the decade.

Here are some ways FCS agents, specialists, and ECA club members are using computers to reach this vast audience:

- *The LiveAbility House*, created by an N.C. State specialist working with faculty at Kansas State University, allows the public to create accessible housing in a virtual world called *SecondLife*.

- Two food and nutrition specialists at NC State University blog about food at *Food Myths and Memes* (foodmythsandmemes.com).

- *Jeannie's Kitchen Tips* has been broadcast on cable TV since 2007, but now people can see those videos and get recipes at any time via FCS Agent, Jeannie Leonard's Facebook page.

- *The Produce Lady*, a.k.a. Rockingham's county director and FCS agent, has videos, stories, and recipes at <theproducelady.wordpress.com>.

- Youngsville ECA Club promotes its annual fall festival and cookbook at youngsvillefallfestival.com/About_Us.html. The club also posts pictures from the annual event, which increases interest.

- ECA Quiltmakers of Gastonia keeps members and the public informed of their activities at www.freewebs.com/quiltmakersgastoniaeca.

Extension's programs for prospective homebuyers have always stressed avoiding unnecessary debt, buying an affordable home, and setting aside money for regular upkeep.

FCS agents worked to help families with lower incomes overcome challenges on the road to homeownership. The FCS agent in Edgecombe County worked with the Individual Development Account Program and Habitat for Humanity to provide education, guidance, and encouragement as families strived to achieve their goal of buying a home. In 2007, five families participating in these programs bought their first home.

Part of homeownership is upkeep on the house. More than 1,100 Buncombe County homeowners and prospective homeowners attended the FCS agent's *Basic Home Maintenance* courses in 2010. The five sessions cover do-it-yourself home repairs like basic plumbing, controlling stormwater runoff, and repairing drywall. The information is so valuable that the course

is required for families being served by several agencies, including Habitat for Humanity and OnTrack Financial Education & Counseling.

Extension programs can also help families increase their financial security. For example, parents of children in Brunswick County Head Start learned to make every penny count through *Money Trackers*, a basic money management program. Families prepared written budgets, learned how to pay bills on time, tracked expenses, set financial goals, established good credit, and saved for unexpected expenses. All 34 participants agreed that tracking their expenses "made life a little easier," the county FCS agent said of her 2009 class.

The state's Latino population is growing four times faster than the Caucasian population and twice as fast as the African American population. Extension was one of the first educational organizations to work with this new audience.

In 2006, Extension FCS was awarded a grant from the N.C. Department of Public Instruction to develop a successful dropout prevention program. They created *Juntos Para Una Mejor Educación* (Together for a Better Education), a program with both an activity-based and a family-based approach, to encourage parents and youth to work together in making academic success a reality.

Juntos has helped 450 parents and youth in 20 locations around the state. The activity-based program gets youth and parents learning together about ways to succeed in school, and helps them set family goals for after high school. *Juntos* is taught in either English or Spanish, and groups meet for 2½ hours once a week for six weeks after a sit-down meal. People from high schools, local community colleges, and college-age mentors also attend the workshops.

Students create plans to improve academic performance, participate in service projects, and develop teamwork and leadership skills.

In 2010, *Juntos* started an afterschool component at six high schools in Caswell, Granville, Sampson, Tyrrell, and Yadkin counties. Afterschool groups are led by bilingual "success coaches", who mentor students and coordinate local resources to meet the educational needs of participants.

Juntos families work together to make academic success a reality.

While citizens were stocking up on batteries and food before Hurricanes Frances and Ivan hit the southwest and northwest parts of the state in 2005, FCS agents were copying pages from Extension's *Disaster Notebook*.

After Frances flooded the area on Tuesday night, September 7, the Haywood County FCS agent took packets on disaster recovery and cleanup to the Clyde and Canton disaster headquarters at their fire departments. Thursday morning, she worried that people wouldn't get packets because they would be overwhelmed with cleaning and wouldn'tstop by the fire departments. So she put together more packets and went door to door delivering the information to Clyde homes. "In most cases that day, I was the first person the flood victims had talked to and I got many, many questions."

On Friday, the agricultural program assistant helped, so they reached more homes.

"The next Monday, just before Ivan," she said, "I returned to the Clyde neighborhoods and distributed what I called 'Phase 2' packets, with Cooperative Extension publications on insurance, going to the FEMA office, dealing with creditors and contractors and such." She also took 500 copies of *Helping Children Cope with Disaster* to Clyde Elementary School, wrote newspaper articles, and gave the local radio station public service announcements. "In my 11 years as an agent, this was the most appreciative and heartfelt response I have had from clientele, and for me,one of the most rewarding things I have done as an agent, although I hope we never have this opportunity again."

In Macon County, the FCS agent also prepared before the hurricanes hit. She faxed storm preparation information to the local newspapers and radio stations and took packets by the schools to be sent home with

In Haywood County, the FCS agent and agricultural program assistant turned to Extension's Disaster Notebook for handouts to deliver to help local citizens recover from flood damage in their county. The photo on the bottom shows damage in Clyde.

the kids. After Ivan had devastated the area, she delivered disaster cleanup information to radio stations and newspapers.

In Avery County, the FCS agent distributed Extension press releases and announcements to the *Avery Post*, the *Avery Journal*, and WECR-AM. That gave the public information on what to do after the floodwater receded and many articles on clean-up, purifying water, getting rid of mold,food safety, and dealing with stress.

Across the state before the start of each hurricane season, Extension agents and volunteers encourage the public to prepare for a possible natural disaster.

Extension encourages the public to be prepared. This display in downtown Raleigh reminds residents that hurricanes, floods, tornadoes, and other natural disasters do strike the state, and that they can take steps to safeguard their families and homes.

Juntos logo.

Leadership has long been a strength of ECA volunteers. The annual Women's Leadership Conference in Union County, co-sponsored by Extension FCS and ECA, began in 2005. The 2007 Union County Women's Leadership Conference, "The Oz Principle" helped 170 women gained skills in networking, diplomacy, relationship building, professional development, leadership skills, and mentoring. Participants included women in business, in local government and public service, entrepreneurs, students, community volunteers, and stay-at-home moms. Other conference themes included everyday

ethics, navigating life's obstacle course, and leadership through a healthy lifestyle.

Many ECA members have become community leaders. They have served as town mayors and county commissioners. Club members have served on the local and state Extension Advisory committees and on the N.C. 4-H Development Fund Board. They have held many leadership positions within the state and national ECA organization. They are watching out for those less fortunate in their communities including nursing home residents and victims of abuse.

Keeping the FCS program strong requires money. As public dollars continue to shrink, private funding helps fill the gaps. In 2004, Dr. Sandra Zaslow appointed a steering committee to oversee the development of a foundation to support FCS programs. The NC Family and Consumer Sciences Foundation, launched in 2005, was the first foundation in the country to support Extension FCS programs.

The following month, the board of directors began *The Founding Circle of Friends* fundraising campaign. By the end of 2007, the FCS Foundation had raised $756,250, and announced its first call for innovative grant proposals in support of FCS county programs.

The Little Switzerland club was the first ECA club in the state to establish a fund within the foundation. Wake ECA was the first county ECA group to fund an endowment in the FCS Foundation when they established their Maude P. McInnes Scholarship. That

Members of the first Board of Directors of the NCECA Foundation.

Wilson County ECA group presenting Lois Rainwater Endowment to FCS Foundation.

was followed by the Frances Turner FCS Endowment and the Wake County ECA Enhancement Fund.

The largest county deposit was $34,317 from Wilson County ECA for the Lois Rainwater Educational Scholarship Endowment.

When Edward Gore established the Dinah Gore Foods, Nutrition, and Fitness Endowment to honor his wife, he wanted to represent her interests in healthy food preparation and fitness. This endowment also served as the largest private gift to the Family and Consumer Sciences program, with $250,000 being invested so that the income might be utilized

in perpetuity. The first program the Dinah Gore Endowment funded was *Cook Smart, Eat Smart*, which was designed to help families learn to prepare foods together and eat at home around the kitchen table.

The NCECA made the second largest gift to date, by transferring $155,740, the NCECA McKimmon, Smith, and Lowe Scholarship Endowment, into the FCS Foundation.

Mrs. Mozelle Parker, a respected ECA member and past president of the association, used a charitable trust to create a fund that will support ECA work in her county of Scotland.

Mrs. Ada Dalla-Pozza, Maurene Rickards, and Sylvia Churchwell unveil the NCECA Foundation logo.

Edward and Dinah Gore, who gave $250,000 to the FCS Foundation to support healthy food preparation and fitness.

Jerry and Martha Hardesty established the first unrestricted fund for FCS with the creation of the Martha and Jerry Hardesty FCS Board Endowment. Like Mrs. Parker, the Hardestys used a charitable trust to fund the endowment that will be managed to support special board initiatives.

In 2008 the NC Extension and Community Association members approved the establishment of a foundation to support NCECA programs. Mrs. Dorothy McCoy, ECA state president, appointed a steering committee to develop the vision, mission and by-laws. The NCECA Foundation, launched in 2010, is the first foundation in the country supporting Extension volunteer programs.

The FCS and 4-H departments at NC State University merged in 2006. Dr. Marshall Stewart, head of the 4-H Youth Development Department was named head of the new combined department. Both programs have traditionally shared some programming initiatives, like EFNEP.

"The merger puts Extension, the college, and the university in the strongest position to address families and youth," Dr. Stewart said. "Statewide, no one has the network of paid staff and volunteers focused on these issues that Extension has."

Dr. Ray McKinnie, administrator of The Cooperative Extension Program at N.C. A&T State University, notes another strength of the organization. "Cooperative Extension strives to make our audiences recession-proof, and when the ravages of this unstable economy cannot be held off, we work to give people new skills, new ways, and new hope."

FCS specialists and agents as well as ECA club members are proud of their rich heritage, but they are especially proud of the impact their programs have on families in North Carolina.

"I am a product of home demonstration clubs. My grandmothers were both leaders in local Martin County (clubs). My love for cooking came through their love for entertaining and extending southern hospitality. Both had very large gardens and worked on the farm. As a child I remember partaking of the fruits of their labor. They would be thrilled to know I help carry Extension traditions by educating and sustaining families in Martin County," said Tanya Wynne, Martin County FCS agent.

FCS in North Carolina is recognized as an organization that, literally, does its research and develops and produces some of the best educational materials in the United States. The woman-on-the-street may only meet the county FCS agent, ECA club volunteer, or pick up an Extension publication from a display at a meeting or event, but the people behind the information are specialists and researchers at NC State University, N.C. A&T State University, and many other colleges and universities.

That team of FCS agent, specialist, and ECA volunteer is a combination that has worked for 100 years.

At the state and county level, programs and program delivery methods have changed to meet the needs of the times. That fact is very clear from the history presented in this book. North Carolina families want up-to-date reliable educational programs to help them improve their lives, just as those women Jane McKimmon worked with in 1911 did, and Extension FCS and its ECA volunteers plan to be there every step of the way.

The Story of Ordinary Women Continues

The following section includes stories about long ago and current Extension programs in each county. There in also an interesting bit of history sprinkled in at times. This is no way reflects ALL the programs and projects. They were too numerous to fit on one page. These are only the highlights chosen by the book committee. There are great stories on every page that illustrate how the dedicated Extension agents and club members have made a difference, and continue to serve the people in their county.

ℐn 1990, Extension Homemakers made batches of soft homemade dolls with a special ingredient...love. These cuddly stuffed dolls went to police and firefighters who gave them to frightened children who needed something to cling to in a crisis. The project was so successful, it was expanded to include homemade sock toys, bears, and clowns that were used to bring smiles to the faces of children at Alamance County Hospital and at the local abuse shelter.

Alamance Extension Homemakers show a batch of care dolls before passing them on to local police and fire departments where they would be given to young children in the midst of a crisis.

The Extension secretary answers a call while the agent and the EH leader discuss a project.

ℰxtension and the Alamance County Landfill provided citizens with a day to dispose of potentially hazardous products that should not go into a regular landfill. In a single day in 2007, county residents brought 53,368 pounds of paint and 1,150 pounds of pesticides to a central location for environmentally responsible disposal.

ℰxtension Homemakers members have always gotten the men involved in their projects, but in the 1980s a group of Alamance county men decided to form their own club. The Honey DO's were full-fledged EH members,

Members of the Honey DO's Mens EH Club are picking up trash as one of their service projects.

attending craft workshops and events and working on community projects. They even taught woodworking and metal craft workshops for women in other clubs. One of the club's projects was construction of a park bench in Graham. A new jail had just been completed and there was one lovely tree left standing. The club built a circular wooden bench around that tree to invite people to stop and rest a while.

𝒜lamance County had 56 Hispanic owned and operated restaurants, and some owners and employees spoke limited English. They had struggled in previous years with Extension's ServSafe foods training program, so the Alamance County center brought in an additional resource, the National Environmental Health Association Food Safety Training, and 87 percent of participants passed.

217

Alexander

POPULATION 36,953

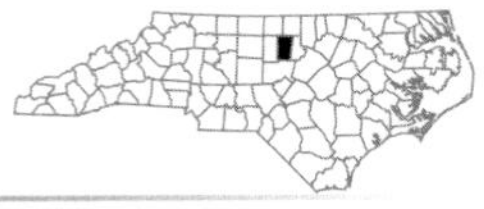

In 1992, two people had died in bike-related accidents, and Alexander County had no bike safety education program. The FCS agent surveyed fourth through sixth graders at five elementary schools. Only 20 percent

After two bike-related deaths in the county, EH members started a bike safety program.

said they owned helmets and only 5 percent actually used them. Extension got the word out via the mass media, EH speakers' bureau, health fairs at elementary schools, and in-store promotions. EH volunteers, local bike club members, and civic club members trained 99 young people at two bike rodeos. Each child at the rodeo was presented an approved, custom-fitted helmet. Police supported the community effort by issuing safe riding citations to 55 youth observed practicing safe riding skills.

When the North Carolina Good Health Association and the Medical Society of North Carolina began a

Alexander County Hospital in the 1950s.

county good health council program in 1948, Alexander County grabbed the opportunity to be one of the first demonstration health councils in the state. The Extension Home Agent was one of the community leaders on that first council. They decided to raise money to complete the hospital-health department first. The Home Demonstration Clubs of Alexander County furnished the reception room. Later, the council took on sanitation, recruitment of medical workers, school health, and hospital insurance campaigns.

After Extension moved into the county administration building, Extension Homemakers members began working on a quilt to represent their group. Each club prepared a block to represent its community or club. The quilt was presented to the county in 1993.

Extension Homemakers Club members prepare Welcome Newcomers buckets in the 1980s, a joint venture with the local Chamber of Commerce.

Alleghany ECA members have offered Alleghany prom attendees an alternative to the typical after-prom parties. They offer food, fun and fellowship and serve as chaperones at an alcohol-free party held at the local bowling alley. Someone dies every 31 minutes on our highways, but since the EH alcohol-free after-prom parties began 19 years ago, there has not been one alcohol-related accident in the county on prom night.

All schools receiving federal funds had to integrate federal food safety guidelines referred to as *Hazard Analysis Critical Control Point* (*HACCP*) into their food program by July 1, 2006. Alleghany County's FCS agent taught site managers from four different schools procedures critical to a successful *HACCP* plan. Site managers have used the information to keep 1,744 children safe.

Alleghany County ECA members put their knitting needles together in

An Alleghany potter throwing a pot in 1979.

2007 to make helmet liners for more than 90 soldiers from the county who were serving in areas with cold climates. Staff Sgt. Brandon Brown of Wellsville was the first to write to thank them. "I work the midnight shift, securing the

Staff Sgt. Brandon Brown of Wellsville, at Kirkuk Air Force Base in northern Iraq, wearing one of the 90 helmet liners knitted and sent overseas to soldiers in 2007. Brown is part of the Security Forces, the equivalent of the Military Police.

base perimeter and I am outside in the elements all night. I have already found them to be very useful," Brown wrote. "Thank you so much for all your support and your prayers." Brown was a member of the 506th Air Expeditionary Group assigned to Kirkuk Air Force Base in northern Iraq.

Roaring Gap Home Demonstration Club members from Alleghany County stand behind products on display in curb market exhibit at North Carolina State Fair in 1956.

In Anson County, the obesity rate is 33 percent for adults and 25 percent for children. Over $2 million Medicaid dollars spent each year in the county are attributed to conditions related to being overweight or obese. The FCS agent held a 10-week program for 65 students in five classes at Wadesboro Primary School, using lessons and demonstrations to increase healthier eating, physical activity, and food safety.

She also involved 21 adults in a 15-week program designed to teach participants to make healthier food choices, increase their levels of activity, and be mindful of their lifestyles. In total, the group lost 150 pounds. Several people were also able to decrease their blood pressure levels.

BARTER DAYS~Farm women traditionally sold butter and eggs for extra money that would be stashed away for an emergency or special purpose. In the late 1950s, Anson County Extension Homemakers also sold delicious cakes, pies, and fresh produce. Clothing and household and farm items were also brought to sell or trade at Barter Days.

Rosalind Redfearn was one of the first home demonstration agents in North Carolina. She organized Anson County's first home demonstration clubs in 1913.

Apron-making contests, unique to rural areas, put cash into the hands of local women in Anson County.

Ashe POPULATION 26,319

Homes in northwestern North Carolina have historically shown the highest radon levels in the state. Radon gas, the second leading cause of lung cancer, can reach unsafe levels in homes. Testing for radon is the only way to know if levels inside a home are unsafe. Working with the NC Division of Radiation Protection, Extension gave 76 free radon test kits to Ashe County families in 2008. Twenty percent of the homes turned out to have elevated levels. Over half of these families asked for information on how to reduce radon levels in their homes.

Ashe County continues to be one of the most economically deprived counties in the state with limited resources, high unemployment and lack of transportation. County human service agencies are faced with tight budgets,

Extension Homemakers are proud of their newly refurbished furniture, a technique learned through Extension.

the domestic violence shelter and local sharing centers.

When Ashe County residents learned that 450 families with children wouldn't be able to afford presents for their children at Christmas, volunteers adopted all the children. ECA volunteers accepted donations and coordinated the volunteer effort to sort,

box, wrap, and distribute about 6,000 gifts to 699 children.

Eight volunteers were trained to help A.S.H.E. (A Safe Home for Everyone) in its work against domestic violence, which includes providing advocates who work on-call shifts. Volunteers have given over 500 hours in support of A.S.H.E.

ECA club members help support higher education by presenting a scholarship check to their 2010 recipient.

so the county is using trained ECA volunteers to help fill gaps in services in tough financial times. ECA volunteers provided services that would have cost taxpayers over $45,000 in 2008. These services include helping with educational programs and providing resources for

ECA members worked with Jefferson Water Services and the county health department to register people bringing in samples of water for testing.

Car crashes are the number one cause of death in North Carolina for children under the age of 14, and they are the number two reason for hospitalizations. The Avery County FCS agent is also the volunteer coordinator of the Avery County Safe Kids Chapter. As such, she helped distribute 42 car seats at half price in 2008 and, more importantly, showed each family how to properly install and use the seat. Studies show that the majority of car seats are improperly installed, and major injury drops by 71 percent when a child is properly secured in a correctly installed car seat.

Each square of this unique quilt made in the 1950s represents a local landmark of the individual Home Demonstration club designing and handcrafting it. The squares were put together and quilted by the Beech Mountain Club. It is still hanging in the Avery County Museum today.

Extension helped 164 Avery County residents keep their 2008 New Year's resolution with Extension's *Eat Smart, Move More, Weigh Less*, a 20-week program to help adults improve their health. At the end of 20 weeks, participants had lost 914 pounds in a safe, healthy manner. One person was able to stop taking acid reflux pills and another talked with his doctor about coming off of his high blood pressure pills.

Cheese Making in the 1940s

At the end of my first summer when the canning season was over, I kept turning in my mind thoughts for a countywide project. Outside my office window there sat Mrs. Barlow. I went out and asked her if she had a milk cow. She said, "Yes, I have three and I get 12 quarts of milk each morning and night from them. I just throw a lot of it out to our pigs." Then I asked if she would like to learn how to make American cheese and she replied, "I shore would." She learned, too, and taught her family and friends in two other communities to make cheese. I took her to the communities but let her do most of the work.

I had a neighbor who lived at West Jefferson, Ashe County, so we took off one day and went to West Jefferson. While she visited with friends I visited the cheese factory. They were very kind to show me the plant and explain the process of making cheese. I secured rennet and cheese coloring, also thermometer and directions given by their manufacturers. I came home, was given milk and so made several runs of cheese.

My equipment for heating milk was a tin lard stand, press was a 4-quart tin can with bottom and top removed. As the weight or press I used a large rock that I had thoroughly scrubbed. At that time many people did not have screens. So I made a frame as for a box 1 foot square by 2 feet high, screened it, then I placed the cheese on the shelves in this container. Neither flies nor mice could get to it. This container was hung from the ceiling in a cool place for the cheese to ripen 6 weeks. Women everywhere requested this demonstration so I made the rounds. Some women made from 20 to 40 pounds of cheese in a season. This protein food was a great help in getting meals balanced as most families had little meat.

Usually a family raised one hog; few used homegrown beef. Chickens were very scarce. When chickens were used they were started in the spring, usually ordered from hatcheries. That meant that gardens were up, so little chicks did not bother. They matured in time to begin laying for fall and winter use. By spring the hens were killed off so they would not destroy the gardens, and new broods were started.

Georgia P. Cahoon
Home Demonstration Agent

The first Home Demonstration curb market in Beaufort County ran from May through September, 1925. Beginning in 1926, the market was open throughout the year. By 1928, the market was so successful that HD clubs no longer needed to sponsor and support it.

———— ∞∞ ————

When one of Beaufort's rural hospitals applied for accreditation in 2008, it received less than satisfactory ratings in the kitchen. The hospital asked Extension to teach a food safety course to the entire kitchen staff. After the staff put what they'd learned into action, the kitchen passed without a single demerit.

———— ∞∞ ————

On May 3, 2010, the FCS agent, was driving her pickup truck down Goose Creek Road heading for an ECA meeting at Polly Cox's house. She noticed a pack of dogs circling

FCS has helped people to become more self-sufficient so they can live successfully on their own.

something on the side of the road. When it raised its head, she realized it was a newborn fawn. She rescued it and drove off to the meeting with a baby deer in her lap. The 76ers immediately fell in love with their new member. They named her Dottie,

An EH club member teaches low-income families how to make their own detergent.

coaxed her to drink milk from a bottle, and were rewarded as Dottie took her first wobbly steps. After staying several days with Beth Allender, sleeping on a bed, chasing after Beth's children and grandchildren, and gaining strength, Dottie was taken to a wildlife refuge in Hatteras where "she" was renamed Little Buck.

At the annual Farm Wives Night Out, FCS provided an educational program on women and heart disease.

The newspaper headline from the *Bertie Ledger* reads "Work of Home Demonstration Club Women at Wakelon is Crowned by Building Church." Members of the Wakelon community held church services in a tenant house for two years until home demonstration club women decided it was time to have a church building. On May 28, 1944, Community Baptist

Bertie residents enjoy a healthy cooking class.

Eat Smart, Move More graduates. The "biggest loser" lost 26.5 pounds and won $300. The 2010 class learned nutrition, calorie counting, and aerobic and strength-building exercises.

Letter from Lorie Odom

"I thoroughly enjoyed the *Eat Smart, Move More, Weigh Less* program and have missed it so much since it ended. Just having that hour to do something for myself was wonderful. I am keeping the weight off and trying to lose more. At work, Viquest has started a challenge for May to exercise at least 150 minutes a week. It's going to be hard but I'm going to try. Years ago, before kids, I was really into aerobics. I loved exercising and even taught some classes at the YMCA. Now I'm so overworked I barely have a moment to myself."

Thank you for bringing this wonderful program to us and please start it again soon.

~Lorie Odom

Church was dedicated. The church name was changed to Wakelon Baptist Church in 1947.

———— ✦ ————

*B*ertie Extension began an in-home breastfeeding support program in March 2008. New mothers signed up in the hospital after giving birth. By the end of 2008, 52 moms had signed up, and 48 were successful at breastfeeding. Half of those continued to breastfeed for more than six months.

———— ✦ ————

*I*n 2008, the FCS agent challenged Bertie County teachers and staff to begin *Step Up To Better Health*, an AARP walking program. Participants were given pedometers, a weekly newsletter, and a walking log. They hit the trails, walking trails built for students, and competed for 10 weeks for a wellness prize. Here's what the winner had to say about the program: "Thank you for organizing this walking program. It gave me the motivation I needed not only to walk but to eat better. I have lost 21 pounds but most importantly, I feel better."

Bladen POPULATION 32,153

Extension Homemakers learn to make baskets in the 1960s.

*A*ny time a volunteer is needed, Extension comes to mind. To use 2005 as an example, ECA had volunteers in Hospice, hospitals, schools, nursing homes, county fairs, county Expo, National Christmas Tree Decoration Project, Parade of Trees, Special Olympics, Bladen We Care, 4-H and Teen Court, rescue squad, Meals on Wheels, Pregnancy Crisis Center, Harmony Hill Historic Site, and area churches.

A few of their fundraising projects include the Turkey Dinner Plate Sale around Thanksgiving, Christmas in July salad luncheon for shoppers, The Rainbow Dinner, an auction, and the Expo Dessert Sale at the County Expo.

*W*hen Hurricane Katrina hit the Gulf Coast in 2005, Bladen County ECA members knew they had to find a way to help. They prepared 85 bags for babies. Members devoted several days to making a baby blanket for each bag. They also included two outfits, diapers, baby wipes, a new toy, soap, shampoo, wash cloths, and information on child development.

*T*he FCS agent teaches healthy eating once a month at each of the two Head Start Centers in Bladen County. The 77 children have learned to discriminate between healthy food and junk food and are willing to try healthy snacks. Recipes are sent home to parents.

*T*he phrase "March madness" took on new meaning for Bladen County students in kindergarten through eighth grade. Extension, working with the public schools, the Bladen County Health Department and Bladen Health Watch, challenged the 4,251 students and 259 staff to eat at least five fruits and vegetables every day with *Gimme 5 Challenge* visits to the cafeterias. One school had 100 percent participation.

Bladen County Head Start students learned about the importance of eating smart and moving more.

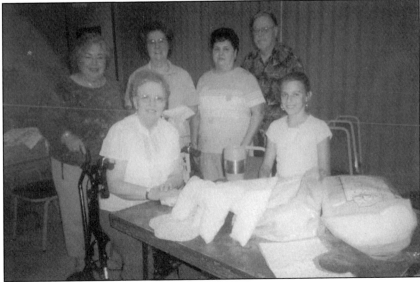

ECA members made 200 mastectomy pillows to donate to breast cancer survivors.

The Brunswick County sheriff received stuffed bears and quilts from ECA members. Law enforcement will use them to comfort traumatized children.

County Habitat for Humanity for families in the homeownership program. To help prepare families for home ownership, the FCS agent developed a series of financial management workshops to help participants get a handle on disposable income, household operations and basic needs (food, shelter and clothing). Participants tracked down money leaks and outlined steps to establish and repair credit. Records were organized, and families learned how to prevent identity theft.

People from all walks of life are being affected by the economic downturn, and parents with children in Brunswick County Head Start are learning to make every penny count. Thirty-four parents completed *Money Trackers* in 2009, learning basic money management. They prepared written budgets and learned how to pay bills on time, track expenses, set financial goals, establish good credit, and save for unexpected expenses. *Money Trackers* helped them eliminate waste in their budgets, especially the money spent on fast foods. All 34 participants agreed that tracking their expenses made life a little easier.

People want to eat healthy foods but only if those healthy foods taste good. The county FCS agent has taught over 500 participants to flavor their foods with herbs instead of extra salt and fat. She printed a 50-page booklet explaining how to grow, harvest, preserve and use herbs. Meg

Shelton of Shelton Herb Farm near Winnabow donated herb samples for demonstrations and offered tours.

Six families were chosen to participate in the *Project Education* curriculum developed by Leadership Brunswick County and implemented by Brunswick

Each year ECA club members collect and donate food to the Volunteer Information Center, Family Assistance, and similar organizations.

During the 1980s and early 1990s, Extension Homemakers members collected hundreds of gently-used dolls. They cleaned them up, combed their hair, and sewed new outfits to make them better than new. Each year, these dolls were distributed to needy children at Christmas.

The Smith-McDowell House in Asheville, a four-story mansion built 20 years before the Civil War, is the oldest surviving house in Asheville and the oldest brick house in Buncombe County. After years of neglect, Francis McDowell and her niece Clare McDowell, members of the Biltmore Extension Homemakers Club, initiated the restoration of the home. Francis' passion for the restoration soon inspired other EH clubs in the county to help. EH volunteers made draperies for the home, assisted with teas, planted bushes and worked in other areas of the renovation.

In 1983 the County Council donated an antique silver punch bowl, tray and ladle dated 1880, in memory of member Genevieve Morris.

Today the home is a museum and is included in the National Register of Historic Places.

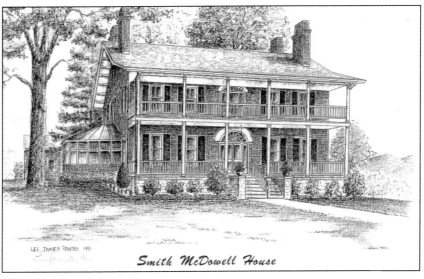

Smith McDowell House

Pen and Ink drawing by Lee Pantas.

Over 1,100 Buncombe County homeowners and prospective homeowners have attended the FCS agent's *basic home maintenance* course. The five sessions, which are offered at least five times a year, cover do-it-yourself home repairs, such as basic plumbing, controlling stormwater runoff and repairing drywall. The course is so valuable that it is required for prospective homeowners by several agencies, including Habitat for Humanity and OnTrack Financial Education & Counseling.

Many mobile home park and campground owners must maintain

EH club members made and presented a county flag to the Buncombe County Commissioners in 1988. The flag remains on display in the chamber to this day.

septic systems and wells to remain in business. In 2006, the FCS agent put together a workshop with experts from Buncombe County Environmental Health, NC DENR Public Water Supply, and NC State University Soil Science Department to help sustain parks and protect the environment. A survey three months after the workshop revealed that the 50 workshop participants had not only put what they'd learned to work, they had shared it with others.

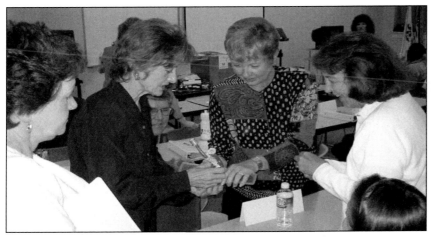

Homeowners and prospective homeowners attend Buncombe County's Basic Home Maintenance course.

227

The 20 Extension Homemakers Clubs in and around Morganton took out their sewing machines in the 1980s to comfort sick children and new mothers. Over the years, they made more than 100 dolls for the pediatric ward at Grace Hospital. Some of the club women also have made diaper bags and donated them to the Health Center for Young Mothers.

—— ❧❧❧ ——

Improving the diet of seniors with limited resources can lead to better health, a sense of well-being and reduced medical expenses. Residents of a local Section 8 housing complex attended a workshop and learned that eating healthier foods can improve

Burke County Extension Club members participated in many environmental and community beautification projects over the years. Here they are planting a tree for Arbor Day.

blood pressure, maintain heart health, and reduce complications from diabetes. Twelve women and two men received a

week of healthy menus featuring basic mixes that could be used to prepare meals. More than half prepared and froze basic mixes or shared them with other residents within the first two weeks following the workshop. Residents made a commitment to eat fruits and vegetables with high nutritional value for better health.

Since 1979, Nouveau ECA Club has supported projects at Options, Inc., the emergency shelter for families in crisis due to domestic violence.

"Options is truly grateful to the Nouveau Extension Club for their ongoing support. When Options opened our new battered women's shelter in 2002, the club furnished a bedroom and bathroom. The club continues to support Options with needed supplies, such as food and cleaning items. They always provide meals for the holidays and make sure all children receive special gifts during the holidays. Options knows

that we can always call on the Nouveau Extension Club when we are in need. They have made a difference in the lives of so many women and children. We are truly thankful to have the Nouveau Extension Club as a supporter."

–Kristy K. Graf, Executive Director

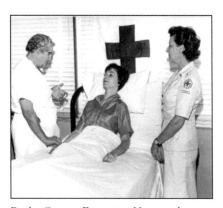

Burke County Extension Homemakers volunteered at community Bloodmobile drives in the 1950s.

Cabarrus POPULATION 170,406

Rimer Extension Homemakers Club members work on a quilt in the 1950s.

In 1976, Extension Homemakers attending a demonstration on seafood saw that Extension's home in the dilapidated county annex was no longer serviceable. They decided to get the county to build a new facility. They visited other county facilities, drew up a proposal and used it to convince the county commissioners. The county commissioners were so impressed with the proposal and the presentation by the Extension Homemakers, they approved the plan. In November 1979 Extension moved into a beautiful new building with a large auditorium for demonstrations and offices for all Extension workers.

Partnering with Cabarrus Family Medicine, the FCS agent offered a series of classes, *Families Eating Smart, Moving More*, each quarter during the year. In addition to moving more and making healthy food choices, families reported they spent less time watching television.

Extension collaborated with the Department of Aging and Carolinas Medical Center - Northeast in presenting the annual Senior Health and Wellness Day in 2008. Over 1,000 seniors benefitted from health screenings, exhibits and demonstrations.

The FCS agent helped county employees improve their health with 12 weeks of *Noonliting* classes held at lunchtime in 2005 and 2006. Fifty-eight graduates lost a total of 370 pounds. Employees report that they are reading food labels, altering recipes to cut back on fat, sugar and sodium, and are much more conscious of the calories they consume.

Poplar Tent members have been decorating Easter eggs for the local soup kitchen since the 1980s.

The Extension FCS agent and Cabarrus ECA club members recently teamed up with Cabarrus Partnership for Children and other children's agencies to offer the 13th annual Coming Together for Children Conference. More than 800 daycare teachers and parents attended.

Cook Smart, Eat Smart class members, assisted by ECA volunteers, cook, chop, and prepare to taste healthy meals.

Caldwell County employees (plus one daughter) participated in Extension's Cook Smart, Eat Smart program, which is funded by a grant. The FCS agent who teaches the class says the most common comment is "I was always busy with my career and never had time to learn how to cook."

After several years of planning and discussion, the Caldwell County culinary program was added to the community college in 2006. The FCS agent is a member of the advisory board for the program and she helps with classes in food safety and the history of the wine industry in North Carolina. Students can earn an associate's degree in culinary technology at Caldwell Community College and Technical Institute.

———————

With high unemployment a problem in 2002, Extension produced two videos for the cable channel that discussed ways to cope when you lose your job. The information was based on the FCS publication series *What to Do When Your Income Drops*. The two videos focused on taking control, creating a plan to pay creditors, and keeping a roof overhead. They gave local phone numbers for additional help. The local cable operator said the shows reached approximately 1,350 citizens.

———————

In 2008 the FCS Agent taught a 10-week program on nutrition to 45 third-graders at one school in

The families of culinary students at Caldwell Community College and Technical Institute enjoy a senior project: a three-course meal.

the county where 80 to 90 percent of the students are receiving free or reduced-price meals. At the end of the program, 96 percent said they were making healthier choices. The greatest improvements were seen in the number of children eating their fruits and vegetables.

———————

When Vance County Social Services Department requested diversity training for its employees, Extension recommended the FCS agents in Caldwell and Granville Counties to lead the workshop. The agents were members of Extension's Diversity Catalyst team. The agents helped 125 employees recognize and find ways to solve issues that might arise.

———————

One of the most gratifying projects of the Half Century Extension Homemakers Club in the last 30 years was helping a child who had juvenile arthritis.

A group of administrative assistants, administrators and professors known as the Thursday Group takes Extension's Eat Smart, Move More, Weigh Less class at Caldwell Community College and Technical Institute.

Camden POPULATION 9,730

The Extension FCS agent has reached many seniors with educational information in the last few years. In 2006, approximately 150 senior adults participated in the multi-county Aging with Gusto Conference, which involved workshops on Medicare Part D, healthy lifestyles, financial planning, living wills, and preventing identity theft. The agent has also taught bi-weekly workshops at the Camden Senior Center. Twenty-five limited-resource adults learned better nutrition and health practices. Fifteen said they are now eating better, being more physically active, handling food safely, and taking charge of their health. More recently some 50 people received help with Medicare Part D at a senior adult health fair at the Camden Senior Center.

—— ❦ ——

In collaboration with More at 4 in Camden County, the FCS agent taught 48 four-year-olds how to properly wash their hands to eliminate germs. Each child's hands were "contaminated" with pretend germs and the children washed their hands as usual. But these germs were "glo-germs," which could be seen when a special light was shown over the children's hands. The children learned how to wash their hands thoroughly to eliminate real germs.

—— ❦ ——

The average age of the nine Belcross ECA Club members may have been 78 in 2007, but that didn't keep these dedicated women from helping their community. They raised more than $5,000 through various fundraising activities. They provided Christmas gifts for four needy children, gave a $500 college scholarship, and donated to the

Aging With Gusto participants learn about healthy lifestyles, financial planning, living wills, and preventing identity theft.

Albemarle Food Bank and Albemarle Hopeline.

—— ❦ ——

Childcare providers are required to participate in continuing education in order for the childcare businesses to operate and remain certified. Camden Extension joined with Extension offices in Chowan, Currituck, Dare, Gates,

Hertford, Tyrrell, and Washington counties to produce the Albemarle Child Care Conference in 2008. The day-long conference offered workshops in curriculum, licensure, handling medicines, safety, and foods and nutrition. Twenty-seven childcare providers participated in the hands-on workshop.

Since 1973, the experienced cooks from county Extension Homemakers clubs have gathered monthly in the N.C. State University Seafood Lab kitchen to test new ways of handling, storing, and preparing fish and shellfish. Their taste-tested recipes have gone worldwide, first in the Seafood Lab's newsletter, Mariner's Menu, then in a 280-page book called Mariner's Menu: Thirty Years of Fresh Seafood Ideas, and now through the web at http://marinersmenu.org/. The group continues to meet and cook every month.

———— 8003 ————

When the curb market began in 1931, 42 Home Demonstration members sold homegrown and homemade items under the trees on Arendell Street in Morehead City. By 1942, they had raised enough money to construct a building on land provided by the county. The Carteret County ECA still owns and operates the Curb Market, which is open each Saturday morning May through Labor Day. Locally grown fruit and vegetables, and flowers, fresh seafood, baked goods, and

Home Demonstration Curb Market in Morehead City in 1950 ... and it is still going today.

North Carolina crafts are sold, and the market also features a demonstration garden.

———— 8003 ————

Could an employee wellness program help hold down the rising cost of employee health insurance? Extension worked with the Carteret County Human Resources Department to test this out. The county offered a free health screening and surveyed employees' interests. Wellness programs were established to meet their needs. At the end of the first year, the county was able to hold the cost of employee

insurance to the same rate as the previous year. This was the first year the county had not seen a substantial increase in employee insurance costs.

———— 8003 ————

The family medicine cabinet is the primary source of drugs for today's teens. Cooperative Extension and other Healthy Carolinians of Carteret County partners joined with the sheriff's department to shut off the source. Sheriff's deputies and local police accepted prescription bottles at the five Food Lion stores in the county. Over 40,000 pills and other drugs, such as vials of morphine, were collected. This campaign increased awareness, provided education about secure storage and proper disposal, and assured that these drugs would not be misused.

Vera Gaskins, former mayor of Emerald Isle and a member of the Emerald Isle ECA, with town manager Frank Rush in front of the quilt ECA made to celebrate the town's 50th birthday in 2007.

The women the Seafood Lab couldn't do without: volunteers from Carteret County ECA clubs who have tested the lab's fish and shellfish recipes since 1973.

232

The FCS agent reports running into one of her Food Stamp Nutrition Education third grade students at the store recently. The child's eyes got extremely big and she said "Mrs. Patterson, I can't believe my dad is making me get this sugar because I know we are not supposed to eat a lot of this!"

"I was so impressed that the classes had made such a huge impact. I told her that it was ok to have a little sugar." In the *Food Stamp Nutrition Education* program, the FCS agent teaches 10 nutrition and food-safety classes to third graders in two of the county's elementary schools. Based on evaluations and parent and teacher feedback forms, more than half of the children are now more active, are making better food and drink choices, and are reading nutrition facts labels.

STATE OF NORTH CAROLINA
OFFICE OF THE GOVERNOR
20301 Mail Service Center • Raleigh, NC 27699-0301

BEVERLY EAVES PERDUE
GOVERNOR

July 15, 2010

Ms. Lesley Stanford
1509 Ridge Lane
Hillsborough, North Carolina 27278

Dear Ms. Stanford,

Thank you for bringing to my attention the *From the Garden to the Pantry* Food Preservation Workshops sponsored by the North Carolina Cooperative Extension. I appreciate you sharing your positive experience with home economists Sonya Patterson, Deborah Taylor and Bess Hester-Whitt.

I am pleased to hear that the program was a success. Basic skills such as canning, freezing and drying foods used to be part of household traditions passed from generation to generation. As our nation embraces "green living" as a part of our 21st Century lifestyle, knowing how to preserve food will be helpful to reducing waste and ensuring that families can stretch their food dollar further.

Thank you for writing and good luck canning, freezing and drying foods.

Sincerely,

Bev Perdue

ABJ/
c: NC Cooperative Extension

"Basic skills such as canning, freezing and drying foods used to be part of household traditions passed from generation to generation. As our nation embraces 'green living' as a part of our 21st Century lifestyle, knowing how to preserve food will be helpful to reducing waste and ensuring that families can stretch their food dollar."

~Bev Perdue, Governor

The Soloman Lea ECA club visits a local rest home at least four times each year. In 2008, the club took each resident a new coat or sweater.

Although it was not cold enough to wear them yet, each resident put on his or her new coat or sweater and did not want to take it off. One of the residents said, with tears in his eyes, that it was the only piece of clothing he had ever received that still had the tag on it.

Home Demonstration Club members reviving their furniture in a refinishing workshop in the 1950s.

An Anderson ECA Club member works on a cooling cloth that will go around the back of the neck of a soldier serving overseas. Caswell County ECA members are also making sand scarves to keep sand out of soldiers' eyes and noses.

In 2000, the FCS agent, who is also a member of the Catawba County Breast Cancer Coalition, took the idea of a comfort garment for breast cancer patients, a t-shirt pattern, and some fabric to an ECA member who was an expert seamstress. The resulting design was a success with cancer patients in a local hospital. Soon other ECA members joined the sewing, and the Camisole Project Group was begun. For the past 10 years ECA members gather the first Monday of the month to cut, sew, and package camisoles which are free to any breast cancer patient in the county. Attached to each garment is a handwritten note to the patient from the group. Over the years, Susie bags (small bags to hold drainage tubes while the patient showers), and tote bags were added. Another ECA group, the Piedmont Piecemakers, constructs mastectomy pillows.

The Camisole Project Group now constructs more than 300 garments, pillows, and tote bags each year. News of the garments has spread and requests have come from Maine to Montana, but the ECA members most appreciate the notes from grateful recipients in

Camisole Project—ECA members have been making camisoles, drainage bags, mastectomy pillows, and tote bags for cancer patients for the past 10 years.

Catawba County. The group has gotten several awards, including the Governor's Leadership Award, and has received donations and grants over the years to buy supplies.

———— ✄ ————

The Jane S. McKimmon Extension Homemakers Club had 15 members when it began in 1948 but the membership quickly increased to 31. Many chicken suppers and other

fundraisers were held so that the group could build its own 28-by-50-foot clubhouse. Mr. and Mrs. Dock Hendricks donated half an acre of land near Lawing's Chapel Baptist Church, others donated building materials, and husbands donated labor. The first club meeting was held in the club house May 28, 1954. But the fundraising didn't stop. Members raised money for the March of Dimes, and they bought a hospital bed and wheelchair that could be used in the community.

———— ✄ ————

The Extension FCS agent taught money management to Habitat for Humanity potential homeowners. Using skills developed in educational sessions, 13 participants were able to reduce their debt by $6,251.93 and save $2,164.95 in just three months. This moved the families a step closer to their goal of home ownership.

Extension Homemakers made United Nations flags in the 1950s.

Chatham   POPULATION 60,881

When the Chatham County School Health Index identified J.S. Waters Elementary as having the highest number of overweight and obese children in the county in 2007, the Extension FCS agent partnered with the school to start *Rowing Across North Carolina*. Ninety-seven fifth and sixth graders participated in the indoor rowing program. One parent expressed enthusiasm with the program and her child's results. And one student said she was now more active at home.

———✂———

Chatham County ECA Club members have a blanket project called Hands and Hearts of Chatham. They have held several workshops, making blankets for local children and families in need. The blankets are distributed to local agencies and to children's hospitals. They also made 30 blankets for Ronald McDonald House in May 2010.

Bottoms up~ Four Chatham County children down healthy glasses of milk in this 1970 photo. Their mother learned how to improve her family's nutrition in an Extension class.

After Pearl Harbor, Extension Homemakers' work shifted to helping win the war in Chatham County. These were trying years. Transportation was a problem. Club women served as neighborhood leaders, organizing 10 to 15 area families to help in such things as home nursing, first aid, food production, and conservation. Many club women went into war work.

———✂———

What does a woman need when she ends up in a shelter? The answer: all sorts of basics. Chatham ECA Club members fill grocery bags with necessities, including towels, a comb, deodorant, lotion, and food. The necessities go to the local battered women's shelter in Pittsboro.

———✂———

Hamlet Milliken ECA Club of Pittsboro may be small with only eight members, but the club has a big heart. It has donated books to children at Pittsboro Primary School, and has made and donated lap robes, cancer caps, fidget aprons, and mastectomy pillows.

———✂———

An ECA club presented a *Parade of Hats* program for residents of a local nursing home and rehabilitation center in Siler City. The moderator was dressed as an 18th century lady. The show began with a story of how hats began as a large piece of fabric

that covered the head and shoulders. ECA members wore hats from their past and some residents also wore hats from times gone by. This brought back memories and smiles as residents reminisced.

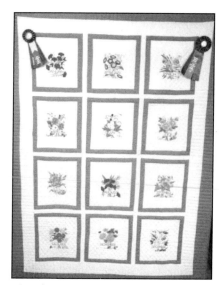

This Flower of the Month quilt, made by Silk Hope EH Club member Beulah Hinshaw in the 1990s, received a blue ribbon and took Best In Show at the National Extension Homemakers' Conference in Portland, Oregon.

The president of the Grape Creek ECA club proudly displays the Grape Creek Quilt. Each member embroidered her name and date of membership.

Students also made a handbag or tote, with trims, embroidery, and embellishments, adding to their sewing skill levels. The skills students have learned can be used to make clothing or home furnishings like curtains and pillows, and to make minor clothing repairs and alterations. Finally, knowledge of sewing will help them be more discerning shoppers.

❦

Don't tell the Cherokee County residents who signed up for Extension's five-week series of sewing classes in 2010 that they would be learning "heritage skills" or that home sewing

Home-schooled students learned basic home sewing skills in 2010, beginning with the parts of the sewing machine, how to thread the machine, and the basic terminology of sewing. They quickly moved on to measuring and selecting their correct size, and then transformed a flat piece of fabric into pajama pants with an elastic waist. Emphasis is placed on the students being able to interpret the guide sheet and follow the instructions. They added their own creative touches like designing a pocket.

The FCS agent teaches sewing to home-schooled students.

is a thing of the past. Participants came with their sewing machines and an eager attitude. They learned basic skills, pattern alterations and fitting. One participant indicated she would use her sewing skills to make Christmas gifts for her family and another said she would convert her creative ideas into marketable items.

Adults who are learning sewing plan to use their new skills to extend family incomes.

Chowan POPULATION 14,687

Chowan Home Demonstration members organized the first rural lending library in their county. At first, the library books were in the Chowan Community Building. Then they received permission to build on county property, but they had to raise the money for actual construction. They did.

HD club members also started the school system's first hot lunch program: pots of homemade soup and bread.

————ᏪᏪᎵᏪ————

The Extension FCS agent works with Social Services, the Community Care Clinic, Social Security and other agencies to help clients with problems or needs related to Medicare and Medicaid. Approximately 120 clients were helped with supplemental plans and consumer complaints in the first half of 2010. These people will no longer have to pay $144,000 out-of-pocket for drug prescriptions, and the value of consumer problem resolution surpasses this amount.

Track Family Day 2006 gets everyone moving, and participants enjoy healthy snacks.

————ᏪᏪᎵᏪ————

Extension, Edenton-Chowan Schools, and the Chowan County Recreation Department partnered to present Track Family Day in 2006 for families of all

students kindergarten through fifth grade. Some 675 people had a lot of fun while they learned economical and easy ways to improve their nutrition and become more active.

————ᏪᏪᎵᏪ————

Unwanted household chemicals are one step away from becoming hazardous waste that could easily be introduced into the environment. Extension partnered with the Regional Solid Waste Authority and NC Department of Agriculture & Consumer Services to offer a household hazardous waste collection in Chowan County in 2007. Hazardous waste was collected from 225 households, including 1,569 pounds of pesticides, 24,368 pounds of paint and related materials, and 10 propane cylinders.

Chowan County ECA provides fruit baskets to past and present members who are no longer active due to health reasons. This is an important remembrance of members who once contributed their time and talents to Chowan County. Each basket is lovingly assembled and delivered to the members, who enjoy the visit as much as the thoughtful gesture.

Children display the fruits of their labor in the Clay County Community Garden.

education series to kindergarten through fourth graders and their parents. Approximately 550 students and their parents learned the importance of living an environmentally friendly life each year. According to the Clay County Recycling Center, since the program was begun in 1998, recycling has increased by 10 percent each year and overall littering has decreased by a total of 45 percent.

The FCS agent also reports that adults facing financial challenges are increasingly interested in classes that will help them with gardening, food preservation, and preparing healthy meals at home. They also took advantage of the Extension's community garden.

———— 🙞🙜 ————

Extension teaches an intensive recycling and solid waste management

One of the founders of Mountain Laurels examines an issue of the newsletter published in the 1950s, which was supported through a series of talent shows.

After five years without a local newspaper, the county's Home Demonstration club women began publishing *Mountain Laurels* in 1951. A retired Baptist minister volunteered as editor and publisher, local citizens subscribed, and the women wrote the stories. They held talent shows to raise money for the advertisement-free paper.

———— 🙞🙜 ————

If they grow it, will they eat it? During the summer of 2010, youth programs were given space in community gardens in Clay County. Over 60 young people dug in, planting, tending, and harvesting their crops. Throughout the summer, the FCS agent taught the children how to prepare healthy dishes from the produce they were picking. Each child took home a vegetable cookbook and produce to cook with their families.

Clay County Extension Homemakers members display four of the hundreds of quilts they have made for the needy. Quilts have been donated to various Ronald McDonald Houses and given to foster children, childbirth class participants, families that have lost their homes due to fire, kidney dialysis patients, and others.

Cleveland POPULATION 97,936

"Our county is very fortunate to have such a caring ECA. Cleveland County has an average of 200 children in the foster care system. ECA members have provided the agency with children's books and stuffed bears to give to the foster children. The most recent projects that ECA participated in were the "My Stuff Bags" to provide duffle bags and personal care items to children. The bags and personal care items helped the children with their transition to a foster home. I have seen personally the difference ECA has made in the lives of Cleveland County foster children."

~Lana A. White
Social Worker III
June 2, 2010

According to Hunger In America 2006, 49 percent of the North Carolina low-income families said they had to choose between food or utilities and heating fuel. "During a shopping trip, a smiling former graduate greeted me,"

The Belwood ECA Club had its start as the Belwood Tomato Club in 1915. The county's first Home Demonstration Agent, Susan Elliot (right), teaches canning to Hattie Bingham, Ora Sain, Carrie Willis, and Jettie Hicks.

The Belwood ECA Club in 2010 has 21 members, three of whom are descendants from members of the original Tomato Club.

The Broad River Grandparents Raising Grandchildren helps relatives access services, expand support systems, and promote family stability. The support group, which meets monthly in Shelby, offers adults information and emotional support while volunteers take care of the children. Shown here, ECA members work with children on a gardening project in 2009.

says the EFNEP nutrition program assistant. "She proceeded to tell me that since graduating from EFNEP, she has been planning, budgeting, comparison shopping, reading food labels, and using coupons, and that she and her family had not run out of food by the end of the month in two months. She also said that not having to worry about not being able to feed her family meant that a considerable amount of tension had disappeared from her family life and her bouts with migraines have virtually disappeared. Then she asked if she might volunteer in the next class held in her community."

In 1963, Columbus HD member Margurite Shaw (now Lennon), was the state Health and Safety Leader. She was also an advisory board member for the NC Safety Council. She was the key player in getting white lines painted on the sides of North Carolina highways.

In 1986, local EH members inquired about using a county flag for the ceremonies at the NC Extension Homemakers Association state meeting. When they learned that the county didn't have a flag, the South Whiteville Extension Homemakers decided to create one using the county seal. With the help of a woman from the local community college, they silk-screened the seal on four flags. They kept one for the county Extension office, gave one to the college, another to the Columbus County Library, and presented the last one to the Columbus County Commissioners. The Commissioners were so impressed, they voted to make it the official county flag.

Extension Homemakers members silk screen the seal on one of four flags.

Many 4-year-olds in limited-resource families do not have fresh vegetables in their meals. The county Extension Center and NC A&T State University partnered with Mt. Olive and Tabor City Head Start in 2008 to build raised gardens and get the children involved in growing vegetables. Then the children helped with planting, weeding and picking vegetables. They also enjoyed tasting the harvest. The 16 pounds of mustard greens harvested in Mt. Olive and cooked at the site were savored. The children not only asked for second servings, many said they wanted a vegetable garden at home.

It's not easy being a parent, and foster parents face special challenges. Extension collaborated with the Department of Social Services and Bolton Health and Wellness Center to provide 30 hours of training for foster parents using Extension's *Parenting Matters* curriculum. The 18 parents in this hands-on, creative program learned how to manage stress, improve their communication skills, avoid power struggles and build a support system so that they could provide a safe and nurturing learning environment for the children in their care.

Columbus County Extension Homemakers hone their money skills with comparison shopping in 1986.

ECA members make snowmen and paint trains for Craven Regional Medical Center Foundation's Breakfast with Santa. Each child who attended got to take home a handmade ornament off the tree.

"Physical Activities for the Golden Age" at the New Bern Senior Center probably doesn't bring boxing to mind, but boxing and bowling became the two most popular physical activities after the county Extension FCS agent taught 32 seniors how to operate the previously unused Nintendo Wii in the center. The lessons in using the Wii were taught at Extension's monthly program at the center, and the senior students are using it throughout the month. Staying active and exercising regularly can help prevent or delay many diseases and disabilities, including dementia.

ECA members assisted the Craven Regional Medical Center Foundation at its 2009 Breakfast with Santa by making Christmas ornaments. Families get a hot breakfast, crafts and photos with Santa, story time with Mrs. Santa,

Kidzone activities, a raffle tree, and each child got to choose an ornament.

In January 2010, the Craven County FCS agent warned of carbon monoxide poisoning in the home at her monthly educational program at the George Street Senior Center in New Bern. During the program, one of the seniors mentioned that she had been ill for a long time. She bought a carbon monoxide tester and found that the level in her home was indeed elevated. The program may have saved her life.

The educator from Extension's Parents as Teachers program was meeting monthly with a military family. The concerned mother said that her daughter didn't always answer when spoken to. Mom felt her daughter wasn't hearing properly, but the family's pediatrician was not concerned. After

using her hearing kit, the parent educator recommended a visit to an ear, nose and throat specialist. That doctor discovered that Mom was right. The child had a hearing loss in both ears. Tubes were placed in the girl's ears, which corrected the problem.

An ECA volunteer teaches children to sew.

After Cumberland County received an "F" on its report card because its citizens were not eating the recommended servings of fruits and vegetables, Extension held *Kids in the Kitchen* classes for 8- to 11-year-olds. The students learned to prepare simple healthy foods, used fresh fruits and vegetables from the county demonstration garden, and learned about the importance of physical activity.

————— ❧❧❧ —————

A young military mom was referred to Extension's EFNEP program by a support program for soldier's families. The social worker referring the young mother told the EFNEP program assistant that this mom had no cooking skills. There was also some concern about how the mother was feeding her 8-month-old baby. Her own diet consisted mainly of frozen pizzas and frozen dinners. After working with the agent for just four weeks, the mom was planning meals and cooking on a

The Cumberland County FCS agent, dressed as a water drop, lets students at Eastover Elementary School know they can conserve water and keep pollutants out of water.

regular basis. She was also introducing vegetables and fruits to the baby.

When her husband returned from Afghanistan, he was thrilled that he and his wife were able to enjoy healthy home-cooked meals.

————— ❧❧❧ —————

Extension Homemakers reveal the Cumberland County history quilt they designed in 1989.

Homeowners in the Eastover area had complaints about their drinking water so they requested water screening. With the help of Eastover ECA members, 20 samples were collected and tested. One sample contained 24 ppb of lead, which indicated a problem.

Nine water conservation programs were presented to 275 third graders, who learned about turning off the water when they brush their teeth, checking for leaky faucets, and taking shorter showers.

The FCS agent teaches a Kids in the Kitchen program.

Currituck Home Demonstration members have sponsored a community Christmas Tree Lighting program from 1952 to the present. In 1989, the holiday celebrations were expanded to include a Christmas Parade. But in 2008, Extension learned that they would not be allowed to close State Highway 168, so the parade was cancelled. Determined not to let the setback spoil the holiday, they put together the 1st Annual Holiday Festival and 56th Annual Christmas Tree Lighting. Approximately

The Extension FCS agent teaches fourth graders the importance of healthy eating.

School children put knowledge into action as they prepare healthy treats.

When Medicare was changed in 2005, seniors had plenty of questions about supplemental insurance, Medicare Advantage, and prescription drug plans. The FCS agent and Senior Health Insurance Information Provider (SHIIP) volunteers made 16 formal presentations, talked with 174 people over the phone and held 346 face-to-face consultations.

Those 442 counseling hours helped Currituck residents on Medicare save an estimated $692,000 dollars in out-of-pocket prescription costs in 2009. One client alone saved $13,500 by changing to a more appropriate prescription drug plan.

200 people attended. It took a lot of hard work, but participants were able to purchase their breakfast, participate in the craft bazaar, create cards for soldiers, make a holiday craft, get their picture taken with Santa, and purchase Christmas gifts from 18 vendors.

Recently, Cooperative Extension, the County Health Department, and Parks and Recreation were awarded a $60,000 grant from the NC Health and Wellness Trust Fund. The *Currituck Gets Fit* program will increase healthy behavior by integrating physical activity and smart food selection. Together, the three

collaborating agencies are developing and building a new walking trail, organizing a mobile farmers' market, and conducting health and wellness programs for county employees.

ECA members put together a holiday celebration for their community.

$\mathscr{D}$*are* POPULATION 33,955

$\mathscr{T}$he Hatteras Homemakers of Dare County erected street signs for their village in 1976. Names of the streets were taken from ships lost on the coast between Oregon and Hatteras Inlets. Monitor Trail was chosen for Main Street. It took about two years to complete the project, beginning with getting permission from the highway department. Fundraisers followed as the women raised money to pay for lumber and materials. The design was a drawing for a three-masted schooner. Salt-treated wood was bought and the Hatteras High School shop class cut out the ships. Homemakers painted the names and then, with the help of high school students, attached the signs to posts.

———— $\mathscr{8008}$ ————

$\mathscr{T}$wenty women completed 14 weeks of nutrition education, physical activity and weekly weigh-ins as part of Extension's *Eat Smart, Move More, Weigh Less* program. The women lost a total of 183 pounds, 70 percent reduced their body mass index by at least one point, 75 percent reduced their waist, and 40 percent reduced their blood pressure. "Since first starting this

In 1976, the Hatteras Homemakers Club prepared and posted street signs based on the names of ships lost between Oregon and Hatteras Inlets.

program last year, I have lost and kept off close to 65 pounds and my blood pressure medication has been cut in half," wrote one participant.

———— $\mathscr{8008}$ ————

$\mathscr{T}$he Dare County ECA members presented an "Antiques Roadshow" type of program offering the community the chance to discover the value of their treasures. But the real benefit to the community was that the club members raised enough money to send a child to 4-H camp for a week.

———— $\mathscr{8008}$ ————

$\mathscr{E}$very year for the past 10 years, the Dare County ECA has lovingly filled shoeboxes with toys, toiletries and school materials for Samaritan's Purse. The boxes are sent to needy children all over the world. Club members estimate they have sent 100 jam-packed shipping boxes so far.

Some of the sucessful Eat Smart, Move More, Weigh Less participants.

244

FCS agent Jeannie Leonard invites Davidson County residents into her kitchen, and they watch her prepare wonderful dishes but they don't get to taste her dishes. That's because she's cooking on "Jeannie's Kitchen Tips", which is broadcast on Hometown TV Today. She has been sharing recipes and information on food safety, preparation, and techniques since 2007. Her healthful recipes include plenty of in-season local fruits and vegetables, and they are available on Facebook. People not on cable can watch the TV segments on the cable channel's web site.

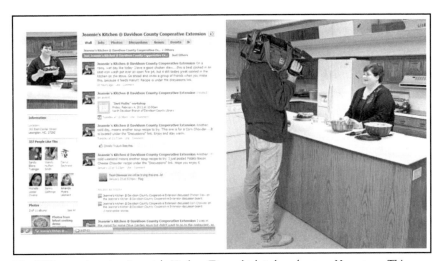

The FCS agent is taping Jeannie's Kitchen Tips, which is broadcast on Hometown TV Today. She's also on Facebook.

When Lucille Koontz joined Welcome HD Club in Davidson County in 1939, the club's theme was "Work, Save and Serve." She remembers creating and maintaining a first aid room at Welcome School that provided linens, blankets and supplies. When a public library branch was opened in Welcome in 1955, the club supported story hours for children and paid rental on space for the library. They also provided band uniforms for the high school and sent boys and girls to 4-H camp every year. She is still an active member at 92, and she is still a faithful volunteer every year in the horticulture exhibit at the Davidson County Fair.

Consumers know Extension is the expert when it comes to food safety. In 2008, Extension tested 26 pressure canners with dial-type gauges.

Of the 72 people attending the third annual Health Fair at Center Hill Baptist Church in Lexington in 1992, 15 were found to have high blood pressure, six had borderline high blood pressure, six had high blood sugars and several had hearing loss. The event was sponsored by the Wallburg Extension Homemakers Club and the Davidson County Senior Services Department.

Extension partnered with the Triad Area Chefs Federation in 2006 to provide a four-day cooking series for 15 children from the Lexington Housing Authority. The children learned about nutrition, food safety, and culinary careers as they prepared meals each day with chefs and culinary students from Guilford Technical Community College. Post-tests showed that 92 percent of the children knew more about safe food handling and preparation and 87 percent knew more about nutrition. Many kids also reported using their new skills to prepare food at home for themselves and their families.

ECA members compile a history of their work in the county.

Extension, the American Culinary Federation, the Chef and Child Federation, and Lowes Foods teamed up to present *Chef and the Child* in 2008. In this week-long day camp, nine children from limited-resource families prepared nutritious meals with the pros. Eight children said they learned more about food preparation, safety and healthy eating and would cook more now. Families that eat dinner together are more likely to get the recommended servings of dairy, fruits and vegetables and consume fewer calories. They also save money by not eating out.

Chefs from the American Culinary Federation help children prepare nutritious meals.

To help grandparents combat the stress of raising grandchildren, the Extension FCS agent taught positive thinking for stress reduction at a local senior center. A few weeks after the session, a local ECA member who had attended the session, called to tell how she was using what she learned. She was using deep breathing, meditation, and daily walks to manage her own stress. After she began making changes within herself, she was able to laugh and relax more with the grandchildren, and began to use a calmer tone when she talked to them, as opposed to yelling and shouting as she had before. She saw the grandchildren change, too; they are much happier, and follow directions better.

The chemicals in many common household cleaning products can cause personal health problems and concerns about safety and the environment. In fact, the EPA estimates that pollution in indoor air can be two to five times higher than outdoor levels. One solution is to use green cleaning recipes to make safer cleaning solutions. Another is to read product labels and be aware of potential risks. The FCS agent offered a series of green cleaning programs to Davie County Senior Services and all eight county ECA clubs.

The East Davie EH Club raised $1,000 with a raffle of handmade quilts. The money was used to support the Red Cross, provide services for cancer patients, help needy families in the community, and support Storehouse for Jesus, which helps with medical, dental, and pharmacy needs in addition to food, clothing, household items, and school supplies.

$\mathcal{D}uplin$ POPULATION 53,431

$\mathcal{W}$hen the first home agent came to Duplin County, she found the Rockfish Home Demostration Club already organized. At a quilting party in 1914, the conversation turned to an article about club work in *The Progressive Farmer*. The women were so impressed with what they'd read, they started their own club.

One of the club's earliest projects was conducting a typhoid clinic. And when the first "demonstrator" agent was hired, the members learned to can in tin cans and glass jars, how to make large fly traps, use fireless cookers and iceless refrigerators, and prepare nutritious meals.

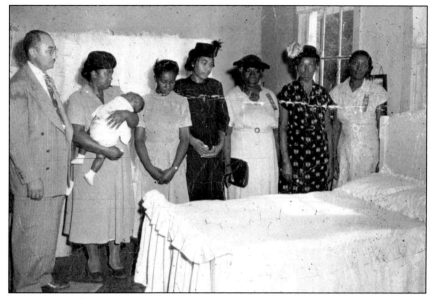

In 1947, members of the Carltontown Home Demonstration Club study home improvement.

Members of Duplin's Rockfish Club, the oldest former club in the county, look over their club's history with the FCS agent and 2010 Duplin ECA President.

———— 8003 ————

$\mathcal{T}$o help people on a limited budget get the nutrition they need, the Extension FCS agent, ECA clubs, and Duplin County Services for Aging co-sponsored a healthy living class. Some 45 senior adults enrolled. Based on what they learned, 70 percent said they were eating more fruits and vegetables each day; 93 percent increased knowledge related to eating well on a budget; 43 percent reported doing 30 minutes or more of activity more days per week; 63 percent said they were eating more meatless dinners each week; 57 percent were using coupons; and 65 percent were reading food labels.

———— 8003 ————

$\mathcal{A}$fter the Duplin County Board of Education report card revealed many youth had low math and reading scores on the end-of-grade tests, Extension and Duplin ECA members partnered with several agencies to conduct a six weeks summer leadership development camp for 32-limited resource youth. Volunteer leaders prepared and presented lessons on leadership development, self-esteem, and health and nutrition, along with activities to improve math and reading skills. Volunteer leaders also helped prepare and serve breakfast and snacks daily.

———— 8003 ————

$\mathcal{A}$ client called the county FCS agent about mold and mildew in her home. The agent was concerned about a possible health risk and contacted Extension specialists from NC State University. The homeowner had replaced a heat pump in the home a few months before the problem was noticed. It turned out that the size of the new heat pump contributed to, and possibly caused, the problem. The homeowner moved out of her home temporarily while the problem was addressed.

During the depression, club members contributed to their agent's salary, paying her themselves for a short time. Early members found time to crochet, sew, and do other handwork while they helped their husbands on the farm, slopping the hogs, milking cows, churning butter, tending flocks of chickens and turkeys, tending gardens, and cooking three meals a day.

During the depths of the Depression, the Saturday morning market organized by Home Demonstration Club members brought cash to farm families. Begun in 1930 with 50 sellers, it had grown to 365 sellers by 1940. Some $291,245 worth of homemade and homegrown goods were sold. Mrs. E.A. Perry used the money she got selling eggs to wire their home for electricity and to install running water. Another homemaker credited the curb market with pulling her family out of the depression. After they had lost all other

The Durham County Home Demonstration Chorus made a joyful sound in the 1950s.

In the 1980s Durham County Extension Homemakers made and presented fidget aprons to Duke Hospital staff that care for Alzheimer's patients.

sources of income, the curb market helped families survive.

In 1941, the Extension Club members went before the County Commissioners and asked for an agricultural building large enough to house the Curb Market, which was then located in the basement of the Farmers' Exchange Building. The Durham County Agricultural Building, built in 1947, included an indoor pavilion large enough for the curb market.

To develop cultural appreciation and encourage and improve rural church

music, the Durham County Home Demonstration Choral Group and the first rural church music school were organized in Durham in the 1950s. The success of the rural church music school in organizing church choirs led to 33 similar music schools across the

state and the Julie Cuyler Foundation. Established by Dr. W.K. Cuyler of Duke University, the foundation created scholarships that were used to send Home Demonstration Club women and 4-H'ers to statewide music camps and workshops.

The FCS agent and the Durham County ECA hold a sewing clinic at a local Wal-Mart in 2000. Participants made mastectomy pillows that were donated to Duke patients undergoing treatment for breast cancer.

248

Cherokee families have a long history of *Gadugi*, the Cherokee word for helping hands. *Gadugi* is a community member who helps community residents, whether on her own, or as part of her community. Extension collaborates with the Chief's office, Cherokee Preservation Foundation, Harrah's Cherokee Casino, and Tsali Care Senior Citizen's Center to sponsor a Cherokee Day of Caring. Each of the 10 communities nominates a household in need of minor repairs, cleaning, and lawn and garden care. Then 125 volunteers spend one day working at 10 various sites, using the $1,500 worth of supplies and materials provided at each site. Volunteers can do carpentry, electrical, plumbing, painting, and general clean up, landscaping and tree planting.

Volunteers at the Cherokee Day of Caring give their time and skills to help one household in each of the 10 communities. Depending on need, they do minor repairs, cleaning, and lawn and garden care.

Youth of the Eastern Band of Cherokee Indians receive money from gaming revenues. This money is put into trust for them until they turn 18. Until recently there has been no financial education program for these youth. The formation of Qualla Financial Freedom, which is a collaboration of Extension, Consumer Credit Counseling and Western Carolina University, is the first program to offer these educational services. Now a financial literacy program begins with preschoolers. *Heads and Tales* helps children identify the difference between a want and a need. Preteens and teens receive training in banking, wise consumerism, budgeting, credit and debt, living away from home, and investments.

Diabetes is very common among the Cherokee population, and 19 percent of all Cherokee people have diabetes. Extension and the Cherokee Diabetes program teach healthy meal planning, proper use of carbohydrates, and heart-healthy cooking with less fat and salt to 16 adults in a four-week series of classes called *Kitchen Creation*. Participants cook familiar foods using spices and flavoring with no salt and less fat than usual, followed by the all-important taste test.

Respect for the environment, an important Cherokee value, has lead people to increase recycling and energy efficiency in their homes and among 1,800 employees who work for the Tribe. Extension coordinated monthly meetings among tribal programs such as tribal recycling, the bottled water enterprise, travel and promotion, tribal housekeeping and environmental planning. The Chamber of Commerce and a local business also participated. The committee held several community education forums that resulted in policy changes and the adoption of more sustainable, energy-efficient practices.

This float carries Extension's message promoting recycling and respect for the environment into the community.

In 1999, the flooding from Hurricane Floyd damaged approximately 900 homes in Edgecombe County. Among Extension's response was the lending of moisture meters so that residents could test the moisture levels of the wood in their homes. As a result of Extension's educational efforts, people learned that they needed to wait until the moisture content was 19 percent or less before rebuilding. Putting up new sheetrock before the wood was sufficiently dry would cause future moisture problems, indoor air quality concerns, and health problems. The moisture meters were in constant use in the months immediately after the flood. An estimated 500 homes and businesses were tested by owners.

ECA club members donate socks for nursing home residents.

Edgecome County's citizen-soldiers and their families face the issues of average citizens along with the additional challenges that result from deployments. Extension provided financial management training for 40 family members in two military reserve units in 2008. Participants rated the classes as "extremely helpful" or "very helpful" to them on a personal level (88 percent) and in their ability to handle deployment (80 percent).

Extension held a series of five parenting classes for 72 incarcerated women who were parents or grandparents of 113 children under the age of 18 in 2008. Ninety-six percent of the women said they believed the classes will help them change or improve their parenting skills. What did they learn? When asked what they plan to do differently as a parent, among the responses were "Listen and communicate rather than fuss," "Discipline in a way that will teach," "Set a good example," "Give my children more words of encouragement," "Be more patient," and "Spend more time with them."

In 1935, home demonstration club members in Edgecombe County began raising money to build a log club house on land donated by J. Albert Brake. The women gathered stones for the foundation, outside chimney, and the mantle from the Tar River at the Falls near Rocky Mount. The clubhouse (above) was completed and the first meeting was held in January, 1937. The clubhouse was rebuilt in brick in 1964 around the original fireplace and chimney (right).

When an outbreak of a deadly disease from an unknown source killed four infants recently in Forsyth County's Latino community, an Extension FCS agent was there to help. Ten cases of listeriosis, which usually stems from homemade soft cheese and raw milk, were confirmed in late November by Forsyth County Health Department officials. Extension got the word out through e-mails to the 111 members of the Hispanic Coalition; Spanish-language PSAs that went into 81,000 homes via TV and that were aired 10 times a day on a 24-hour Hispanic radio station; a live call-in show on the city's cable TV channel; and posters.

In the 1970s, the Forsyth Extension home economics agent taught techniques that could be used to make or modify clothing for the disabled. One popular approach transformed a round tablecloth into a tent dress, which could be worn backwards or forwards. The agent also taught about using pressure tape instead of ties, buttons, and hooks and eyes.

Knowing you can't work if you can't get to work, the Extension FCS agent

With a $14,000 grant that ECA members got from the Winston-Salem Foundation, volunteers held a Paintfest to brighten the walls and ceilings at the Children's Center for the Physically Disabled. Volunteers also brightened up the Sticht Center on Aging at Wake Forest University Baptist Medical Center.

collaborated with Family Services and presented *Ways to Work* program to 39 limited-resource adults. Before the classes, they didn't manage their money. After the classes, they were tracking their money and making a budget. They understood the difference between needs and wants, and had learned about credit and various bank accounts. They also paid their loans on time to avoid late fees and penalties that would affect their credit ratings.

With a 7.2 percent rate increase for electricity coming in 2010-2011, Extension responded to requests from the Housing Authority of Winston-Salem, Experiment in Self-Reliance, Habitat for Humanity, and various churches for information on using energy wisely. In 2009, the FCS agent taught residents to change furnace air filters regularly, to seal up holes, cracks

Mrs. Betty Friddle of the Peace Haven ECA club has headed up the construction of 11,723 From Our Heart to Your Heart pillows since 1997. The pillows are donated to Forsyth Medical Center, where they are used by patients who have had heart or abdominal surgery. The pillows are used to ease the pain when coughing or moving.

and crevices, and to switch to compact fluorescent lights. She also taught about weather stripping, leaving the thermostat at a comfortable setting, not blocking vents, and insulating pipes, attics, crawl spaces and basements. Half of participants said they planned to buy products that would help them implement at least one suggestion.

The home demonstration agent teaches home canning in 1941.

Youngsville ECA Fall Festival, held the third Saturday in September, has grown over the years to include a craft show, car show, children's area, bake-off contest, and lots of food. Over 2,000 people attend the event, which is the club's major fundraiser.

Over the years, the women have used the money raised to improve two parks. They provided sidewalks, trash receptacles, benches, flowers, trees, and a park sign at Mitchell Park, and a children's playground area, basketball court, and park sign at Luddy Park. They also participate in the annual Halloween Carnival, the Old-Time Christmas, and the Christmas Care program.

For more information about Youngsville ECA Club and their projects, see http://youngsvillefallfestival.com/About_Us.html.

Franklin County's annual Farm Foods and Crafts Tour held in late spring lets people see day-to-day life on nine working farms and buy fresh eggs, produce and meats directly from the farmers. Local heritage arts and crafts, such as wrought iron garden gates, paintings, pottery and handmade quilts, are also sold over the weekend. Other fun events include a children's fishing rodeo, dinner on the green, and a farm to river Fun 5K Run/Walk. Extension sponsors the weekend event with the Franklin County Tourism Development Authority, Whole Foods Grocery, and the Franklin County Arts Council.

The Youngsville ECA Fall Festival draws over 2,000 people each year. An ECA member dressed as a clown delights children, folks check out the old cars, and shop for bargains.

Four Bridges ECA Club adopted two rest home residents who had no family and few visitors. The club helps each woman celebrate her birthday, Easter, Mother's Day, and Christmas with a gift bag. And "sometimes we fix a bag just because we want them to know someone is thinking of them," says Gladys Aycock.

Gaston Population 204,971

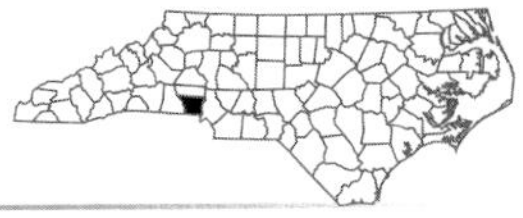

In the 1930s, Miss Lucile Tatum, home demonstration agent, told the County Commissioners, "I need a place to show how to do things." The Armstrong House on South York Street became the first Home Center for the Gaston County Home Demonstration women. Over the years, they would move from place to place before finally settling into the Lucile Tatum Extension Homemakers Center on Osceola Street. Built just for home demonstration, the 5,054-square-foot building opened in 1974 with a kitchen, dining area, multi-purpose room, sewing room, foyer, living room, ceramics room, kiln room, and office.

The Tatum Center, the only ECA Club center separate from the County Extension Center in the state, was named for Lucile Tatum, home demonstration agent from 1936 to 1963.

The FCS agent partnered with the Health Department to provide *Weigh Less* to FMC Lithium employees. Eight employees completed this 12-week program during the summer 2008. The total group weight loss was 59 pounds. Five participants reported a decrease in blood pressure, and two were able to stop taking blood pressure pills. All of the participants say they still exercise at least 30 minutes a day. Almost all reported eating fewer calories and being more mindful of how much they eat.

Extension Homemakers were instrumental in establishing the first "Meals on Wheels" in Gaston County in 1972. Hot meals were prepared and delivered five days a week by Extension Homemakers volunteers. The successful program was then funded by the county.

The signing of the Eat Smart, Move More healthy foods policy. ECA has supported several related programs, such as Cook Smart, Eat Smart.

After 10 years of rallying support for a branch library for the Union Road Community, ECA club members sponsored a reception at the library dedication in 2000. Two acres of land were donated by the Union Road Community Club specifically for construction of the new library. Members from the county's ECA clubs had advocated for the project and helped raised funds to support it. Fundraisers were held to buy a podium, two flag stands and a display cabinet. ECA volunteers also donated hours of their time processing books. The new library is off the road, so ECA decided to raise money for a sign. In less than three months, they had $3,000.

Union ECA Club members and a library supervisor are outside the Union Road Library dedicated in 2000.

$\mathscr{I}$n the late 1930s, home demonstration club members decided they needed a public library. In 1938, they asked the State Library Commission what would be involved. After much work in 1939, the county's first public library was begun. The home demonstration agent began collecting books and housed them in the Extension office. She would take 15 books to several reading centers set up throughout the county.

———&cΩ3———

$\mathscr{I}$n a rural county like Gates, it can take more than 20 minutes for emergency workers with advanced lifesaving skills to arrive. Having someone trained in CPR can mean the difference between life and death. The Gates and Hertford FCS agent certified 36 people in CPR, recertified 16 in CPR, and certified or recertified 29 in first aid.

———&cΩ3———

$\mathscr{T}$he home demonstration clubs became "soldiers on the home front" in the 1940s during WWII. In addition to the traditional programs, workshops

The FCS agent meets with a SHIIP client.

and activities, they collected scrap metals, fats and newspapers. They sewed and knitted for the Red Cross, planted victory gardens, sold war bonds and manned aircraft observation towers.

———&cΩ3———

$\mathscr{C}$ooperative Extension's *New Choices* program for the unemployed and under-

employed in Gates County drew a DSS client who was receiving $236 a month in 2008. After workshops on how to apply and dress for a job, interview, how to find daycare, and manage money, she went out and applied at seven different places. The next week, she had a job working 20 hours a week for $6.15 an hour. Another client went to the local tax office to see what was involved in starting a business. Then she started her own eBay business.

The FCS agent holds a breakfast workshop with young people in Gates County.

The FCS agent teaches CPR classes.

"*Times* in the 1940s were extremely hard. Most residents lived on farms with no electricity or indoor plumbing and heated their homes with wood. Miss Nellie Jo Carter, the home demonstration agent, spent nearly 30 years educating the Home Demonstration Club members on food safety and food conservation methods, family financial and resource management, the importance of good nutrition for themselves and their children, and health issues. They learned how to make their own mattresses, construct their garments and home furnishings, such as draperies and quilts, and even how to make their own hats. Everyone grew to love this talented agent who taught them skills that would help them cope in difficult times. Nellie Jo retired in 1963."
~Laurie R. Stevens, retired FCS agent

—ૹ☯ૹ—

*W*ith 49 percent of local children in school eligible to receive free or reduced

Middle-school students learn financial skills.

lunches and one of every five families living in poverty, the Extension advisory committee made economic education an objective for Graham County staff in 2008. The FCS agent collaborated with the GEARUP coordinator at

Robbinsville Middle School and taught 90 students financial skills, including the importance of budgeting, timely bill paying, money saving, and responsible spending. Twenty of these middle school students thanked Extension and requested more information so they could continue building their financial skills.

—ૹ☯ૹ—

*G*raham County Cooperative Extension created a newsletter in 2004 on disaster preparedness in the event of a terrorist attack. The newsletter provided basic information about keeping safe in the event of a biological, chemical, nuclear, or explosive attack. The feedback from clients was very positive and several clients said they would put together disaster preparedness kits for their home and automobile.

The Graham County FCS agent helped bring out the "inner chef" with a Men in the Kitchen class.

255

Working with Durham Technical Institute in 1965 and later Vance Tech, Extension home agents publicized class offerings and registered students for classrooms in the county. The assembly room of the Extension office was full morning, afternoon, and night. Eighteen to 20 classes were offered each fall and spring with enrollment ranging from 500 to 700 students.

Popular classes were high school diploma (GED), driver's education, driver safety, sewing, tailoring, knitting, crocheting, cross stitch, basketry, wicker repair, shorthand, typing, ceramics, bookkeeping, physical fitness, cake decorating, tractor maintenance, small engine repair, bridge, and guitar.

The most valuable class was home nursing. It prepared women to work in health care in hospitals and nursing homes. Sixty-five percent of the 175 students found employment for the first time.

—————

For three years Granville Extension has partnered with Area Congregations in Ministry and the Oxford Housing Authority to offer a family money management series called *Get the Money*

Extension Home Agent, Mary Irene Parham and Home Demonstration club members meet at the Extension Center for Blacks before integration.

Monkey Off Your Back! As of September 2010, 192 county residents have identified their financial values, learned how to communicate about money, tracked their spending, set long- and short-term goals, identified spending leaks, developed a budget, and learned how to use credit wisely and buy more nutritious foods.

One participant said, "I feel like I can finally take control of my money and what I do with it." One mother said she had learned to say 'No' to her teen-age daughters. Another said she had stopped going to yard sales after the first class and started saving money. And one man started packing his lunch

EH members made and raffled this quilt to raise money for their scholarship fund.

daily after realizing how much it was costing to eat out.

—————

Two FCS agents, members of Extension's Diversity Catalyst Team, presented four two-hour workshops on respect in the workplace. All of the county's 111 Department of Social Services employees attended.

—————

Extension's *Listening to Our Kids: A Dialogue about Completing High School in Granville County* was completed in May 2008. The report has become the focus of *LiveWell*, Granville's Youth Issues Workgroup action plan. The group's goal is to keep children in school through graduation.

Graduates have gotten the money monkey off their backs.

Greene POPULATION 21,205

Three- and four-year-olds at Aaron's Playground Center in Snow Hill grow tomatoes, cucumbers, basil, oregano, and dill weed in their "pizza garden". At harvest, they enjoyed pizzas made with flatbread and English muffins.

Twenty Greene County residents started 2008 by joining an AARP walking club sponsored by Extension. Each member received a pedometer to track his or her steps and was encouraged to walk 10,000 steps every day. The group met Thursday evenings for an hour-long walk and a 30-minute nutrition program. Each walker also had a buddy, and they encouraged each other to walk every day. By the end of April, members had lost a total of 214 pounds.

Medicare beneficiaries face challenging decisions when selecting prescription drug coverage. Fortunately, the FCS agent in Greene County is also a SHIIP coordinator. SHIIP volunteers have helped more than 400 seniors since the beginning of 2010. Forty limited-income beneficiaries who were automatically enrolled into the Fox plan that was then cancelled in early February were particularly discouraged. SHIIP volunteers helped them enroll in a new plan and get their drugs through the LI-NET drug assistance program.

SHIIP (Seniors Health Insurance and Information Program) is sponsored by the Greene County Senior Center and Greene County Cooperative Extension.

Ten people attended Extension's *Caring for Those You Care About* training in May and June, 2008. They learned about home safety, hiring home care workers, balancing work and caregiving, housing options, transportation needs, legal and insurance issues, Medicare, end-of-life issues, and advance directives. Seven requested more caregiver classes and all 10 said they wished they'd had all the information they'd gained before they started caregiving.

Extension and the Greene County Health Department helped Discovery Land Daycare start a gardening project. Teachers and children built three garden boxes and planted vegetables, fruits and herbs. As the harvest came in, they picked and ate it. Children and teachers ate more fruits and vegetables because they could pick them from their garden, and children learned how fruits, vegetables and herbs grow.

Extension is also teaching children nutrition through its *Project Eat Right, Add to Life* and *Read Me a Story*, a series of books with food themes and activities. Extension partners with the Greene County Health Department and offers the classes through Greene Lampe Head Start and private daycare centers.

Members of the Lindell EH Club at a hatmaking workshop in 1967.

257

The Guilford County Solar Communities Program, begun by Extension in Guilford County in 1982, has provided information to about 6,000 people, face-to-face, via telephone, e-mail and its Guilford Energy Resources blog. Extension also offered monthly renewable energy workshops on topics including residential energy efficiency, commercial solar design, solar hot water, passive solar, biofuels, and xeroscaping. It sponsored tours of over 20 energy efficient homes in the area; a poster contest for young people; public service announcements to local TV and radio; use of an electric tiller, trimmer and mower for the Community Garden and construction of a "red barn" for photovoltaic pad and storage of equipment.

The 1954 Guilford County Home Demonstration Club Chorus with Donald Trexler, director.

Consumers know Extension is the expert when it comes to food safety. They train people who prepare food professionally, but what about the average family cook? Guilford County has a Consumer Food Safety Hotline. Of the 421 calls received last year, most dealt with food storage and safety and home food preservation, especially canning.

Extension partnered with St. Paul Baptist Church in Greensboro to explain why everyone should have a living will and health care power of attorney. Thirty-six senior citizens participated in two sessions in 2008. Ninety-two percent said they gained new knowledge. Twelve now have a living will and seven now have a health care power of attorney. According to the group coordinator, "We were wondering where we could get reliable information on these two documents, and Extension had exactly what we needed!"

The county FCS agent answers the Consumer Food Safety Hotline.

Women's Health Focus 1999, sponsored by the Guilford County Extension Homemakers, began with blood pressure checks and weight and height measurements. Then participants attended classes on aging health concerns, supplements, aging with gusto, and physical activity.

Extension has a solar-powered shed to power electric tools at the community gardens.

The forerunner of today's bookmobile program in Halifax County was started by home demonstration in the 1930s. Local clubs served as centers for lending, and the home demonstration agent transferred books from club to club every three months.

━━━⋘⋙━━━

In 2007 and 2008, the FCS agent and county health department dietitian trained a total of 38 dental hygiene students at Halifax County College to use Extension's *Color Me Healthy* program for children. The students all said they would use elements from the program in patient and parent education. *Color Me Healthy* encourages children to make healthy choices by eating more fruits and vegetables and being active.

━━━⋘⋙━━━

Training in customer service is helping Halifax Regional Medical Center put "Patients First." After hearing positive reports about customer

ECA members show off handmade bears for Victory Junction.

service training offered by the Extension county director and FCS agent, the hospital asked them to train the vice presidents and department heads. Of the 36 participants, 34 had never attended an Extension program, but all 36 said they would attend future programs and asked that Extension continue as the lead agency in providing customer service training at the hospital.

━━━⋘⋙━━━

Twelve ECA volunteers showed area 400 area fourth graders what life was like at the turn-of-the century at the annual Halifax County Harvest Days activities. Children toured the farm house and saw how space was shared in a large family. They also learned about old-fashioned appliances and furniture.

━━━⋘⋙━━━

EFNEP had a tremendous impact on one first grade class in Halifax County. After six lessons with Professor Popcorn, the children understood the importance of eating smart and getting daily physical activity. They decided that their end-of-the-year celebration would include healthy foods from recipes received during the lessons. The menu included turkey tortilla wraps, fruit kabobs, salsa and chips, fresh vegetables with dip, and yogurt sundaes. Parent volunteers set up stations for physical activity during the celebration. All of the first graders agreed that this was better than sitting in the classroom watching a movie.

This old farmhouse is visited during the county's annual Harvest Days celebration. ECA volunteers conduct tours and explain what life was like in the early 1900s.

Harnett County Cooperative Extension was selected to share its teen pregnancy prevention program during the 2007 fall session of the American Public Health Association Conference in Washington, D.C. Their program supports pregnant teens' efforts to keep prenatal appointments, stay in school or at work, and practice birth control to prevent a second pregnancy. In 2006, the repeat pregnancy rate for

Ambassadors Extension Homemakers Club helped restore the county's last remaining traditional late 19th century one-room school, the Williams Grove School. The building was relocated to Angier's Yesteryear Park and is open by appointment.

Parents as Teachers (PAT) gets the message across with fun, hands-on activities.

program participants was zero, very much lower than the county's previous repeat pregnancy rate of 32 percent. That decrease was enough to move the county's teen pregnancy rate from 46th in 2005 to 78th in 2006 in the state. All the 100 teens in the program in 2005 made their prenatal appointments and all had healthy babies.

At the end of the school day on Friday, some 200 elementary school children take home Buddy Back Packs, backpacks filled with ready-to-eat, nutritious food so that they don't have to go hungry over the weekend. Teachers report these children do better

in class when they've had nutritious food over the weekend. Harnett ECA provides the financial support and manpower for the program.

In 1988, Extension Homemakers partnered with Cooperative Extension to hold the first *Girls Are Great* program. Each year since then, some 250 girls between the ages of 9 and 14 and their mothers or female guardians

have met to discuss the special physical and emotional changes associated with puberty. The program was also designed to help mothers open the lines of communication between daughter and parent, so important during the teen years. Not many programs 21 years old would still be going strong, but Extension receives calls every year from concerned parents asking when "this year's program would be held."

As part of Cooperative Extension's Child Care Resource and Referral program, Extension has taught 1,300 persons safe sleep practices to help prevent sudden infant death syndrome since 2003. The FCS agent also consults on site on all kinds of topics related to caring for children in daycare.

Haywood POPULATION 57,108

The Cooperative Extension FCS agent helped participants *Shake Off the Holidays* with a 10-week nutrition program designed to help people lose weight gained by overindulging over the holidays.

After the first class, participants were encouraged to record everything they ate. The second class offered participants a chance to make observations about changes they could make in eating or exercise pattern changes. Other class topics included physical activity, facts about fat and cholesterol; water, fiber and sleep; grocery shopping, holidays, and restaurant dining. They wrapped up with a class on "shaking it off: how to keep it up."

Twelve participants completed the entire program in 2006, losing an average of eight pounds each.

—&❧—

The FCS agent helped more than 100 people make plans to transfer favorite family treasures to the next generation. Disputes over family items like "Grandma's yellow pie plate" can lead to much unhappiness and even result in lawsuits between family members.

—&❧—

Participants weigh in for Haywood County's Shake Off the Holidays program.

In 1975, the Haywood County homemakers' clubs began raising $50,000 to build a handicraft museum. It took three years but after many dinners, cake sales, cookbook sales, and other fundraisers, the museum was established in the Shelton House.

Haywood Extension started a food safety education program for restaurant employees in 2007. Using a program based on Extension's ServSafe course, the FCS agent taught 58 employees. Now a local professional teaches the program and also consults on food safety issues with area restaurants, schools, and community groups.

—&❧—

The Haywood County FCS agent chairs a committee that coordinates specialized supportive services for caregivers and individuals suffering from dementia-related illnesses. In 2008 the group provided family members with care packages that included information on services and organizations that can help.

—&❧—

The first area Extension craft workshop in the western part of North Carolina was held in 1950 at Schwab 4-H Camp, and Haywood HD agent Mary Cornwell chaired the event. Cornwell also served as superintendent of the popular Village of Yesteryear at the North Carolina State Fair for many years.

—&❧—

For many years, a Christmas ideas exhibit was one of the most popular and successful projects of the Haywood County homemakers clubs. Each club displayed ideas and crafts to thousands of local people, and they also collected hundreds of gifts for patients at Broughton Hospital.

In 1924, Rachel Everette served as home agent for a year. She was one of the supporters of the formation of a curb market that still exists today on Church Street. In 2010 the curb market is celebrating its 85th anniversary. Extension continues to hold annual Old-Timey Days with displays of many arts, crafts, food and plants.

In Henderson County, EFNEP teaches nutrition education to WIC recipients. One Hispanic farm worker, recently diagnosed with Type II diabetes, wanted to learn how to eat more nutritious foods. With work during the day and family responsibilities in the evening, her time was limited. So the EFNEP program assistant taught her during the farm worker's lunch hour. As a result, the farm worker now plans healthy menus, makes grocery lists, and checks food labels for fat, sugar and sodium content. She is storing foods properly at home and boils, steams or bakes, instead of frying. She said, thanks to EFNEP, not only is she eating healthier, but her family is also!

Programming in the Family and Consumer Sciences (FCS) has come full circle. In the past ten years one of the major focuses during the summer months has been on food preservation. Some 700 participants have attended workshops to learn the current researched-based techniques to preserve foods purchased from a local farmer or grown in their own garden, so that their families can savor the taste of summer during the winter months.

In 2010, Henderson County's ECA clubs supported many organizations and agencies in Henderson County, including MainStay, a battered women's shelter; Open Arms, a shelter for

women with an unplanned pregnancy; and Interfaith Assistance Ministry, which helps people in crisis by offering emergency funds, food, clothing and counseling.

Extension taught *Steps to Health* in an elementary school that had a high percentage of students receiving free and reduced lunches. The 150 students learned to use the USDA MyPyramid food guide to healthy eating and to read food labels.

A boy checks his hands under the black light in the box to see how well he washed off the "glow-germs".

FCS agent teaches quilting to young students.

At the Kindergarten Resources Rally in the Hendersonville mall, the FCS agent shows healthy snack examples.

"I never turned the stove on before attending *Families Eating Smart, Moving More*. Now I am cooking at least four meals a week at home," said one of the Murfreesboro Head Start parents who completed the FCS agent's program. All of the parents reported learning new information on eating healthier and being active, and 40 percent have made at least one positive change since the program ended in 2008. The program stressed eating more meals at home, choosing healthy foods when eating out, moving more, and watching less TV.

Other programs promoting healthy eating and physical activity offered in Hertford County include *Dining with Diabetes; CyberShop; Workable Wellness; Steps to Health: Adult Component;* and most recently *Eat Smart, Move More, Weigh Less*. The FCS agent has helped more than 350 people gain knowledge and skills needed to improve their health and to lead healthier lives.

———— ✃✄ ————

The county FCS agent worked with seven families who wanted to make purchasing their first home a reality. The families began by taking a hard

Home demonstration club members learn to fit a garment in the 1930s.

look at their finances. With the help of Extension, they cut their debts, raised their credit scores, and increased their savings. One family was able to buy a foreclosed home in 2008.

———— ✃✄ ————

The Cooperative Extension FCS agent taught 287 first graders about nutrition, health, and exercise. They were taught about MyPyramid, grains, calcium, fruits and vegetables, protein, physical activity and food safety. They prepared simple nutritious snacks. After the series of classes, more than half said they understood what it meant to be physically fit and could cite examples of activities that could help them become more physically active. They especially liked dancing as an indoors physical activity.

———— ✃✄ ————

In a three-year period, some 144 childcare providers received CPR and first aid trainings at a reduced cost thanks to Extension.

———— ✃✄ ————

"ECA clubs taught me how to sew and can food for my family. Being a part of ECA not only helped me but my entire family."

~Mrs. Dolores Benthall,
longtime ECA member

The FCS agent leads school-age kids in a Power Up activity, which encourages children to get up and move.

The adolescent pregnancy prevention class enjoy a variety of learning activities.

The Hoke County Home Demonstration clubs worked to get electric lines in the rural areas in 1939-1940, telephone lines in 1958, the health center, and a new library building along with a bookmobile to carry the library to the people.

───── ✦ ─────

It's All About You, a 16-week series of classes offered in 2009 and 2010, helped 50 people lose a total of 466 pounds by eating healthier, and exercising at least 30 minutes a day. They also reduced their blood pressure and cholesterol levels. The program was offered by Extension and the Hoke County Health Department.

───── ✦ ─────

In 2009 and 2010 the FCS agent hosted the Women's Health Symposium. At the 2009 symposium, 52 people received cholesterol and blood pressure screenings and they got the CD titled *Women Living Healthy, Women Living Well*. The information they received at the symposium and the information contained on the CD

The community garden helps kids learn where food comes from. Children are also more likely to eat what they have helped to grow.

could be used to encourage the women to eat healthy, exercise more, and get enough sleep. In 2010, 46 people attended. A doctor from Hoke Family Medical Center spoke on disease prevention, controlling cholesterol and blood pressure, healthy eating and maintaining a healthy weight. Both symposiums encouraged lifestyle changes to help prevent chronic diseases.

───── ✦ ─────

It's All About You graduates successfully lost weight and exercised more in Extension's 16-week series of classes.

Hoke County had 43 children in foster care in 2009. By partnering with the Department of Social Services, the FCS agent taught a class in parenting skills that could reunite families. As an example, one of the parents referred to a parenting class was the mother of a 4-year-old who had been removed from the home as a result of neglect. After the FCS agent taught eight sessions of parenting classes, and the mother met the requirements for change by the Department of Social Services, the child was returned to her mother. This saved the county the $5,700 it would have cost to keep the child in foster care.

ECA club members prepare a spaghetti dinner as a fundraiser.

After Hurricane Floyd, many people were stressed and depressed by the damage done to homes, communities, and lives. Cooperative Extension decided that a fun evening with dinner and a humorous motivational speaker would help the stressed couples. Some 150 people attended the dinner program, and participant feedback indicated that laughter was indeed good medicine. Later, a square dance was held at the Mattamuskeet Lodge for the entire family to attend.

From two-room schoolhouse to community center, thanks, in part, to Rose Bay Home Demonstration Club.

Rose Bay Schoolhouse was almost lost during World War II, but the Rose Bay Home Demonstration Club members stepped in to preserve it until a community committee was formed to carry on the project. The former two-room schoolhouse is a community building now, and the money raised by a fish fry held on the grounds every Labor Day provides the money to preserve it forever.

The Bell Island pier has been destroyed twice by hurricanes, and it has been rebuilt twice by popular demand. The shelters and picnic tables put in place by Extension Homemakers have not been replaced, and steps down into the water are gone, but the pier, rebuilt with federal funds, is a popular fishing spot today.

When Soule Cemetery was abandoned and overgrown, Swindell Fork ECA Club organized to clean it up and have it mowed. Club members baked goods to pay for the upkeep.

Hyde EH Clubs helped the highway department establish Hyde Memorial Park on Mattamuskeet Lake Road and placed picnic tables and shelters at the wildlife refuge at Bell Island. The park has been used for countywide Labor Day picnics enjoyed by hundreds each year.

When the Albemarle Craftsman's Guild was organized in 1966, seven Hyde County HD club women were accepted as charter members. Those members had the privilege of using the Guild's identification on their articles. Three Craftsman's Guild members also had articles on display at the State House of Representatives in Raleigh.

Home demonstration club members helped support community literacy.

When the FCS agent in Iredell piloted the AARP's new *Prepare to Care* program for employed caregivers of older adults, she taught the class in front of a film crew. The Centers for Medicare/Medicaid and AARP wanted more than 1,900 Extension and other professionals across the United States to view the program. The program helps the family develop a plan, which reduces stress and time away from work when caregiving actually begins.

Tight production schedules often make a worksite wellness class difficult, but in 2008 a local company asked Extension to be part of its wellness fair. The wellness coordinator told the FCS agent he was concerned when he saw the unhealthy choices employees made when they ate in the company cafeteria. Extension set up an exhibit on healthy food choices. About 400 employees participated and many expressed surprise when they saw how unhealthy some of their favorite foods were.

In 1932, the 500 home demonstration club members worked to get hot lunches in schools with free lunches for needy children. Club members canned surplus food for the

ECA club members donate bears and blankets to Victory Junction (above) and supplies to My Sister's House Women's Shelter (below).

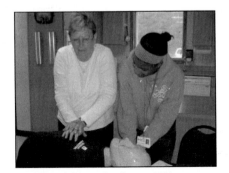

An ECA club member learns CPR.

hot lunch program. The Shepherd, Amity, Oakdale, and Scotts Clubs were particularly active in the school lunch program, providing funds, equipment, and canned food.

In the 1970s the Iredell County Extension Homemakers were instrumental in getting a new Extension Center built. They met and took their idea to local policymakers. The new center was completed in 1978 under the leadership of County Extension Director Ken Vaughn.

Today the former Extension Center serves as a Hall of Justice Annex and Extension has a new building.

In 1944, the Cashiers home demonstration members saw a need for a community health center and decided to start a fundraising campaign. By 1945 they had enough money to start construction of a building in the corner of the school yard. The building was erected by husbands of the club members with materials contributed by the community. The clinic was geared around preventive medicine: immunizations, dental care, eye examination, prenatal and well-baby clinic, home nursing and child care.

Members of the Jackson County ECA Craft Club admire a hand-braided rug. The club has monthly workshops. Some people in those workshops have sold items generating additional income for their families.

The Jackson County FCS agent regularly offers cooking classes based on the various needs of different groups of people.

In 2007, the FCS agent held two special-request nutrition and health programs. A county employee wellness program in cooperation with the health department and recreation department, reached over 100 employees, and a monthly diabetes clinic was started for patients of the Good Samaritan Clinic in cooperation with the health department's dietitian.

During the summer of 2010, ECA members lent support to a new project, the Appalachian Women's Museum, which is being planned for the Monteith Family Farmstead in Dillsboro. Members met for sewing bees or sewed at home, creating vintage-looking aprons from an original design worn by the Monteith sisters. The aprons are being sold with all proceeds going to benefit the museum, which will spotlight the important role women played in the history of the mountain region.

The FCS agent holds monthly cooking classes, limited to eight students because of the space in the kitchen. Class members vary. For example, a recent class had a mother and son and his girlfriend and her mother. "When families take time to eat together, they eat more healthy meals and it builds good healthy family feelings and inspires conversation," the FCS agent said.

Other recent classes included *Food Preservation Made Easy*, and a four-part series called *Cook Smart, Eat Smart*. Also, throughout the year, the agent has local cooks demonstrate their signature dishes.

In the 1960s a "Birthday Pot Fund" was started by the Cullowhee Home Demonstration Club and home demonstration club members across the county contributed to it on their birthdays. For years, money received was used to provide equipment including an IV cart, pacemaker, and weight scales for the C.J. Harris Hospital in Sylva. A large black pot was also placed in the hospital lobby so the public could make donations.

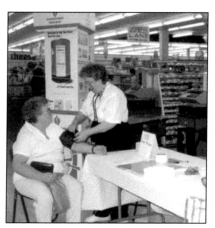

Members of the Glenville Extension Homemakers provide blood pressure checks and health information at a local grocery store during Heart Month in the early 1990s.

Johnston Extension partnered with the USDA's rural development program in 2009 to teach a homebuyer education program to 11 individuals and three couples. The course was required as part of the loan process to qualify for the government's guaranteed loans to low- to moderate-income borrowers. In 2010, the FCS agent helped 28 people, and they later closed on their homes, taking advantage of the federal homebuyer tax credit.

Knowing that one quarter of all teenagers 16 to 18 years old already have a debt of $1,000, the FCS agent took home-schooled students through a seven-week *High School Financial Planning Program.* By the end of the course, students were able to write financial goals and understand the terms on credit card statements. They were thinking about how they would spend money and start to use budgeting as a tool to achieve future financial goals. All of the students said they would begin to save money immediately.

ECA held its first Heritage Quilt Show in the fall of 2007. Over 100 quilts were registered, some dating back to the turn of the century. Some 50 home-schooled youth studied the quilts, and one of the students decided as a senior project to study the use of quilts to direct slaves on the Underground Railroad. The students also presented a quilt created by the junior historian home schoolers for their advisers.

The FCS agent helped 23 young people 8 to 14-years-old learn proper nutrition, menu planning, cooking, and

ECA hosted its first Heritage Quilt Show in 2007. Students and adults enjoyed seeing the different designs and students learned how to create a design with paper.

food safety in a summer class called Chef in the Kitchen. Now the students can make good nutritional choices and put those choices into practice by preparing their own meals and analyzing the nutritional benefit.

Walking briskly for 30 minutes is an inexpensive way to improve overall health, raise spirits, and clear the mind.

Walking strengthens bones and can help control weight. During the ECA Spring Extravaganza, a representative for AARP presented their *Step Up to Better Health* walking program. After just six days, one participant reported she had increased her daily activity, reached her goal of walking and felt her spirits lift as she envisioned herself making her way across the Appalachian Trail.

A county home demonstration club Flower Show, started in the early 1950s, was the first countywide integrated event, with planning committee members from all races, professions, civic and church organizations. The flower show showcased local talents, and included art, crafts, antiques, horticulture, flower arrangements, and performing arts by county people of all ages. Admission was free. This event shortly evolved into the Jones County Arts Council, which continues today. These events were instrumental in smoothing integration in the county.

Jones County Extension is the only one in North Carolina with a Senior Center under its jurisdiction and a county director who also has FCS and Community and Rural Development responsibilities.

In 2007, the county government asked that a committee be formed to address communication and to help coordinate events in the county in hopes of creating more county pride and unity. The Jones County Communication and Coordinating

Festival-goers tested out old-fashioned farm equipment.

Council was formed to create an event that would unite the county, create economic impact, instill pride in county residents and provide a venue for local organizations to raise funds for their causes. Two years later, the Jones County Heritage Festival became a reality complete with a parade, heritage skills demonstrations, entertainment, vendors and exhibitors, heritage interviews, and a car show. Festival goers loop tobacco by hand, make butter, shell corn, milk a cow, dig for fossils, and display their prized canned

goods. They also learn to quilt, make baskets, make lye soap, and learn about beekeeping and taxidermy. Youth engage in old-fashioned potato sack races, three-legged races and watermelon seed spitting contests.

Aside from the community spirit and pride generated, seasoned Jones County residents were interviewed about how life used to be in the county. These videotaped interviews will be used by the Jones County Arts Council in conjunction with high school students to craft a theatrical production depicting how life was in Jones County during the early 1900s.

Some 4,500 people attended the 2010 festival, up from 1,500 in 2009.

In the 1930s the Home Demonstration agent was the librarian, borrowing books from the State Library and taking them to club meetings. In 1948, club members started working toward getting a local public library and kept taking their request to the county commissioners until the first library was built in the early 1960s.

The Jones ECA club members worked with Pollocksville Rotary Club in 2006 to make soccer vests to allow an inner city team in Brazil to compete. The soccer vests had the ECA and Rotary logos screened on the front. The team was thrilled to be able to compete and ECA club members were rewarded with a photo of their Brazilian team wearing their new vests.

In 1986 Lee County Extension Homemakers and farm women not involved in EH clubs held the first Farm City Ladies Luncheon. The guest list has been expanded over the years to include other women's organizations in the county. Today the annual luncheon brings together more than 100 women, rural and urban, working outside the home and at home. One thing hasn't changed. Each year club members compile some of their best recipes into a small cookbook. Many women joke that they attend the luncheon primarily for the cookbook but also say they enjoy the fellowship and the program, which currently focuses on the family.

—————&⟨⟩⟨⟩3—————

Extension Family and Consumer Sciences worked with the Lee County Health Department, providing two 18-hour food safety certification classes and one food safety certification class taught entirely in Spanish. Some 39 foodservice employees completed the

Lee County residents learn how to preserve local tomatoes in a home canning class at the county's Extension center.

class with 31 passing the certification exam.

—————&⟨⟩⟨⟩3—————

The FCS agent teamed with the county schools and the health department in 2008 to involve over 700 students in *Fit for Life*, a program that focused on making healthy eating choices, learning about where food comes from, eating fruits and vegetables and getting plenty of exercise. Students kept track of the fruits and vegetables they ate and of their physical activity.

Based on the journals completed, over 70 percent of students ate more fruit and vegetables and were more active.

—————&⟨⟩⟨⟩3—————

Eighty percent of Lee County's mothers are employed, and 64 percent of these mothers have children younger than five who need safe childcare. Extension provides CPR and first aid classes for child care providers. One hundred twenty-five providers were trained in one year alone.

Extension Club members sold $3 tickets to Foods With Finesse, a cooking school, to raise money to restore the Temple Theatre in Sanford in the 1980s.

In the 1990s, EH members assisted with one of the first collections of hazardous household waste events.

In the 1980s, Extension Homemakers club members petitioned the County Commissioners to have fenced, manned trash drop-off sites established around the county with covered boxes and separate receptacles for recycling. Before that, the trash boxes were not covered and a lot of trash ended up on the ground.

※※※

In 2008 the FCS agent started *Home Solutions*, a weekly newspaper column that reaches more than 13,000 readers of the real estate section of the local newspaper. The column shows readers different aspects of energy conservation and recycling so they can choose a "home solution" that is environmentally friendly, cost-effective, and keeps recyclable waste out of the landfill.

※※※

Lenoir Extension has two *Parents as Teachers* programs, one in English and the other in Spanish. The children are taught primarily in English. Their Spanish-speaking parents are not only learning how to be their child's first and best teacher in Spanish, they are also learning English from their children. Thus, parents and children help each other to succeed. Forty Latino families were reached each month.

※※※

EFNEP partnered with Lenoir Community College to provide a series of EFNEP lessons to parents who were unemployed and seeking to learn skills that would help them get new jobs. The EFNEP program assistant emphasized skills that would

EH club members at a basket workshop in 1995.

enhance their resumes and also help them provide healthy meals for their families. After completing the series, one participant got a job right away. He credited Extension with making that happen. His food preparation experience, his food safety knowledge as well as his certificate helped him get a job in food preparation. He thanked EFNEP for helping him provide healthy food for his family in difficult times and for helping him learn skills that opened the door to a new job.

County council leaders picking up trash for recycling.

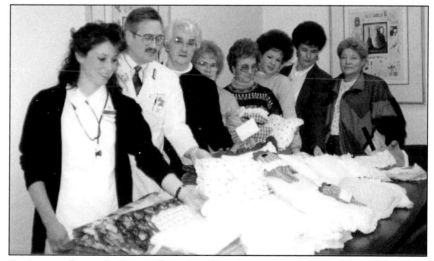

Dr. Barry and nurse look over pillows, lap robes, shirts and caps Lenoir County clubs made for cancer center.

When HE agent Melinda Houser came to Lincoln County, she suggested the county start an apple festival similar to the strawberry festival she had assisted with in the eastern part of North Carolina. The first Apple Festival was held at the Boger City Methodist Church in 1972 and 300 people attended. Today, the festival takes over downtown Lincolnton, includes 30 booths, an Apple Queen, and draws a crowd of between 40,000 and 60,000.

For more than 25 years, Lincoln County ECA volunteers have sold 2,000 fried apple pies. In fact, the old-fashion hand-held pies sometimes sell out. Volunteers ranging in age from 10 to 90, work all day long at the demonstration center, but the process actually begins the previous fall when 25 to 30 bushels of apples are bought, dried, and then frozen.

In response to a demand for local food, the FCS agent convened and facilitated a focus group from which emerged the Lincoln County Farmers Market @ Denver, now thriving in its fifth year. The agent also coordinated a local food and farm marketing program, FoothillsFresh.com, covering six counties, over 50 farms, and involving Extension agents from all disciplines. The agent received over $10,000 in grant money to help produce a traveling display, web site and brochures touting the importance and availability of local food. Additionally, she has used social

The public enjoys the annual Apple Festival in downtown Lincolnton, sponsored by Extension.

ECA members with some of the 2,000 fried apple pies made each year.

media (Facebook, Twitter, blogs) to connect with over 500 customers weekly during the farmers' market season. By receiving and implementing the 21st Century Farmers Market program, she has enabled customers to use EBT (electronic food stamps), debit and credit cards at the local farmers market. This increases income for farmers and makes accessing healthy fresh foods easier for the public.

National Pie Day in January is celebrated by the Lincoln County ECA members. The community is invited to come hungry and get free samples of all kinds of homemade apple pies. The apple pie recipes are compiled in a small cookbook, which is sold to the public at cost.

The FCS agent demonstrates a healthy vegetable stir fry at the farmer's market.

In the 1940s, the home demonstration clubs started the Franklin Curb Market. The members sold eggs, dairy products, dressed chickens, pies, vegetables, canned foods, and crafts. Nine regular sellers kept the market open on Saturday morning for a number of years. This extra income helped many families.

❧❧❧

Some 47 participants learned the basics of putting up food in an Extension class called *Food Preservation 101*, and demand for the information was such that the class was repeated. The FCS agent also demonstrated putting up green beans and held a peach jam workshop for the 22 participants who wanted more than the basics. The classes were offered in partnership with Extension Centers in Jackson, Swain, and the Cherokee Reservation.

❧❧❧

One WIC mom in an on-site EFNEP class declined a sample of chicken and

County EH members win a TVA Demonstration Garden award in the early 1970s.

spinach quiche. She said she didn't like spinach. No, she had never tried it but she had heard how horrible it tasted when she was growing up. After learning how nutritious spinach was, she decided to take a little taste. It was good! She admitted that she'd been guilty of not cooking foods at home (or even encouraging her children to try a food) if she didn't like it herself. She realized that as a parent she was not being fair to her family when she failed

In Food Preservation 101, the FCS agent teaches participants canning in a water bath (high-acid foods), a pressure canner (low-acid foods), and freezing or dehydrating the bounty of their own garden or from local markets.

to offer foods she didn't enjoy. She decided she would now prepare foods for her family that she didn't care for personally. She would let them try the new foods and decide for themselves.

❧❧❧

The Extension Homemakers clubs in Macon County have always supported reading. Starting in 1962, memorial books were purchased for the county library for many years. Local clubs have also purchased books for their school libraries. When a new library was built in the 1970s, the homemakers contributed $2,000 for construction.

A retired FCS agent volunteers with Extension, teaching Macon County residents how to weave chair bottoms.

What can you do with $25? In 1954, Home Demonstration club women decided to use a $25 *Progressive Farmer* award to begin a library fund. They added in a $500 award that was to be used for the benefit of the community. The state told them that $3,000 should be allotted to begin a library, so Mrs. Dorothy Schupe, a strong Home Demonstration leader, met with the County Board of Commissioners. County officials said they couldn't put that amount in the budget but would the next year "if the ladies managed to raise the $3,000 in a year." A year later, they had raised $3,344. The library was opened in a used bookmobile.

Extension values literacy and the Extension Homemakers, now called ECA members, are still promoting it. Most recently, they used a grant to distribute books at childcare centers.

ECA members perform Green and Growing, a play about the history of home demonstration work in North Carolina.

With concern about rising energy costs, slim profit margins on farms, and budget considerations, the Madison County FCS agent partnered with various organizations to offer a class on alternative energy for farm and home. Farmers and homeowners learned how to stretch every energy dollar. Sixty-two people attended this 8-hour workshop, which featured eight experts covering solar, thermal, photovoltaics, hydro, wind, residential energy conservation, and the North Carolina Farm Bureau's Farm Energy Efficiency Program.

The need for public exercise facilities was identified by several communities during *Community Voices* leadership training in 1997. As a result, three walking trails were established in three isolated rural communities, thanks to a $14,000 grant from Mission Hospital Foundation to the Madison County Health Consortium. These trails provide citizens with a safe place to walk, and they support other Extension programs, such as *Fit for Life*. Extension worked with the Hot Springs Health Program and Madison County Recreation Department on the project.

One-year-old Braydon began to choke and turn blue. Fortunately, the caregivers knew just what to do because they had taken CPR training sponsored by Extension. "I have been a childcare provider for 25 years and have never had a child choke in my care. Because of this CPR First Aid workshop, I did not panic but had the confidence and skills to help Braydon," said the caregiver. Extension coordinates monthly in-service childcare training for 61 childcare providers, including the training that helped save Braydon's life.

Putting knowledge to work, local library staff members weatherstripped the door and wrapped the library water heater after an Extension workshop on stretching energy dollars.

Madison County's library began with a used bookmobile purchased with funds raised by Home Demonstration members in 1954. Today, club members are still promoting literacy.

Martin POPULATION 23,870

After attending an Extension Family Community Leadership Institute in the 1980s, Martha Jean Daniels of Dardens decided to convince the telephone company to extend the service area for local calls for Williamston and Plymouth. She said it was a difficult but worthwhile task. The Institute taught her how to communicate effectively with officials and the support of her Dardens EH Club kept her going as she put up posters, and sought the support of mayors and other public officials. All citizens in both communities appreciated her efforts as they could call friends and family without having to pay long-distance fees.

Martha Jean Daniels reviews the paperwork that enabled her to convince the telephone company to extend its service area for local calls.

The Building Quality Child Care Conference at Martin Community College in Williamston in 2008 offered a day of learning for 112 childcare providers, owners, and operators. The focus was on creating safer learning environments with stimulating learning materials. Eighty-five percent of participants indicated that the conference helped them provide quality educational programs.

Martin County Extension and the Smart Start Agency hosted the event, which also was co-sponsored by Extension and Smart Start agencies in Beaufort, Bertie, Chowan, Gates, Hertford, Hyde, Pitt, Tyrrell and Washington counties.

Extension homemakers display the quilt that allowed them to donate $6,500 to help restore the old Martin County Courthouse. Names of local people were embroidered into the quilt.

An Extension Homemakers Association fundraising quilt honoring 561 people and 17 non-profit organizations is displayed at the old Martin County Courthouse. Quiltmakers "sold" the right to have names embroidered into the quilt by local EHA members. The center rectangle is a replica of the front of the old courthouse surrounded by 32 blocks of the "courthouse steps" pattern. Within these steps, names have been embroidered by local EHA members, who then assembled and quilted the quilt. The border of the quilt is half of the "brick walk" pattern. A few names have been included in this section of the design, too. The quilt took four years to complete and raised almost $6,500. In addition the quilt will always be a "living" history of people and organizations in the county in the 1990s.

The number of people preserving food at home is growing as gardening becomes more popular. The most frequent source of foodborne illness in home canned foods is botulism, which is caused by preserving foods unsafely. The Martin County Extension office received 100 phone calls from first-time and long-time home preservers last summer. Fifteen pressure canners with dial gauges were inspected and tested for accuracy. Thirty participants attended 11 food preservation workshops and were taught current research-based recommendations for canning, pickling, freezing and making jams and jellies. Based on evaluations completed by participants, over 95 percent adopted at least one new safe technique in food preservation.

McDowell

POPULATION 44,562

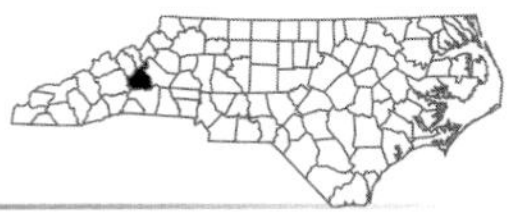

Since 2003, the FCS agent has taught a hands-on, creative learning program call *Parenting Matters* for parents mandated to take the class by the court or referred by Social Services. Parents were referred for various reasons, ranging from custody issues to issues related to child abuse or neglect. The classes help parents gain the knowledge and skills needed to enhance their parenting. This program, funded by grants from Smart Start and the Department of Juvenile Justice and Delinquency Prevention, is free to parents. Extension FCS has reached over 300 parents and their children during the seven years that the classes have been offered in the community. These programs fulfill a great need and no other agency in McDowell County provides these programs.

McDowell Extension Homemakers dressed in costumes representing the 13 original states when they hosted the Re-Living Our American Heritage celebration held at the 1780 Carson House. About 1,700 people attended the event.

The FCS agent offered weekly healthy cooking demonstrations at Historic Marion Tailgate Market. Beginning in May and running through October, she showed how people could incorporate more local fruits and vegetables in their diets.

Old Fort ECA has held fundraisers each year from 1990 to 2010. Each year it donates $500 to the Old Fort public library and $500 to the Old Fort Elementary School media center, providing 20 years of donations and $20,000 in support of literacy efforts.

In 2006, a Family Caregiver's Assistance Network was formed with leadership from the FCS agent. Committee members were recruited from several local agencies serving older adults, and a local resource directory for caregivers and their families in McDowell County was created and distributed.

"Little did Sheriff Robinson think when he captured a copper still from a blockader's hideout that some day it would be transformed into vessels of beauty and usefulness. But he had not reckoned with the resourcefulness of a woman's mind. Copper is expensive and no matter how much we Home Demonstration women wanted to decorate our homes with the lovely copper vases, flower containers, and fruit bowls, our budgets would not permit all we needed.

"Then somebody thought about the copper stills the sheriff's department had stored away in the courthouse, and turned loose their power of persuasion, and we got some of them!"

~1955 McDowell News

Members of Zion Hill Extension Homemakers Club were there when the county began to recycle glass, encouraging others to do the same.

Extension work in Mecklenburg County began in 1912 with home canning. In 2004, despite the efforts and the substantial impact of the FCS program throughout the years, the Mecklenburg Board of County Commissioners voted to drop the FCS program in the county. However, in 2010, the position was reinstated, in part due to the high demand for an agent who could address issues related to local foods, food preservation and food safety. The FCS agent is now the face of Mecklenburg County's local foods initiative, helping to promote a local food economy. Now, the county has an expert to teach canning to a whole new generation.

———— ✽✿✽ ————

The 150 members of Federation of Home Demonstration Clubs of Mecklenburg County celebrated its first anniversary on May 26, 1920.

Extension's Successful Family newsletter is available to anyone on the web at http://www.ces.ncsu.edu/successfulfamily/index.htm.

FCS agents from Mecklenburg, Gaston, and Cabarrus counties began a newsletter called *Families First* in 1998 with articles about home, family, nutrition, budgeting and parenting. Over the years the publication grew and the name was changed to *Successful Family*. As the years went by more counties became involved with the newsletter and eventually the publication went statewide. Today *Successful Family* is available online.

———— ✽✿✽ ————

In 2003 members of the Mecklenburg Extension and Community Association (ECA) clubs collected and donated supplies and money to the county's battered women's shelter. The members collected toiletries, clothes, paper goods, office supplies and $200. The money was earmarked to buy a vacuum cleaner, something particularly requested by the women at the shelter.

———— ✽✿✽ ————

Partnering with WBTV community news reporter, Bernie Simmons, FCS agents in Mecklenburg presented weekly television segments during 1999. The segments, titled *Keeping it Simple*, were broadcast during the station's morning news broadcast. FCS agents were frequently invited to host call-in shows at the station and to provide expert comment on topics of the day.

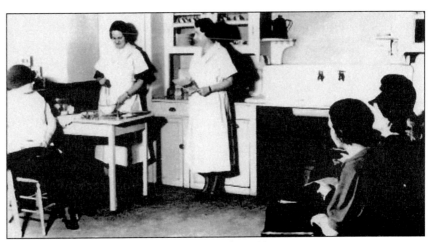

Club women attend a cooking demonstration in the 1930s.

Mitchell County ranks as one of the highest counties in North Carolina for radon that could infiltrate into homes. Radon exposure is the second leading cause of lung cancer. The FCS agent taught radon awareness and testing to every 6th grader and sent them home with radon test kits. Students set up radon kits in their homes and reported results back to the classroom. Households with high radon levels were given additional information on retesting and mitigation. The FCS agent also distributed another 200 free test kits to citizens of Mitchell County.

———— ৪০৫ ————

Sometimes grandmother's recipes aren't the best, at least not when it comes to home canning. Improper canning procedures can lead to food spoilage or illness. The FCS agent explains proper procedures via newspaper articles, radio interviews, and classes. Information on canning fruits and vegetables and preserving

The Little Switzerland ECA club gives $1,000 to a deserving college student every year for four years. Each year they try to add an incoming freshman to the group as another graduates. That is $3,000 to $4,000 each year in scholarships. Their biggest fundraiser is a yard sale held in late July every year. Here members get ready for the 2010 yard sale, which was a huge success.

For many years the ECA Clubs have held their annual Homemakers' Handmades two-day sale at Geneva Hall in Little Switzerland. They sell arts and crafts made by members of the clubs, home canned goods, cookies, cakes, pies, and other treats. The money earned provides income for the individual members and a portion of the sales supports ECA activities throughout the year. Here EH members get ready for the sale in the 1970s.

jams, jellies and pickles is available through the county center and online at the county's web site.

———— ৪০৫ ————

Mitchell County ECA members have motivated 4-H youth through the years by allowing them to present programs at monthly meetings and to present demonstrations before going to district or state competitions. The members were complimentary and helped build confidence in the 4-H presenters while also preparing them for the tough questions they would be asked.

"The Little Switzerland Club was especially encouraging to 4-H youth. In addition to inviting youth to present demonstrations, they also created

intrigue in learning about the larger world since more than half of the members were summer residents who had come from all over the country. Stories about life in Florida or New York helped inspire 4-H'ers to dream about seeing other parts of the country. Receiving a college scholarship from the Little Switzerland Club was a real encouragement and challenged me to achieve excellence at UNC-Greensboro so that I could become a 4-H agent. Reporting back to the club was especially valuable each summer," says Sharon Runion Rowland, who is now Executive Director of Development with the North Carolina Cooperative Extension Service Foundation.

Montgomery POPULATION 27,651

During the 1940s, Montgomery County HD Agent Martha McKinnon worked with prisoners at Troy Prison Camp, teaching them how to can. One year they had such a terrific crop of beets, the prisoners got "sick" of canning them.

⁂

The FCS agent taught a 10-week program on good nutrition and food safety to 61 third graders in an elementary school where greater than 85 percent of students receive free and

Children celebrate healthy choices with a fruit and vegetable parade.

ServSafe classes teach food handlers practices that ensure safe, quality foods.

reduced lunches. Four out of every five students said they had made positive changes based on the classes. According to the teachers, students discussed the different foods while eating lunch and noticed the food labels during snacktime. They wash their hands and are taking more time to do so.

⁂

Montgomery County Extension Homemakers held their first Tastin' Party in 1972, raising funds for local projects and the Boys and Girls Homes of North Carolina. Tastin' Parties were a way of getting people to try new and different foods and to show people

what different clubs were doing. The best recipes from club members were compiled into a cookbook, and the cookbook was sold. Tastin' Parties were again held in 1975 and 1977, and Extension Homemakers furnished a room at Girls Haven near Asheboro with the proceeds.

⁂

Food borne illness is more common than most people realize. Approximately one in every four Americans

suffers each year from a foodborne illness. Most reported cases of foodborne illness are tracked to food service establishments. The FCS agent taught two 16-hour *ServSafe* courses for public food service handlers. Of the 38 participants all but one passed the ServSafe exam and were certified for three years. After the classes, several food service managers indicated they had made changes in their establishments and others plan to make changes in the future.

Participants are "tastin' and raisin'" money in 1972.

In the 1920s, Dorthea Cowgill recruited local women to do needlework for The Woman's Exchange, now known as The Sandhills Exchange. The shop opened in 1924 and 125 people grossed $2,500 the first year. Women who made products for the Exchange earned money for the first time in their lives. The Sandhills Exchange still sells homemade items.

In 1928, the Eureka Home Demonstration club established a "Library Day" over the summer months so people in the community could borrow books. Over 100 books were borrowed the first year. Their emphasis on literacy has continued throughout the club's history with members tutoring adults, tutoring prisoners, and donating books to schools and prisons.

In fact all ECA clubs in Moore County have been actively involved in fostering reading among children. ECA helped the Rotarians provide every child in one grade with a dictionary of his own. They have also donated funds and labor for a yearly awards luncheon for children and parents through the county library reading program and they also helped provide money for books to a South American library.

EH sponsored a "Kitchens ... and Moore" tour that opened six houses to the public in 1993. Since then the annual home tours have raised more than $124,000, which has been contributed to groups such as Moore County 4-H, Boys & Girls Homes of North Carolina, Master Gardeners' youth program, the county library reading program, Hillcrest Park for

youth at Carthage, and the new History Center and 4-H Museum.

What would make the Moore County horticulture agent dress up like a large bespeckled aardvark? He was portraying children's literary and PBS TV hero Arthur for the county FCS agent's story hour at the Moore County Library. She uses characters like Arthur as part of the *Ready to Learn* program.

Ready to Learn, which includes educational programming for childcare providers and parents of young children, is sponsored by UNC-TV. "We get excellent curriculum, free children's books and the privilege of using familiar Public Broadcast System characters such as Arthur, which helps us to get parents into workshops," the FCS agent said.

ECA Club hostesses on Kitchens ... and Moore greet guests at recent fundraiser.

Sandhills Extension Homemakers Club members pick up trash.

280

In 1960, a program to eradicate illiteracy in the county was sponsored by the HD members. Twenty-five volunteer members were trained to teach reading using the Laubach method. Seventy-five people were enrolled the first year. This successful program was later taken over by the superintendent of schools and became part of the Nash Technical Institute's adult education program for a number of years.

Nash County students "bought" supersized fast food meals with sweetened drinks using SyberShop, a FCS program on an interactive CD that encourages teens to make healthy nutrition choices. Then they were taught to make choices that would decrease the salt, sugar, fat and calories. Before the class, 83 percent said they always had fries with their sandwich, 79 percent always had a sweetened drink, and 20 percent always added salt. After the class, 58 percent said they would drink unsweetened drinks, 55 percent would choose something other than fries, and 62 percent would not add salt. "You will see me in here (school) with water tomorrow," said one Nash County student.

This home demonstation club celebrated freedom from household drudgery in this 1950s parade.

The FCS agent taught handwashing techniques to 1,748 students in 82 classrooms in 2009. Each student rubbed fake "glow germs" on their hands. Then they washed their hands as they normally did. They placed their "clean" hands under a black light and were able to see how many "germs" remained.

The FCS and 4-H agents in Nash County started a Chef School & Cooking Club, teaching 402 young people how to prepare healthy snacks and meals. Some of the students used their skills at the county's Annual Holiday Extravaganza, making and selling their own baked goods.

Extension worked with the Nash County Health Department in 2009 to train 15 childcare providers to use Extension's *Color Me Healthy* program.

An ECA member demonstrates old-fashioned clothes washing techniques at Heritage Days.

These providers then taught 161 children to make wise food choices and be more physically active.

Hazel Valentine compiled *I Remember When*, a collection of stories written by Extension Homemakers aged 65 and older. She donated $1,000 to D.H. Hill Library at NC State University from the sales of her book. She was the mother of Tim Valentine, former member of the U.S. House of Representatives.

With SyberShop, students learn to make healthier food choices when eating out.

New Hanover POPULATION 192,235

The FCS agent is keeping firemen in shape. Some 87 New Hanover County firemen completed her six-week health and wellness class *Shape Up for Life* in 2008. Based on their evaluation of the program, 75 percent have increased their physical activity levels. They also are preparing healthy meals with less salt, fat, and sugar, and are not overeating. Ninety-five percent are reading food labels, and over 80 percent have lost weight.

The Masonboro ECA Club adopted students in the pre-kindergarten program at the William H. Blount Elementary School in Wilmington. They provided the staff with school supplies for their classrooms at the beginning of the year and spent one day each month in the classroom, helping children with reading, subject matter projects, and school activities.

New Hanover County Cooperative Extension participated in Festival Latino for the first time in 2008. Agents assembled a booth with Spanish-language materials, including pamphlets, flyers, CDs, and DVDs. Homeowners and business owners were offered information about agricultural worker safety, safe use of pesticides, nutrition and diabetes awareness. Also general information was presented about life in North Carolina for people new to the area, and information about preparing to attend college. Ten thousand visitors became aware of Extension as a resource.

When the Extension instructor in an EFNEP class noticed how many of her students were bringing sugary soft drinks to class, she presented the lesson *Making Smart Drink Choices* early in the series. After the class, a small refrigerator was donated to the classroom. Now participants bring

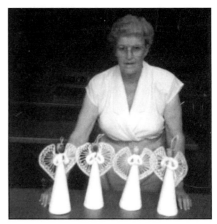

An Extension Homemaker displays angels made for Christmas trees in Washington, D.C., in 1995.

bottled water to class—a much smarter choice and obvious application of what they learned during the EFNEP class.

A health assessment by the New Hanover County Human Resources Department indicated that 85 percent of county employees were overweight in 2008. The county began a one-year health and wellness program. The Extension agent taught a class called *Cooking a Healthy Way*. The 26 participants prepared a healthy lunch during the class. Since then, 85 percent say they are cooking more meals at home and taking lunches to work.

From 1949 to 1955 the Home Demonstration clubs in New Hanover County were represented by a float in the Azalea Festival parade. The float shown here is from the 1950 parade.

In 1916, Tomato Clubs were organized in 10 Northampton communities. Home-canned tomatoes provided nutrition in the winter and also could be sold. Mrs. Walter Bryant, a Tomato Club member, reported one year that she had canned over 500 cans of tomatoes. She sold all of her canned products that summer with the help of her brother, who operated a local grocery store.

—— ༄༅ ——

The Extension FCS and livestock agents turned fourth graders at Northeast Academy into home energy investigators in 2008. In an Energy Conservation at Home class, students were challenged to go home, and with parents' help, perform their own home energy audits. What did they find? A total of 161 light fixtures in their homes, and only 17 had compact fluorescent bulbs. Seven of the students found drafts coming in around the doorframe. To wrap up the study,

The sale of homemade goods and crafts supplemented the income of many homes in the 1970s. The Extension Homemaker pictured here is the owner of Under the Elms, a small craft shop in Severn.

students developed posters to show ways they could help their parents retrofit their home to save energy, increase comfort, save money, and reduce carbon emissions.

—— ༄༅ ——

Fourteen Northampton residents completed training in the *Individual Development Account* program, which is part of Extension's economic literacy training for people who would like to buy homes in the future. Class members made budget plans, set achievable goals, and worked to improve their credit ratings. The class was especially motivated because the Choanoke Area Development Association received a grant from

the Department of Labor that would provide $2 for every dollar saved by participants during the program.

—— ༄༅ ——

Foodborne illness is nearly 100 percent preventable when safe food handling practices are used. The *Hazard Analysis Critical Control Process* (HACCP) system is designed to control risk and hazards in the food service environment. Extension partnered with the Child Nutrition Services of Northampton County Schools to provide three hours of HACCP Update training to cafeteria managers and school food service workers before the 2008-09 school year. The school system feeds 3,200 students.

Christine F. Brown was the first home demonstration agent in the county.

In a Partners for Readiness program, FCS agents from Onslow and Craven counties and five Marine employees were trained in 1996 to use the *Command Financial Specialist* train-the-trainer program at Camp Lejeune and the air stations at New River and Cherry Point. The information and educational resources helped prevent personal financial problems, and it referred people who already had problems to appropriate military or community services. The goal was to reduce problems like bounced checks, debt, and repossessed cars, all of which stress and distract military personnel.

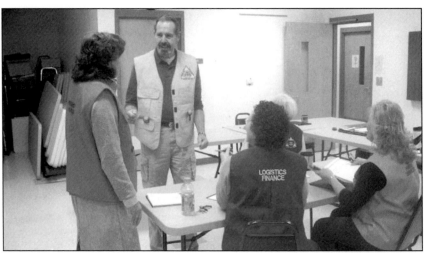

Extension ECA members made safety vests for county employees, saving the county the $5,000 it would have cost to purchase them.

When used properly in a home, solar energy can reduce energy use by 50 percent. Eastern North Carolina's climate provides 225 to 230 days of sunshine annually, making solar power a viable option. Recognizing the opportunity for alternative energy education, Onslow County Cooperative Extension received a donation of 30 solar panels from Arizona State University's Photovoltaic Testing Lab. Once installed at the Onslow County Farmer's Market Building, these panels will run lights and ceiling fans and provide Onslow County Cooperative Extension agents a hands-on solar energy demonstration site. Educational programming will include hands-on demonstrations of the efficiency of solar energy and guidelines on installation and use in homes.

Mold is a fact of life in southeastern North Carolina. A local resident had been having a terrible time controlling mold in her home. She was spending a lot of time in the doctor's office because her respiratory system was being affected by the mold spores in the air of her home. At an Extension class, she learned cleaning methods to kill mold, how to provide ventilation along all walls to keep the mold from growing again, and how to use the proper filter for her heating and air conditioning system. After putting what she learned into practice, she is no longer bothered by respiratory infections.

Extension Homemakers offer Southern hospitality, a wonderful meal, and a warm welcome on Sundays at the USO in 1980.

Between 2002 and 2008, Extension and other community members of the Orange on the Move Coalition held countywide events promoting physical activity and better nutrition at the Chapel Hill YMCA and the Triangle Sportsplex. A total of 600 to 700 people attended each year. According to their parents, children who attended the nutrition workshops held at these events did improve their eating habits.

One state legislator who attended a 2003 event sponsored by the Coalition for parents, agencies and policy makers used the information and data to support one of the first state bills for more physical activity in the schools.

What happens if you pair four families with volunteer fitness and nutrition experts for 10 weeks? The local newspaper printed more than 20 articles as the families worked to

ECA members in front of the green boxes at a county recycling center. These centers exist in large part as a result of the members' efforts in 1973 to establish trash collection centers around the county.

improve their health. Families reported eating more fruits and vegetables, drinking more water and fewer sugar-sweetened beverages, getting more physical activity, losing weight, lowering blood pressure, and other healthful changes, thanks to Extension instruction.

In 1990 when the garbage drop off sites were expanded to include recycling centers, several county Extension Homemakers clubs sponsored and monitored the sites for garbage overflow and vandalism. They also educated people on recycling.

Orange County Extension was the first in the state to offer *ServSafe* food safety training for food service managers. Since the program began in 1997, a total of 28 classes have trained 1,458 managers and certified 1,234. They were also the first in the state to offer a six-hour ServSafe Employee class in Spanish. Seven classes reaching 229 Spanish-speaking employees have been held since the program began.

Powerful Tools for Caregivers were provided in 2008 in the form of six 2 ½ hour sessions sponsored by Extension and the Orange County Department on Aging. Caregivers reported improved coping skills and enhanced communication skills. They also said they liked being able to share their personal challenges and that the emotional support they received from the class leaders and group members was beneficial.

Families (above) exercise and learn to read labels in the grocery store (right) as part of Extension's Family Challenge.

*M*rs. Elsie Jones and Mrs. Bela Carawan of the Mesic Extension Homemakers Club were among the 724 dedicated club members in the county in 1935. Pointing out to the County Commissioners that these two women walked three miles and then rode 17 miles in an open truck in 12-degree weather to attend a home demonstration meeting helped convince the commissioners to vote to furnish the site and build an agricultural building as a W.P.A. project.

---

*E*xtension's *Out for Lunch*, a four-week hands-on nutrition program, was begun in 1996 in Pamlico County. With Social Services Food Stamp Division as co-

Using a circle game, the FCS program assistant tests children's knowledge of nutrition.

sponsor, the group taught 80 mothers, grandmothers, and children how to prepare nutritious meals on a budget.

---

*E*xtension offered *Powerful Tools for Caregivers*, a course that teaches caregivers how to take care of themselves in a difficult time. One participant got so much help from the course that she wanted to help others going through a similar challenge. She attended a two-day facilitators' training session in New Bern, became a certified facilitator and volunteered at the next six-week course in Pamlico County.

---

*E*xtension offered *Partners in Wellness*, a nutrition education program for senior citizens. The FCS agent had just completed lessons on meals on a budget and variety matters for a group from a low-income housing area, when one woman volunteered that she was now a whole lot more calorie conscious, was eating better, and had lost 10 pounds. She said she had not bought a package of snack cakes in two months and had been eating apples and grapes instead.

The Extension FCS program assistant teaches third graders from Fred Anderson Elementary School in Bayboro about healthy snacks.

286

In the 1980s, when young members of the local Coast Guard were experiencing financial problems, the Coast Guard called Washington, DC, to learn where to send those having trouble to receive financial training and counseling. They were told to contact their county Extension Center for counseling. A number of the young Coasties were required to seek the HE agent's help. Coasties who improved their financial problems were allowed to stay in the Coast Guard. Those who failed to improve after counseling were relieved of their duties.

Extension teaches babysitting basics to help young people safely care for infants and children, communicate effectively with parents, and market themselves as babysitters. The class includes six hours of CPR and first aid training, so that the babysitter can act should an emergency occur. Role-playing, handouts, hands-on activities, and lectures are used to complete the 14-hour training.

—————

U.S. soldiers serving in the Middle East are a lot cooler thanks to the Pasquotank ECA members. Recently the ECA club members sewed 130

ECA club members sew reusable neckbands that will go to soldiers in the Middle East and to firefighters in Tyrrell County.

reusable neckbands that hold moisture-retaining crystals. When soaked in cool water and worn around the neck, the neckbands cool the wearer. In addition to the 100 bound for the Middle East, 30 neckbands are destined for those fighting wildfires in Tyrrell County. Since the original batch of neck wraps was made in 2006, ECA members have constructed more than 600. Other organizations have contacted them for information on starting this project.

—————

Extension works with SHIIP, the Senior's Health Insurance Information Program, which is a consumer information division of the North Carolina Department of Insurance. SHIIP volunteers help people understand Medicare and the options they can select. They also help citizens recognize and prevent Medicare billing errors and possible fraud and abuse. In 2009, the Extension FCS agent and volunteers helped about 300 people. A change in the prescription drug plan and pharmacy helped one individual save $309 a month on out-of-pocket prescription costs.

—————

Pasquotank had one of the last operating home demonstration curb markets. Money from the sale of the building continues to be used today for scholarships and for grants to local nonprofit groups that apply for the funds.

The Inter-County Public Transportation Authority van promotes Extension as one source for help with Medicare questions.

Pender
POPULATION 28,855

On a Monday morning in October 1996, 20 homemaker club members picked up protest signs and divided into two groups. Half marched in front of the York Agricultural Building and the other half stood in front of the library where the county commissioners would be sure to see them. They were protesting the proposed move from the agricultural building in the county office complex to the York Building on Cowan Street. At stake was a large demonstration kitchen where groups could see cooking demonstrations. The kitchen available in the proposed spot

Rocky Point Extension Homemakers sell crafts at Holiday House Bazaar. Clubs use the money from sales to fund a variety of community projects.

Members of the Silver Bells ECA Club serve lunch to Habitat for Humanity workers in 2008.

was intended for the average family, so demonstrations before large groups would not be possible. They went to every commissioners' meeting, and finally the Commissioners agreed with them.

◦∞◦

The Extension FCS agent used kids' fascination with computers and computer games to teach healthy food choices in 2007 using SyberShop. Students made virtual visits to a Food Court to learn about the nutritional

content of fast food. They learned how to select healthy options in cafeterias, use the food guide pyramid, count calories, and incorporate physical activity into their daily routines.

◦∞◦

Extension helps sponsor the blueberry recipe contest at the NC Blueberry Festival held each June in historic downtown Burgaw. Contestants are challenged to use these healthy, locally grown berries in any delicious way, from entrees, jams, to beverages. There's

even a competition for kids ages 9 to 15. Cash prizes are provided by the Wilmington Star-News.

◦∞◦

ECA club activities in 2010 included Holiday House Bazaar, Cultural Arts Spring Show, volunteering, craft workshops, Christian Services Scholarship, and a Senior Recognition luncheon. Between 300 and 400 people attend the Holiday House Bazaar each year, and money raised goes back to assist the needs in each community. Club members also provide Binky Patrol with 300 handmade blankets each year. Binky Patrol is a national organization that provides handmade baby blankets to needy parents.

Burgaw Bells ECA Club members show eight of the 21 homemade teddy bears donated in 2005 to Victory Junction Gang Camp in Asheboro.

"*T*hrough Extension Homemaking Leadership Training, I've learned when to be a leader and when to be a follower. I've learned to be active, be humble, and aspire to leadership roles at home, school, church, community and abroad. Through leadership training my husband and I have learned to train our children to be respectable citizens and to love, trust and be leaders themselves. Extension Homemakers will help you to say 'The greatest leaders are positive, constructive, creative human beings,'" said Mrs. Emma Burke.

Mrs. Burke's son joined the Pasquotank Extension staff after graduating from NC State University. In 2010, this dedicated and well-respected Extension professional became the Northeast District Extension Director for the NC Cooperative Extension Service. His name is Dr. Travis Burke, and he is an example of the impact of Extension in Perquimans County.

*P*erquimans ECA volunteers have been sending handmade pillows to the patients at Chowan Hospital since 1995. These small, unusually shaped mastectomy pillows comfort the tender area under the arm following

"*Mrs. Emma Burke poses with her family*"

lympectomy surgery. Twice a year, volunteers gather to wash, press, cut, sew, and stuff pillows. Then they attach a special label to comfort the recipient.

We made this pillow just for you.
We care about what you're going through.

Use it on a trip to rest your head.
Or prop it around you when you're in bed.

Some choose to use it under their arm.
Or behind the neck, it works like a charm.

If it gets dirty and you want it clean,
It's fine to wash & dry in a machine.

Donated by:
Perquimans Extension & Community Association

2010

Perquimans Extension is the "go to" place to find someone who can explain the legal jargon and sort through the detailed paperwork involved with Medicare, Medicaid, and Medicare Part D. Between 1995 and 2010, the FCS agent, working with the NC Department of Insurance, has saved Perquimans County Medicare beneficiaries approximately $950,000 in out-of-pocket expenses.

The Person County Extension FCS agent gets several calls each year about mold and mildew concerns. In 2007, one of those calls came from a church. The agent met with church deacons. She used the office moisture meter to take readings at various places in the building. The church members were then loaned a hygrometer to measure the relative humidity in the air at various points in the church. Readings ranged from 38 to 43 percent, depending upon open doors and heat.

According to a church member who runs a mold inspection system, it would have cost the church between $10,000 and $12,000 to hire someone to do what the church was able to do for itself with the help and expertise of the county agent.

—————&⛯3—————

A child uses SyberShop, an Extension educational program on CD, to learn about nutrition.

Forty-eight EH club members from seven local clubs helped the county schools register preschoolers in 1992. They provided snacks for the 400 children. They also gave parents a "Safety Bag" with recipes for nutritious snacks and lunch ideas; information about bicycle-related head injuries and bicycle helmets, bicycle laws and safety tips; a safe environment checklist for the home; information on the proper way to wear seatbelts; and a list of

The FCS agent works with preschoolers at the public library as part of a wellness and literacy program called Read Me a Story.

publications and magazines available at the Person County Library.

—————&⛯3—————

*P*erson County FCS has a major focus on health and well being. In 2010, the 13th annual *Aging With Gusto* conference, the 14th annual *Give Your Heart a Healthy Beat* program, and the first *Cook Smart, Eat Smart, Move More, Weigh Less* programs were held. FCS is working with the local health department, Council on Aging, Partnership for Children, the

local hospital and schools to build cohesive wellness and health promotion programs for county citizens.

—————&⛯3—————

*P*erson County ECA clubs sponsor an annual arts and crafts bazaar. For the past 20 years, the bazaar has helped home-based businesses in the area. ECA also supports five county workshops to carry on the tradition of home-based businesses and preservation of quality heritage skills.

Reamstown ECA members stuff goody bags with back-to-school items to help county children at the beginning of another school year.

In 2000, the FCS agent partnered with Brody School of Medicine at ECU to train volunteers for *The Food Literacy Partners Program*. The volunteers learned about the role of food and nutrition in health promotion, disease prevention, and effective weight management in adults and children. Volunteers then provided 20 hours of service in schools, churches, and at health fairs and worksites. Almost 400 volunteers have been trained, and they have given more than 7,000 hours of service to the county.

ECA club members donate presents for Operation Shoebox. The shoeboxes go to needy children.

Finding health care in a new country can be a challenge, especially when you don't speak the language. Extension teamed up with Catholic Social Ministries to host a Hispanic Health Fair at the county's Agriculture Building in 2003.

A man at the Hispanic Health Fair is tested for diabetes.

Fifty-six vendors representing 25 agencies provided information about health care topics such as second-hand smoke, lead poisoning, AIDS, child development issues, mental health issues, pregnancy issues, dental health, substance abuse, nutrition, first aid, asthma and car seats for children. Diabetes and blood-pressure screenings also were available to participants. Hundreds of free resource guides, featuring all agencies taking part in the event, were distributed.

While parents visited educational exhibits, children enjoyed face painting, puppet shows, a fire truck and smoke house and recreational activities provided by East Carolina University.

An ECU dance exhibition and live band entertained all participants. Some 120 Hispanic people attended and 67 volunteers, including Spanish-language interpreters, participated.

Pitt County EH projects have reached out to help the community and have extended the efforts of the HE agent. Club members have made cozy caps for cancer patients and fidget aprons for Alzheimers and dementia patients; dressed dolls for the Salvation Army Christmas project; collected recipes and compiled cookbooks; provided scholarships for youth; and participated in Operation Shoebox. They assisted the HE agent by serving as group leaders for women's financial planning services; distributing cheese and butter to needy families; promoting Extension-approved canning and freezing procedures, conducting craft workshops, encouraging home safety and security; promoting food safety and reading labels; and volunteering at county and state fairs.

Children's activities were offered at the Hispanic Health Fair, making the event attractive to the whole family.

In the 1920s, with the Lanier Home Demonstration Club's help, an office library of 200 to 300 books was made available to the county. When the Polk County Library Association was organized in 1931, those books were turned over to them. For many years the club women talked about the need for a county library, but they could not get the project to move forward. Then in 1959, Extension Homemakers decided to focus on getting a library and a bookmobile and do whatever was necessary to make it happen. They raised support by speaking at PTA meetings and to civic clubs. They showed what was possible by borrowing a bookmobile from Henderson County and taking it to all the schools. They distributed information sheets on the topic. A special tax election was held, and the measure passed.

On April 30, 1967, the ground-breaking ceremony was held with Daisy Feagan representing Extension

Extension Homemaker Daisy Feagan turns the shovel (right) at the 1967 groundbreaking for the Polk Public Library (above).

Homemakers. The library opened on Nov. 7.

⸻ ❧ ⸻

Twenty-five years ago, Gene Parks, a state Kiwanis leader, had a simple request: help men learn to cook. Parks noticed that local men who had lost their wives had no idea how to cook after many years of having someone else doing it for them, and the seeds of the program were planted. The program was geared to local Kiwanis members who had been thrust into the role of caregiver or who had become widowers. The HE agent responded. In the early days the class focused on basic cooking skills.

Today the course is called Learning the Culinary Art: A Man's Touch, and

Men need to take a turn in the kitchen, and the FCS agent teaches how to prepare tasty, healthful, safe dishes.

it's open to any man. Many men take the class for the fellowship or to prepare for the day their wives may not be able to cook.

⸻ ❧ ⸻

To reduce waste, Polk County Extension Homemakers brought their own china and utensils from home along with their covered dish to their spring luncheon in 1991.

*H*omemakers from 13 clubs prepared 750 pounds of fudge, peanut brittle, pulled mints, coconut bonbons and other delicious candies, which were sold Oct. 3 and 4, 1993, to the thousands who attended Asheboro's first Fall Festival. Today, club members are still filling the shelves with homemade candy sold during the festival at Granny's Candy Kitchen.

The money they've raised has been used to provide $2,000 college loans to students in need of financial assistance, to purchase Lifeline units for Randolph Hospital and to support Girls Haven.

ECA volunteers prepared candy to sell in their booth at Asheboro's Fall Festival.

*M*ore than 2,000 grandparents in Randolph County were providing primary care for their grandchildren in 2007. The FCS and 4-H agents joined forces to offer a six-week class to help them cope with their new roles. Grandparents learned new skills in communicating with the grandchildren and appreciating one another. They also learned about community resources.

In addition to the grandparents, 10 children between 6 and 10 attended each two-hour class. A hot meal was served each evening and homework assistance was provided. Children learned new techniques for handling stress, communicating with their grandparents, helping out at home, and getting along with their siblings. At the end of the series of classes, each

family received digital photos to create a family scrapbook.

*"T*he Community Voices* program is helping us become organized as a group and showing us how to bring our ideas to fruition. It also teaches leadership skills, goal setting, decision making and consensus building techniques," said Cathy Clark, a participant in the St. Peter Community Center group. *Community Voices,* an Extension leadership development program developed at N.C. A&T State University, nurtures grassroots leadership and teaches people what they need to become part of community affairs. The St. Peter community near Randleman had decided to incorporate in 1997 so that it would be eligible for community improvement grants.

ECA club members served soup to raise money for Habitat for Humanity. They also constructed and hung window treatments in the Habitat house.

293

At the 11th annual Richmond County Wild Game Cookery contest in Ellerby, area residents brought their best dishes and Extension judged the entries. The categories were big game; small game and other mammals; wild fowl; fish, reptiles and amphibians; and dishes prepared with wild fruits, nuts and vegetation. Over the years, a catfish casserole has proven to be the most popular dish, and venison recipes have been the most numerous. Some of the less common ingredients have included snake, porcupine, beaver, bear and groundhog.

~~~~~~

In the early 1930s, pellagra was a problem in Richmond County. The agent reported visiting 147 people with pellagra in 1930. Only two of those people died and they were "in extremis" when found. Pellagra was found mostly in mill villages and was deemed to be due to economic conditions to a great extent. Club members contributed milk and eggs to the pellagrins, and nutrition was a main topic studied by clubs. In 1932 a goal for club members was to have "no deaths from pellagra in the county."

~~~~~~

Cooperative Extension collaborated with Richmond County Environmental Health to teach 23 foodservice managers ServSafe, an 18-hour certification course developed by the Educational Foundation of the National Restaurant Association. Through role-playing, group discussion, and lecture, the managers learned the principles and safe food handling practices that reduce the risk of foodborne illness. Twenty passed the certification exam.

In 1923, Mrs. Anna Lea Harris and the county agent, W.H. Barden, organized a curb market open every Saturday morning that let town residents get fresh produce and farm families increase their income. In 1937, the curb market moved inside, to the Richmond County Country Market built by the county.

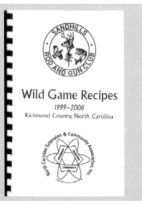

Richmond County's Wild Game Recipes cookbook was published in 2010. It contains winning recipes from the county's wild game cookery contest, including the most popular Catfish Casserole. The book is published by Sandhills Rod and Gun Club and ECA club members.

In 1933, Home Demonstration club members were making hats of braided corn shucks. Miss Glenn Caudle of Gibson Mill community took orders from Burlington, Clinton, Wilmington and Raleigh. She charged one dollar for a hat finished and blocked.

More than 1,962 grandparents are the primary caregivers of their grandchildren in Robeson County. These families face unique challenges. To address the issue, Extension partnered with the Lumber River Council of Government's *Family Caregiver Support Program* and the City of Lumberton to begin a Grandparents Raising Grandchildren Support Group in 2005. In addition to sharing problems and support, each meeting had an educational component. For example, the grandparents took Darkness to Light Training, designed to help them recognize and protect their grandchildren from sexual assault. They also heard from a local legal aid attorney, who talked about issues related to senior citizens and grandparents providing care for their grandchildren.

Seventeen percent of Robeson County residents are illiterate. To encourage reading in the home, the Extension FCS agent partnered with

County residents attend a hands-on home canning workshop (above and below). Food preservation classes have filled as people want to put up the surplus from their vegetable gardens.

a local church youth group and a local transitional housing program for mothers receiving substance recovery services. The mothers were given books for preschoolers, and each youth read the book aloud before leaving. As a result, 24 families received at least one book.

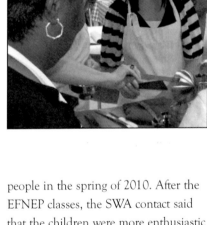

Extension Homemakers sponsored the Snowflake Shoppe in 1979. Quality crafts that had been made by homemakers and master craftsmen were on sale to the public. Items that were sold were needle crafts of all kinds, woven baskets, feather crafts, wood carving crafts, plants and flowers, and baked goods.

The EFNEP program assistant partnered with the local Strength, Wisdom, Achievement Youth (SWA) organization to teach a series of six nutrition education classes to 307 young

Children in the Grandparents Raising Grandchildren group create family shields.

people in the spring of 2010. After the EFNEP classes, the SWA contact said that the children were more enthusiastic about eating vegetables as a snack and they talked about using EFNEP recipes at home. They also wanted to play outside more and were choosing to do so instead of playing video games. The program was such a success that the EFNEP program assistant decided to teach EFNEP afterschool groups in the fall.

Rockingham POPULATION 86,064

County commissioners discontinued funding the home demonstration agent position in 1929. Local people, including farmers, farm women, Mr. and Mrs. Jefferson Penn, Mr. and Mrs. Charles Penn and Mrs. Frank Mebane, donated money to fund the position. Extension Homemakers pleaded with the commissioners to fund the position. They also went to the State Legislature and had a law passed to the effect that Rockingham County would always employ a home agent. Rockingham is the only county in the state with such a law.

~~~

Beginning in 1951, the county's home demonstration clubs published its first cookbook and started a cookbook fund for education. In 1974 they advertised their second cookbook nationally and sold copies all over the US and in some foreign countries. The most recent cookbook borrows favorite recipes from the older cookbooks and adds new recipes, including heart-healthy choices. Profits for the

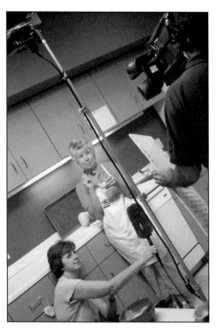

The Produce Lady is Extension's director and FCS agent in Rockingham County. Good quality local foods are her passion and she loves developing and sharing ways to select, store, prepare, and preserve foods. Her videos on North Carolina foods are on the web at www.theproducelady.org and on YouTube, and she also has a blog.

cookbook fund and wise investment of the money continue today to provide scholarships for Rockingham County students attending colleges in North Carolina.

~~~

When the newly formed county Weavers and Fiber Arts Guild decided to join Extension's Volunteer Fall Fair in 2008, both organizations benefited. The number of vendors doubled and the number of shoppers dramatically increased. ECA netted over $2,000 from table rentals, quilt raffle tickets, cookbook sales, and foods, which enriched the county's scholarship fund.

~~~

Extension Homemaker Anne Boyd enrolled in a district crafts workshop in 1976 and made two small egg baskets in the two-day class. She's been making baskets in her spare time ever since and has taught basketry to others in Extension and to the public through Rockingham Community College Continuing Education program. Although she considers this a hobby, she has sold many baskets, adding to her family's income.

In 2008, volunteers began a quilt scholarship fund to help students in Rockingham County. The sale of cookbooks has supported college scholarships for local students since 1951.

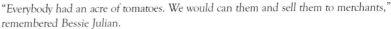

"Everybody had an acre of tomatoes. We would can them and sell them to merchants," remembered Bessie Julian.

Rowan County Extension Homemakers were instrumental in getting the county's agricultural building, which currently houses Cooperative Extension, Farm Services, Soil and Water Conservation, Forestry Services, the Fire Marshal, and EMS. In 1986, the women began writing letters, speaking to the county manager and at commissioners' meetings, and raising money. In a year's time, the Rowan County Agricultural Center became a reality.

The Extension FCS agent regularly gives short talks to groups of women on the importance of regular medical checkups, preventive screenings, and warning signs that require immediate help. A few weeks after one talk, she got a call. One of the women realized she had several of the warning signs of a heart attack. She went to her doctor and asked him to check her heart. After performing cardiac catheterization, the doctor found five blockages. She has since had triple bypass surgery and is doing well. She insists it was the information she received from the Extension agent that made the difference, and was calling to say thank you.

Catherine Safrit of St. Paul's ECA Club was a retired schoolteacher who couldn't forget several boys in her classes. They were the boys who couldn't read. "With 35 others in the room, you couldn't do much to help them." After she retired, she began a literacy program using the Laubach reading method. Since starting the program, she has taught more than 600 people to read. Although Catherine Safrit died in 2001, volunteers are still in her literacy program teaching people to read at the Rowan County Public Library.

For over 30 years, beginning in 1949, the Extension club women made a total of 20,647 garments to give to the Welfare Department for needy children in the county and contributed almost $5,000 for new shoes.

The Rowan County Quilt, presented to the county in 1998, was a joint project of the Rowan Extension Homemakers and the Salisbury-Rowan Quilters Guild. The quilt features historic landmarks taken from original art and the county seal. It was framed and hung in the county commissioners' meeting room.

When the Depression set in, the recently developed hot school lunch program faced a food shortage. Home demonstration members took food to the schools and even helped to prepare it because of employee shortages. The hospital also suffered from a shortage of food but in the Ellenboro Club report, Miss Cleo Burns says " ... (we) donated to the hospital 66 cans of fruit and vegetables, one can of sausage, one bushel of sweet potatoes, half-bushel of field peas and one gallon of molasses." The ladies were providing food to combat the more than 250 cases of pellagra in the county.

___

To let people know about the Foothills Grandparents Raising Grandchildren, Extension sponsored a

Children work on a crafts project while their grandparents attend a support group.

Grandparents Raising Grandchildren conference. As a result of the one-day conference, attendance at the monthly support group meetings tripled.

___

In 2008, students attending an alternative high school took Food Preservation Made Easy classes taught by Extension's FCS agent. As his or her final project, each student preserved a food and created a recipe book based on what he or she learned. Before the class, no student had any food preservation experience.

___

In the 1930s the county commissioners voted to cut the home agent's position. Afterwards 675 men and women held a mass meeting. Mrs. W.P. Dorsey gave a ringing plea on the need for an agent. A vote was held and the results were 500 votes to continue the agent and 25 votes against. The commissioners rescinded their action, and not only hired the agent back, but added an assistant.

Young people at Extension's Kids & Chefs day camp learn about local foods at the farmer's market. Parents reported that their children are now careful about washing hands, choosing healthier foods, and helping with meal planning and cooking at home.

Sampson POPULATION 65,396

$\mathscr{B}$ecause of the political situation in 1929, the county didn't appropriate any money to pay a home demonstration agent that year. However, in January 1930, the county promised to reinstate the money in July. Clubs used their local funds to finance the county's part of the agent's salary from January until July.

———— ✣ ————

$\mathscr{T}$he Sampson County Coalition for Healthy Children brings together organizations that are addressing the issues of childhood obesity and health. A special project of the group was to sponsor an Eating Smart, Moving More Contest in 2008. Third-graders could construct a display board promoting the concepts of healthy eating and physical activity. Participating classes spent a *Super Fun Day* at the park, where they rotated through seven activity stations: relay races, tag games, dance aerobics, parachute games, poison ball, quick-start tennis, and soccer. At the farmer's market, students had the opportunity to

More than 100 Eat Smart, Move More, Weigh Less participants lost a total of more than 1,000 pounds in 2010. Many reported reduced joint pain, some have had their blood pressure or diabetes medicine either reduced or discontinued. Here, participants taste test a variety of smoothies while learning how to make them at home.

taste some new fruits and eat a healthy lunch. Tony the Tiger and Flex the Health Hound also stopped by. Over 350 students and teachers participated.

———— ✣ ————

$\mathscr{D}$uring a 2008 visit with a senior citizen who was also a widow, the question of home repairs was raised. The woman already had a mortgage with Rural Housing and could not afford to borrow more money to repair the plumbing, roof, overhangs, electrical problems, and paint. The Extension FCS agent talked with Rural Housing and the homeowner received a $12,000 grant to make the needed repairs.

———— ✣ ————

$\mathscr{I}$n 2008, a gentleman was talking with the Extension FCS agent about the possibility of home loans for low-income people. He revealed that he had filed for bankruptcy in the past. When asked if there might be any other problems in his credit history, he said no but agreed to get reports from all

three credit reporting agencies. The Extension agent reviewed his credit reports and he started working on raising his credit scores. Seven months after that, he had a household budget in place and was taking steps to fix negative items on his credit reports. He decided to become debt-free before applying for a house loan.

The FCS agent teaches healthy cooking to area teens.

Extension Homemakers created this quilt shaped like Sampson County in the 1970s.

Mary Odom was one of two women to serve as Scotland County's representative in the state House and the state Senate. She continued her service to the community as a member of Extension Homemakers. As an Extension Homemaker, she campaigned for waste management, promoted citywide recycling, and successfully lobbied to protect North Carolina rivers. In 1986, she spearheaded a series of candidate forums with the Laurinburg/Scotland County Area Chamber of Commerce and the Junior Service League. Candidates spoke on three consecutive Mondays to a packed room and the forum was broadcast live by a local radio station.

———— ❧ ————

Scotland County Extension and Extension Homemakers co-sponsored three Leadership Development Seminars for Minority Women in 1991, 1993, and 1996. Approximately 115 women attended the 1996 seminar

at St. Andrews Presbyterian College. The keynote address was given by Rev. Shirley Hines, pastor of Zion Campbell A.M.E. Church, who reminded the audience of the time when they had no rights—minority or otherwise. "Now women can do anything they want to. We, as women, cannot afford to go half stepping. Today's woman has to invest in herself and realize she can make a difference."

———— ❧ ————

In the 1990s, Extension sponsored Easy Meals for Mature Men, a cooking class taught by Colin McArthur of Laurinburg, owner of General McArthur's Restaurant. Under his guidance, the men prepared a 20-minute oven meal.

Extension, Scotland ECA club members, and the Shred-It Company held a Community Shred program that allowed 200 citizens to have 9,700 pounds of personal documents shredded. The shredded paper, representing 48 trees, was delivered to a secure bailing facility and then recycled.

Scotland County Extension Homemakers assisted the local Sheriff's Department in launching a countywide Neighborhood Watch Program. EH club members distributed 168 leaflets that explained the program and included safety precautions.

———— ❧ ————

The Extension FCS agent got retired men into the kitchen on Friday mornings for a series of classes called Men's Basic Survival: Know Your Kitchen. The series was offered in 2008 by St. Andrews Institute for Lifelong Learning and held at St. Andrews and Scotia Village Retirement Community. The county agent taught her students nutrition, food safety and easy food preparation. She also took them on a field trip to visit local grocery stores to learn the basics about food shopping.

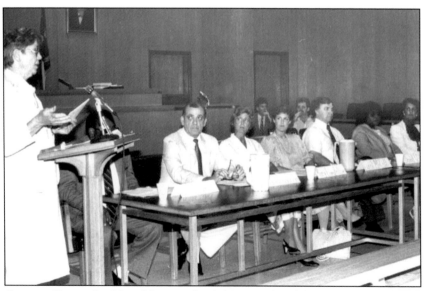

Extension Homemaker Mary Odom spearheaded a series of candidate forums in Scotland County after serving in the state House and state Senate.

$\mathcal{S}tanly$ POPULATION 59,714

As has been the trend when the economy goes down, interest in gardening and home food preservation goes up. A recent visitor to the Extension center learned that she had been using a pressure cooker instead of a pressure canner to can green beans. She had wondered why half the green beans spoiled. In 2009, more than 60 canner gauges were checked, compared to a handful in previous years.

———— ✄✄✄ ————

Funds for the Betty Watson Memorial Scholarship were nearly depleted after years of awarding a scholarship to a deserving student from the county. ECA club members held two Serendipity Afternoon Teas in 2009 and 2010 to rebuild the fund. As a result they made enough money to continue the scholarship for at least five years. The tea has become so popular, ECA members want to make it a yearly

ECA club members held Serendipity Afternoon Teas to raise scholarship money for a Stanly County student.

fundraiser. Betty Watson was a beloved Stanly County home economics agent between 1953 and 1976.

———— ✄✄✄ ————

Twelve middle school children took The *Balancing Act*, an Extension class about the financial responsibilities of life. They learned how to create a budget and how their level of education will greatly affect their future financial well-being.

———— ✄✄✄ ————

Home demonstration work began in 1913 in Stanly County. Thirteen clubs were formed that year. By 1926, club women were traveling to Raleigh to attend farm women's short courses. Early club records for 1928-1929 speak of rat-killing contests and explanations about how a proper diet could cure pellagra. Pressure cookers became popular the next year, and 25 homemakers bought one. By 1932, there were 15 organized clubs with 397 members.

The FCS agent teaches canning and safe food preservation.

Stokes POPULATION 46,638

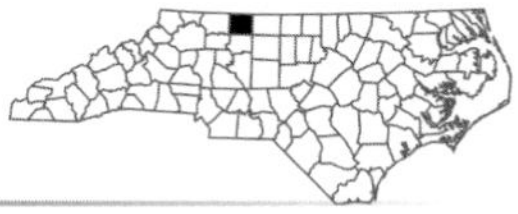

During the war years, clothing conservation was stressed with the motto, "Use it up, wear it out, make it do, or do without." However, the home demonstration club members made sure that was not the case for the Red Cross. They made 1,200 garments and bandages to meet their demand for assistance.

In the early 1950s, health and safety programs were the emphasis. Stokes County led all counties in the state in home nursing work with 150 home demonstration women receiving home nursing certificates.

Stokes Extension Homemakers display the hats and dresses they made in a revue called Members on Parade.

The FCS agent taught 42 elementary students food safety and nutrition in a 10-week program. Children tasted several new foods and practiced reading food labels. Parents were surveyed after the class and they reported that their children were eating more fruits and vegetables and drinking fewer soft drinks. A teacher commented that students were bringing healthier snacks, and another teacher said her class planned a healthy Valentine party, which included fruits and vegetables.

In 1952, the HD club women of the county pledged $4,000 to help build the Stokes-Reynolds Hospital. They wrote a cookbook and after selling 5,000 copies, they had $4,000 for the hospital. Here, club members admire the new stove purchased when they furnished the kitchen at the hospital.

ECA volunteers in 2009 helped "extend" the educational efforts of the Extension FCS agent by assisting or teaching *Chef & the Child*, basics of canning, and sewing classes.

In 2007 Extension sponsored a 10-week program called *Moving Towards a Healthier You*, with Meadows Baptist Church, Healthy Carolinians of Stokes and Stokes-Reynolds Memorial Hospital. Fifty women were enrolled in the program. Some 86 percent lost weight, with the average loss of 9 pounds per person. The group also logged 61,619 minutes of walking.

In 1989, Walnut Cove EH Club had volunteered 10,000-plus hours in recycling, work with the Cancer Society, the local library, a Centennial celebration for the town of Walnut Cove, a radon survey, the Red Cross, and efforts to get extended area telephone service for two exchanges in the county.

Stokes County students learn to check the nutritional value of foods by reading labels.

Surry Home Demonstration clubs began a reading program in 1941. Practically all the books came from Raleigh. The members ordered them and then returned the books when they were finished reading them. The club women were instrumental in getting the first county library which opened in 1949. Soon after, the bookmobile began its journey along the highways and county roads.

⁂

Surry County residents joined Extension and ECA club members in Celebrating Agriculture, an annual day of celebration and education begun in 2007. One grandfather said the day has become a tradition for his family. He has children who live outside of the county, and they make a special effort to come back to enjoy the day together. This year as they were looking at the chickens and he was telling the grandchildren about how he had helped with chickens when he was a boy, his granddaughter had the chance to reach under a hen and find an egg. She'd never experienced that before and now she knows that eggs don't just come from the grocery store. In Surry County, agriculture is responsible for 28 percent of county income and over 24 percent of the employment.

⁂

The fun at Celebrating Agriculture included riding a barrel train and dancing with a chicken and a cow.

Assisting Medicare Part D participants in choosing a prescription drug plan is an important role for Family and Consumer Sciences in Surry County where Cooperative Extension serves as the coordinating site for the North Carolina Department of Insurance Senior Health Insurance Information Program (SHIIP). Between 2007 and 2010, six trained SHIIP volunteers have conducted over 1,200 individual counseling sessions with Medicare recipients. The North Carolina Department of Insurance estimates that an average of $2,000 will not have to be paid out-of-pocket when a person selects the best plan for his particular prescription needs, resulting in an estimated savings of $2,400,000 for Surry County residents.

⁂

During 2008, Surry County ECA members volunteered 8,525 hours to Extension and an additional 9,919 hours in the community to make the county a better place. If a volunteer's time is worth $19.51 an hour, that's a gift of $359,842.44. ECA members do make a difference.

Mrs. Robert Marr remembers when a Mrs. Jane Cobb came to Swain County and taught women how to can green beans and tomatoes in glass jars. They were canned in wash tubs over an open fire in the early 1920s. Mrs. Jura Miller remembers a similar demonstration in the early 1920s, this one at the old County Home on Deep Creek. Green beans were canned over an open fire in wash tubs that were used to wash clothes.

※❦❧

Eighty-five people attended Beginner Food Preservation 101 in 2008. FCS agents from Swain, Jackson, Macon counties and the Cherokee Reservation taught the class.

※❦❧

Extension used an *Out for Lunch* program consisting of eight two-hour lessons to teach 270 adults to get the most nutrition from their Food Stamps in 2002. Adults learned to buy, prepare and store nutritious foods, to handle food safely, and to manage a budget. The program also taught 122 preschool children about food safety, fruits, vegetables and milk.

※❦❧

In 2008, Extension partnered with the Healthy Lifestyles Task Force and Partnership for Health to present a weeklong event called *Moving in the Mountains*. The purpose was to encourage people to try new forms of physical activity. Thirty-four people tried yoga, hiking, dance, kayaking, biking, judo and swimming. They also used a local fitness center and took healthy cooking classes.

Extension Homemakers make brooms and learn Swedish darning in the 1950s.

Transylvania

During the summer of 1918, when the vines in the gardens hung heavily with beans, Lula M. Cassidy, home demonstration agent, came to the valley of Pisgah Forest. Miss Cassidy visited in the homes, speaking of canning methods. The schoolhouse was the center of community activities, so this was the meeting place for women to take their homegrown beans, and here they learned safe methods of canning.

The first home demonstration club began in the valley of Davidson River. Mrs. J.P. Cheek was a charter member and first president. "Words cannot express what the home demonstration program has meant to me. It has given me a new way of life."

In 2006, the FCS agent explained nutritional management to 24 diabetic patients who had no health insurance. All were able to better control their blood sugar, and their hemoglobin A_1c scores improved by at least 2 points.

Club members get in shape together and work with Extension to beautify the environment.

With the help of an EFNEP program assistant, Junior Girl Scout Troop 177 learned about nutrition. The girls took the lessons to heart, trying new foods like soybeans, spaghetti squash and papaya. At sleepovers, they cooked instead of making crafts. Mothers were so excited about their daughters' new interest in nutrition at home, they began helping with the EFNEP sessions. An unexpected report came from the troop leader, who said she had been inspired to start walking for an hour every night during the five-week series. She was also reading food labels with her daughter and making a conscious effort to improve her family's diet. From series beginning to end, she had lost 10 pounds.

Little River club women work for certificates in food preservation.

Transylvania County has many summer camps staffed by college and high school students. The week before these camps opened in 2005, FCS offered food safety training for kitchen staff from three camps.

305

During the 1950s the home demonstration clubs assisted with the cancer fund, the heart fund, tuberculosis fund, crippled children's fund, Red Cross and the blood mobile. Not only did the homemakers support these organizations financially, but they also provided transportation to and from the bloodmobile and registered people.

——— 🙲🙵🙲 ———

Tyrrell County's ECA membership is growing and the club members are getting younger and younger. In 2007, a Teen ECA club was formed which currently has 12 members ages 12 to 17. Another group of Hispanic teens has formed the Jovenes Con Suenos Grandes (Youth with Big Dreams) ECA Club.

——— 🙲🙵🙲 ———

The Extension FCS agent works with Juntos, a six-week program to help Hispanic teens and their families explore college options. With the Tyrrell County Hispanic/Latino Advisory Council, she has helped set up English, health and driver's education classes;

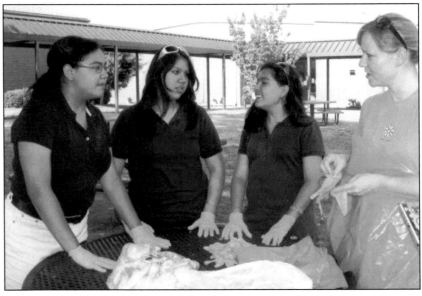

Members of the Jovenes Con Suenos Grandes ECA Club pick up trash around Columbia.

distributed health kits for workers; and make La Posada part of the River Town Christmas celebration. La Posada is the traditional musical re-enactment of Mary and Joseph's quest for shelter in Bethlehem.

——— 🙲🙵🙲 ———

To encourage citizens to vote, Tyrrell County ECA members began a voter registration campaign in the spring of 2008, using letters to the editor,

Young ECA Club members make baskets for The Lost Colony outdoor drama to replace those lost in a fire.

newsletter articles, and posters. They also worked with the local Board of Elections to hold a voter registration drive.

——— 🙲🙵🙲 ———

In 1977 the Extension homemakers began collecting stamps for the Bangladesh food project. By the time they were done, they had collected over 300,000 stamps.

Tyrrell County residents learn how they can improve their health in the FCS agent's series Give Your Heart a Healthy Beat. The Extension series includes information on choosing nutrition-packed foods, controlling portion size, and getting the healthy amount of exercise.

𝒞CA club members hold a weeklong summer enrichment program for second through fifth graders. Campers paint, draw and express their creativity in the visual exploration class. In science frontiers, they may go on plant scavenger hunts, study earthworms, or dissect owl pellets. Cultural expedition campers learn about Latino culture, learn to play dominoes and sing in Spanish. Each year brings something different. In creative expressions, students hone writing skills one year and acting skills another. *Discovery in Motion* class keeps them moving and exploring lots of activities. At the end of the week, the children put on a program for friends and families. The ECA members in Union County have conducted this program each summer for the past 15 years. Money raised through the camp goes toward local scholarships.

Kids enjoy themselves and learn a lot at ECA's Summer Enrichment Program.

𝓔xtension collaborated with the Union County Council on Aging and the Ellen Fitzgerald Senior Center in Monroe to bring healthcare service providers and screeners under one roof, so that seniors could get health-related information in one place, at one time. On average, 400 seniors have attended the Senior Wellness Expo each year since it began in 2006. In 2009, 75 vendors and screeners set up informational booths or provided cholesterol, blood sugar, blood pressure, dental, eye, and spinal checks. Pharmacy students from Wingate University answered questions on medications, and representatives from assisted living, long-term care facilities, hospitals, and Senior Health Insurance Information (SHIIP) were available to assist the seniors. If problems were detected from the screenings, the individual was referred to appropriate healthcare providers for follow-up. Some doctors in the community are even recommending it to their patients as a good source for health information.

𝒰nion County's *Turn Off TV Week* was established by the Extension FCS agent working with partners from Partnership for Children, including Union Regional Medical Center, *The Enquirer Journal*, The Union County Public Library and the Monroe Aquatic and Fitness Center. Schools, churches, United Way agencies, More at Four and Smart Start all supported the effort, and many area merchants provided discounts for families who signed a TV-free pledge.

Seniors get information at the Senior Wellness Expo.

The Extension FCS agent worked with the Smart Start evaluator to organize the Vance County Parenting Task Force in 2004. The task force is a working partnership of 22 agencies and individuals. The task force has netted over $280,000 in grant funding to support parenting educator salaries, parenting classes, and training for 64 area professionals in the *Parenting Matters* curricula. The task force has put a weekly parenting tip in *The Daily Dispatch* newspaper since 2004.

A team of task force members is working with pastors convened by the Vance County Schools church/school involvement committee to establish parenting education satellite centers at churches in targeted communities. Church participation may vary from offering printed information to facilitating interactive parenting classes.

Youth mentoring volunteers are being trained by the Friends of Youth Coordinator at two churches. The pastors became aware of this opportunity during the church/school project work. The parenting task force

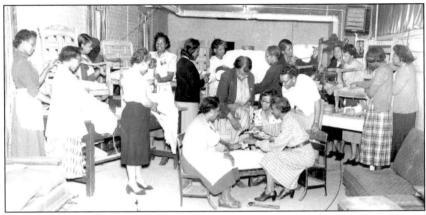

The Black Vance County Council was honored in 1958 for the best refinishing furniture project in the state. The NC State specialist used the photos taken during this workshop as illustrations in the publication called New Furniture from Old. The publication was used throughout the state. The furniture was also featured in an article in Extension Review, a national magazine.

meets bimonthly and is facilitated by Extension's FCS agent.

Fifty court-referred or -mandated parents took the eight-week *Parenting Matters* course between January and June, 2008.

— 8003 —

A dream of the Vance County Negro Home Demonstration Council was building a community center. However, that was not to be and in 1989 the

Vance County ECA members visit nursing home residents.

former council president donated $9,589.95 from the sale of the lot to the Henderson Institute Graduates and Former Students Association Library.

— 8003 —

Through the 1980s, the Pine Haven Convalescent Center Extension Homemakers Club collected 400,000 stamps for the *Stamps for Food Program* and 5,167 soup labels which were donated to Aycock Elementary School for purchasing supplies. They also donated 281 pairs of glasses to the Lions Club.

Parents role-play to explore ways to communicate with children.

Extension helped Gethsemane SDA Church in southeast Raleigh encourage exercise by renovating a playground and creating a walking trail to connect it with the community garden and the neighborhood. The project was funded by the John Rex Endowment. Other partners included the School of Design, Parks and Recreation Department, NC State University, and the city of Raleigh.

Wake County EH members celebrate holidays around the world.

Heritage Days, started as a fun-filled day showcasing heritage crafts demonstrated by EH people, has evolved into an event with Wake County Parks. A member of the Driftwood Club demonstrates basketry at Heritage Days.

Wake County ECA members demonstrated heritage crafts and sold food at the county's Heritage Day Celebration and Youth 4-H Fair Day for 10 years. The group earned $10,000, which was given in scholarships and used to set up the first County ECA Endowment within the Family and Consumer Sciences Foundation at NC State University.

The First-Time Home Buyers' Program, begun in 1990, taught hundreds of people about budgeting, credit, and closing on a house. Attorneys, mortgage lenders, and consumer counselors were guest speakers, and participants who attended all four sessions received a certificate which helped with securing a mortgage.

To celebrate holidays around the world, ECA club members decorated 17 Christmas trees and made more than 50 window swags, window treatments and greenery arrangements to decorate at Historic Oak View County Park. Each tree or display was accompanied with the story of the customs and practices of the country celebrated. At each display, an ECA member explained the country's holiday traditions to hundreds of children, helping them understand and appreciate diversity. As many as 4,000 people attended a Saturday night candlelight celebration, followed by a week of tours. After the celebrations, the 17 trees were donated to needy families.

Extension in Wake County helped pilot the *Women's Financial Information Program* for the AARP. The program taught more than 100 women money management, estate planning, investing, and local resources. Each of the eight sessions was 2 ½ hours long. The first half was teaching and the second half allowed each woman to work on her particular situation.

Wake County Extension Homemakers club members show cased their organization with an exhibit shown at the Southern Women's Show throughout the 1980s.

For seven years, the FCS agent taught teens in foster care about budgeting, credit, insurance and banking.

Prospective home owners learn the ins and outs of buying for the first time.

Warren POPULATION 19,918

*H*ome demonstration volunteers mended linens and made gowns and aprons for Warren General Hospital. They also furnished two rooms for $1,000 and gave shrubbery for the hospital grounds when the hospital opened in 1951.

———— 8003 ————

*P*regnant by age 15...young boys calling young ladies unthinkable nicknames...unreported abuse... Warren County teens were going down the wrong path. Extension worked to get teachers, DSS, Library and Health Department workers, a nonprofit agency, and church and community leaders trained in its new program: *Healthy Marriage Matters* for teenagers. Within six months, HMM's coordinator reached more than 500 youth. Participants said the program taught them to decide rather than to slide into a relationship, the difference between healthy and unhealthy relationships, and the importance of friends, family, and setting goals in life.

Graduates of the Healthy Marriage Matters class for teens celebrate.

The *Healthy Marriage Matters* program is for youth ages 13 to 19. This FCS program impacted more than 800 youth, with more than 350 of them taking a full 8- to 12-hour research-based course.

———— 8003 ————

A young mother with two daughters said her food stamp dollars just didn't last the whole month. Then she took

The Healthy Marriage Matters coordinator teaches a lesson to 150 youth.

part in Extension's *Expanded Food and Nutrition Program* in Warren County, and realized she had saved $37.67 on her last weekly shopping trip by putting what she learned into practice.

———— 8003 ————

*M*any *Parenting Matters* participants admitted that they would never have set foot in a parenting class if attendance hadn't been required by the court. But after attending, they said they would recommend the class to their friends.

FCS Agent teaches effective communication by explaining how to make a peanut butter sandwich.

Watermark Association of Artisans was chartered in 1978. Extension homemakers had a strong role in developing this member-owned craft cooperative for the Albemarle area. The sales of crafts supplemented family income.

———❦———

Sales at the Washington County Home Demonstration Curb Market in 1931 were $3,500 but dropped to $1,042 in 1932 due to the Depression. The mill had closed in Plymouth, making money tight in the community. General sales, which included poultry and eggs shipped to commission merchants, sold to trucks passing through and delivered to merchants, brought in another $1,516. Sellers wore white cotton dresses, and used standard scales to ensure correct weight for each customer. Some of the sellers were able to buy all their groceries and provide for their families on the proceeds from the curb market. They declared that they couldn't get along without the market.

Members of two early Home Demonstration Clubs in Washington County. The names of the clubs and dates the pictures were taken are not known.

Frances (Misenheimer) Darden was home demonstration agent from 1935 to 1966. She recalled her car getting stuck in the mud following home demonstration meetings. Club women had to push her out, getting mud splattered all over themselves.

———❦———

The Extension HE agent got an enthusiastic response from 19 mothers of preschoolers in 1972 with her series of classes entitled the Preschooler and His Clothes. One mother said, "I needed this lesson on shoes two years ago, but I can still benefit before the children's feet are ruined." To reach low-income audiences, mini-lessons were given at the Health Development Center. Lessons included Clothes and Your Preschooler's Physical Development; Oh, My Aching Feet; and Teach-Me Clothes.

———❦———

The Precious Past, a collection of reminiscences about life as it used to be, was written and published by Extension homemakers in Washington County in 1992.

When the Courthouse Annex, originally built in 1939, was renovated in 1979, the refurbished area included a kitchen for demonstrations and a meeting room that would hold 60. Extension homemakers volunteered their sewing skills, and saved the county $224 by making draperies for windows throughout the renovated area.

———❧———

Of the 2,560 Watauga County residents who had been diagnosed with diabetes, 44.5 percent had no diabetes education, 84 percent were overweight or obese, 78 percent didn't eat the recommended number of fruits and vegetables each day, and 71 percent were not active enough. In 2007, Extension

Watauga County Extension coordinated English as a Second Language classes for children and adults.

Happy Hearts ECA members show their beautification project at Watauga Opportunties, an Applecart bus stop.

partnered with Watauga County Health Department to offer two 4-day-long diabetes workshops. A nurse educator, pharmacist, diabetes educator, podiatrist, endocrinologist, registered dietitian, and the Extension FCS agent (who is also a registered dietitian), covered all aspects of diabetes complication prevention. A daily cooking lesson demonstrated health promoting cooking techniques, and the 37 participants learned how to monitor and control their blood

glucose levels. Proper control of diabetes improves health, increases lifespan, and reduces medical expenses.

———❧———

The Watauga FCS agent and an ASU nutrition intern taught four classes for 6- to 9-year-olds in 2008. One class focused on greens. When children entered the classroom, they smelled kale sautéing in olive oil and garlic. The children tasted the kale and two types of lettuce and spinach. The kale was a hit. One student wanted kale for a birthday dinner; his father requested the recipe. A mom said her daughter demanded kale in the grocery store, telling other

An Hispanic women's group learns sewing skills from the FCS agent and ECA volunteers.

Kindergarteners work in a school garden. After they grew the vegetables, they enjoyed eating them.

customers how to prepare it. And a third picky eater asked her mom to add kale once a week to family meals.

———❧———

Extension taught *Low Impact Living* in 2008. Participants built rain barrels, started backyard composting, and detoxified their home by switching to watershed-friendly home cleaning products. The class also offered information on backyard chickens, rain gardens and home weatherization.

Wayne POPULATION 115,696

In 1988, plans were made to transform the porch at the Wayne Center into a room for Extension homemakers. It became quite a room, with a kitchen, storage space, and furnished space for meetings and projects. When the home economics agent retired in 1994 the totally transformed porch was named the Evelyn Raper Learning Center.

———— ✦ ————

Men at the Neuse Correctional Facility in Wayne County take parenting classes, hoping to learn how to re-establish or improve ties with their children. Since 1996, the FCS agent has conducted a series of six one-hour sessions, reaching 372 inmates. One unique aspect of these parenting classes is that the agent teaches letter writing to help inmates stay in touch with their children.

———— ✦ ————

In 1996 and 1997, EH clubs purchased 70 *Kids for Character* videos for schools, day care centers, and churches. The focus was on developing the six pillars of character: trustworthiness, respect, sharing, responsibility, caring, and citizenship. Songs, skits, activities and discussions reinforced the idea that character counts. In addition, 11 club members were trained and used these videos in their communities with neighborhood groups.

———— ✦ ————

Extension's *Parents as Teachers* program held its annual *Creating Happy Holidays* event with a celebration they called On the Farm with Mrs. Claus. Holiday activities were available

Best Grove ECA Club members clean up the roadside in their community.

Mrs. Claus (the FCS agent) posed with children at Parents As Teachers' annual holiday event.

based on children's ages, and children alternated singing songs in English and Spanish. The "parents' corner" disbursed tips, including information on reducing stress during the holidays.

Mrs. Claus read a story, children had their pictures taken with her, and then everyone enjoyed a hayride to see the lights in downtown Goldsboro.

———— ✦ ————

ECA Clubs donated $5,000 to refurbish a room at the Ronald McDonald House in Greenville.

———— ✦ ————

The Wayne County Livestock Association relies on over 35 dedicated ECA volunteers who serve each year at the Wayne Regional Fair. Volunteers accept, record, and oversee judging in a number of categories.

ECA members at work in the kitchen at the Evelyn Raper Learning Resource Center.

*F*CS leads the Wilkes Family Caregiver's Council, which provides education and support to caregivers. Over 30 family caregivers participated in the county's fourth annual caregivers' retreat in 2008. Extension also offered a four-week program called *Tools for Caregivers.* Participants learned about the negative effects of stress and tried stress reduction activities. Pre- and post- blood pressure assessments showed that blood pressure readings dropped significantly after participation in the activities. All the caregivers said they had an increased understanding of the importance of managing stress and would use the skills gained at the retreat.

*W*ilkes Extension Homemakers through the years have staffed the bloodmobile, the cancer clinics, and had volunteered at the crippled children's clinic. They have been strong supporters of Heart Fund drives, March of Dimes campaign and the United Fund.

*F*CS reached 70 households in 2008 with basic money management programs for students at Wilkes Community College, at Smart Start Family Resource Centers and for parents of Head Start children. All participants learned basic money skills, such as tracking spending and developing a spending plan. The majority said they would reduce credit card debt and build savings.

*F*CS partnered with Wilkes County Environmental Health to teach food

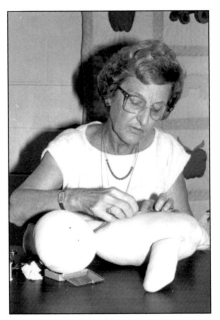

Marianna Foster, Wilkes County Extension Homemaker, making a soft sculptured doll in 1985.

safety certification programs for food service employees in restaurants, schools and medical facilities. Some 68 people working at restaurants, nursing homes and schools attended, and 90 percent of those attending passed the certification exam.

A new EH club was formed in Wilkes County in 1992. They called themselves the Career Homemakers ECA club, and they met during their lunch hour because they worked outside the home and that was the only time they could get together.

*O*ld Times Around Pores Knob, a collection of local history, individual reminiscences and over 200 old-time recipes handed down by mother and grandmothers of the Pores Knob EH club members, was published in 1984.

Wilkes County ECA members celebrated their 2009 achievements and kicked off June Dairy Month with the theme ECA is Mooving On! Mozelle Shumaker received a gift in recognition of her 59 years of perfect attendance. Ferguson Extension Homemakers Club, organized in 1938, is the oldest club in the country.

In 1941, Mitchell HD Club members became interested in some type of roadside market in which to sell their produce. A countywide meeting of all interested people was held at the high school and on May 10, 1941, a curb market was opened on East Nash Street.

❦

In 1944, the Wilson County Extension club members established the Lois Rainwater Educational Scholarship Loan Fund. Clubs each put $10 in the fund, and held fundraisers through the year. Each year, Wilson County students borrowed money and repaid it interest-free after graduation. In 2007, the ECA members placed $34,318 with the Family and Consumer Sciences Foundation at NC State University to establish an endowment to continue the program as a scholarship fund.

❦

Home demonstration club members make United Nations' flags in this 1950s workshop.

The FCS agent and SHIIP volunteers met with 68 Medicare recipients. One person saved an estimated $23,000 in out-of-pocket drug costs by appropriate selection of a drug plan. Another person who was getting Medicaid and Medicare and living in a low-income, high-rise apartment complex got $1,000 back in premiums paid for a Medicare Part D plan. The gentleman could not read and write and was not aware that he had been entered into this coverage by a salesman. Getting the refund involved several phone calls and an appeal process.

❦

The FCS agent and Wilson County Smart Start provided monthly classes to 213 childcare workers. They taught classroom interactions; infant toddler milestones; hands-on science experiences; sanitary standards for childcare centers; preventing child abuse; math and science mania; classroom safety practices; and social and emotional development in infants and toddlers.

❦

Children learn the steps to healthy eating in this class taught by the FCS agent.

ECA members let America's soldiers know they are appreciated by delivering 146 handmade cooling neck wraps, supplies and cash to Give 2 the Troops, an organization headquartered in Greenville that mails items to the military overseas. The members also helped supply and pack goody bags to mail to the soldiers.

An Extension homemaker fingerprints a child for his parents. The fingerprints were part of a kit to record information on the child. This was a statewide program for Extension homemakers in the 1980s.

The Yadkin County Home Demonstration Club Chorus sang on WSJS radio and television in Winston-Salem in 1957. In addition to singing, two club members shared what home demonstration work had meant to them.

        —❧—

Yadkin County Extension Homemakers, the NC Department of Transportation, and Yadkin County Chamber of Commerce erected "Welcome to Yadkin County" signs on highways entering the county in 1989. Extension homemakers designed the signs and raised almost $3,000 from cookbook sales to cover costs. Clubs also helped pay for signs for Community Watch.

        —❧—

Extension sponsored *Putting Your Best Foot Forward*, a three-day 'mini-camp' for 5- to 11-year-olds. Instruction and food preparation emphasized the importance of healthy, low-fat foods as well as food safety. The second day included a partnership with the local YMCA which placed emphasis

Extension homemakers raised $2,884 through sales of the Extension homemakers cookbook. This money was used to buy eight signs in 1989, which were placed at the county line on highways 421, 601, 67, and I-77. The Chamber of Commerce paid for the posts. Clubs also paid for Community Watch signs.

on the importance of physical activity in building and maintaining healthy bodies. All participants reported an increase in understanding of the importance of nutrition and exercise for an improved lifestyle.

        —❧—

After hearing about a successful fundraiser in Gaston County, Yadkin ECA members decided to raise money with homemade pies for lunch. For just $5, each person could have a slice of any pie. The ECA members made chicken pie, shepherd's pie, railroad pie, spaghetti pie, vegetable quiches of all sorts, pub pie (potatoes, onion, cheese), pumpkin pie, pecan pie, coconut pie, chocolate pie, lemon pie, egg custard pie, and this list doesn't even come close to describing all the pies. There was even a purple sweet potato pie.

ECA members raise money with a pie tasting.

Extension homemakers volunteer at Yadkin Christian Ministries, which helps feed the hungry.

During the Depression, the county home demonstration agent taught people to use a canner, a treadle sewing machine, and later the electric sewing machine. She taught them how to make clothes for the family, and taught cooking classes and arts and crafts to beautify the home.

Yancey ECA has given scholarships, supported local charities, helped the sick in the community and elevated quality of life for women in the community.

One ECA member in the county said that ECA provided her with the opportunity to do more, learn more, and go more than she ever imagined when she retired from teaching.

Students at Bald Creek Elementary School's after-school program attended the Extension FCS agent's *Dealing with Anger* class. In 2010 students brainstormed techniques to improve thinking and decision-making skills. They learned to recognize anger and the importance of finding a positive outlet for anger and other negative emotions, and to cooperate with their classmates and work together to find peaceful solutions. Finally, they learned to take responsibility for personal actions and handle negative emotions in a positive way.

The Yancey FCS agent teaches mountain heritage to a group of 4-H'ers at a day camp in 2010.

The EFNEP program assistant teaches nutrition to parents and children so they can share what they learn and encourage each other to eat healthy. Recently, a mother told the program assistant that as a result of what they learned, her daughter was now actively involved in the family meal planning and grocery shopping, and the two had agreed to eat less fast food, more fruits and vegetables, and follow other *MyPyramid* guidelines. The mother stated that since practicing more healthy eating habits, she had lost 13 pounds and both she and her daughter felt healthier.

The FCS agent held a nutrition class in 2010 at Valley Place Apartments in Burnsville, helping people with chronic diseases. As a result of what they have learned, participants have reported having lost weight and lowered blood sugar and triglyceride levels.

Burnsville Extension Homemakers marked their 50th anniversary in 1970 with a quilting party at the home of Mrs. Ralph Jacks.

Families will always be our highest priority

Family & Consumer Sciences and its Extension & Community Association volunteers have been local leaders since inception.

Beginning with curb markets to add income for your families, to raising money to fund hospital ships during World War II, to speaking out for those who would have never been heard, you have been the leaders in your communities since 1911.

One hundred years of selfless service to the families of North Carolina is the highest of achievements. Thank you for allowing us to be your partner along the way.

Together, we will grow the next generation of leaders.

FARM BUREAU INSURANCE ®

SOUTHERN FARM BUREAU
LIFE INSURANCE COMPANY

Farm Bureau and Family & Consumer Sciences growing together in every community across North Carolina

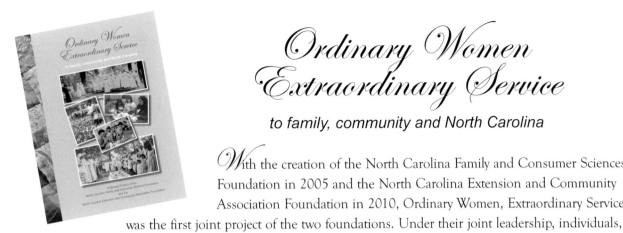

Ordinary Women Extraordinary Service

to family, community and North Carolina

With the creation of the North Carolina Family and Consumer Sciences Foundation in 2005 and the North Carolina Extension and Community Association Foundation in 2010, Ordinary Women, Extraordinary Service was the first joint project of the two foundations. Under their joint leadership, individuals, families, businesses, and corporations have joined together to support the production of this outstanding publication. Provided below are persons who believe in Family and Consumer Sciences and see the book as a way to tell stories of yesterday and today . . . launching extraordinary service for the next century.

Sections for both honorariums and memorials have been provided by giving levels (found at the end of the sections). The contributors are listed in a state-level section if they did not identify a specific county or if their programs are statewide. Other contributors have been identified under the county of their choice. Please note that the entries are worded as they were submitted. Enjoy looking at the list and please express your thanks for each person's generosity in sharing the story.

Honorariums From Across the State

BLUE RIBBON SPONSORS

Frances J. Cope by Dr. Pauline Calloway

The History Book Committee:
Wilma Hammett, Chair, Jan Christensen, Wanda Denning, Joan Gosper, Carol Cox, Judy Mock, Ada Dalla-Pozza, Jerry Hardesty, Sue Counts, Frances Turner, Jeannie Leonard, Dr. Sarah Shoffner, Nancy Young
by Kay, Dale & Kat Saville

The History Book Editing and Proofing Team: Dr. Wilma Hammett, Jan Christensen, Joan Gosper, Sarah Nixon, Murray Nixon, Cathy Wilkins, Beth Howell, Dr. Sarah Shoffner, Dr. Carolyn Lackey, Dr. Judy Mock
by Kay, Dale & Kat Saville

 T. W. Garner Food Company

 North Carolina Cooperative Extension

BUTTER AND EGG SPONSORS

Albemarle Bank & Trust –
  A West Town Bank
Ada Dalla-Pozza
My Wife, Martha by Jerry Hardesty
Dr. Judieth Mock

Maurene Rickards, Executive Director FCS
  & ECA Foundations
Kay Saville, Executive Director FCS & ECA
  Foundations
The Winston and McKimmon Families
  by the Bell Family Foundation

CORNERSTONE SPONSORS

All Previous State Home Demonstration, Extension
  Homemakers, Extension and Community
  Association Leaders and Specialists
  by Dr. Marshall Stewart, State Leader
Wilma Scott Hammett by Betsy Uzzle Meldau

Martha and Jerry Hardestry by Maurene Rickards
Mack & Juanita Hudson by Betsy Uzzle Meldau
Cheryl Lemay Lloyd
Carolyn Rouse Register by Betsy Uzzle Meldau
Lizzie Mock by Judieth Mock

Ada Braswell Dalla-Pozza

North Carolina Assistant State Home Economics Leader and
North Carolina Extension Homemakers Leader

visionary leader, mentor and friend

In appreciation for over 70 years
of servant leadership to
Family & Consumer Sciences and
the Extension & Community Association.

Jean C. Bowen
Jan Christensen
Dan & Fairley Bell
  Cook, Bell Family
  Foundation
Genelle Dail
Doris Davis
Dr. Mike Davis
Helen H. Dosier
Duplin NCCE,
  Family & Consumer
  Sciences
Donna B. Edsel
Curtis D. Fountain
Wanda J. Hardison

Juanita O. Hudson
Mrs. Elmer B. Lagg
Betsy Uzzle Meldau
Sarah M. Nixon
Pamela C. Outen
Isabelle M. Fletcher Perry
Alice L. Pettitt
Maurene Rickards
Sharon Runion Rowland
Dr. Dale Safrit
Kay Saville
Elizabeth G. Thompson
Mae H. Troublefield
Frances G. Turner
Marguerite Whitfield

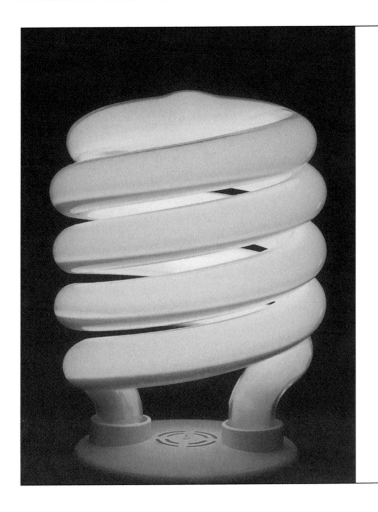

Here's to 100 years of lighting the way.

Honoring the women of
Family & Consumer Sciences and the
Extension & Community Association

North Carolina's Electric Cooperatives salute the women of Family & Consumer Sciences and the Extension & Community Association for providing 100 years of leadership and service to North Carolina communities. We're proud to be a partner in your vision for the future.

North Carolina's Electric Cooperatives

Your Touchstone Energy® Cooperatives

www.ncelectriccooperatives.com

FRIENDS & FAMILY SPONSORS

Zeda Bashford by Driftwood ECA Club
Betsy, Ronnie, Sharon & Kay by Ada Dalla-Pozza
Dr. Edgar J. Boone by Richard Liles
Pat Brafford by Wilma Hammett
Susan Brame, Devona Beard, Crystal Green, by Sharon Rowland
Isabelle Buckley by Joan Robertson
Emma Burke, Perquimans County Extension Homemaker by Dr. Travis Burke
Dr. Pauline Calloway by Sharon Rowland
Charles L. Campbell, Jr.
Centennial Steering Committee by Sarah Ray
Jan Christensen by Jean C. Bowen
Dr. Karen B. DeBord, Department of 4-H Youth Development and Family & Consumer Sciences
Dr. Carolyn Dunn, Department of 4-H Youth Development and Family & Consumer Sciences

Extension Workers by Charles Averre
Thomas Hobgood, Jr.
George R. Hughes by Vivian Hughes
Dr. Sarah Kirby, Department of 4-H Youth Development and Family & Consumer Sciences
Dr. Carolyn J. Lackey, Professor Emeritus by Kathryn Kelly
Lorna Langley by Dr. Myrle Swicegood
Betsy Meldau by Helen H. Dosier
Dr. Betsy Meldau by Sharon Rowland
Betsy Meldau by Wilma Hammett
NC Extension Association of Family and Consumer Sciences
North Central District by Jim Cowden, North Central District Extension Director
Our Future by I. F. Parker
Justine Rozier by Jan Christensen

From Our Corner to Yours...

Family and Consumer Sciences thrives as North Carolina's families seek locally produced, nutritional foods for their dinner table.

Originally founded on an idea born from local businessmen over a bumper crop of cucumbers, Mt. Olive Pickle Company appreciates all that Family and Consumer Sciences has done, and continues to do for North Carolina's food industry.

Mt. Olive
CUCUMBER VINE

Mt.Olive
SINCE 1926

Sarah Ray, by The History Book Committee
Sharon Rowland by Dr. Pauline Calloway
Frank D. Sargent
Annie Stewart by Marshall and Jan Stewart
Maidred M. & Reginald Stroud

Jane Stuart
Nadine Tope by Jean C. Bowen
Lenore Walston by Linda Boyette
Elizabeth B. Wilson
Dr. Sandra Zaslow

Memorials from Across the State

BLUE RIBBON SPONSORS

Anamerle Arrant by Dr. Pauline Calloway

Eloise Cofer by Dr. Pauline Calloway

BUTTER AND EGG SPONSORS

Mrs. Cora Bailey by Jim and Agnes Goldston

Mrs. Margie Goldston by Jim and Agnes Goldston

CORNERSTONE SPONSORS

Eloise Snowden Cofer by Betsy Uzzle Meldau

Herberta Stuckey Uzzle by Betsy Uzzle Meldau

FRIENDS & FAMILY SPONSORS

Jack Barnes by Betty Barnes
Roy R. Bennett by Alice Bennett
Dr. Eloise Cofer and Dr. Emily Quinn Pou by Dr. and Mrs. Edgar Boone
Eloise Cofer by Jan Christensen

Eloise Cofer by Martha Keravuori
Marjorie Donnelly by Jan Christensen
Nell Kennett by Dr. Rebecca M. Smith
My Parents by Charles Averre

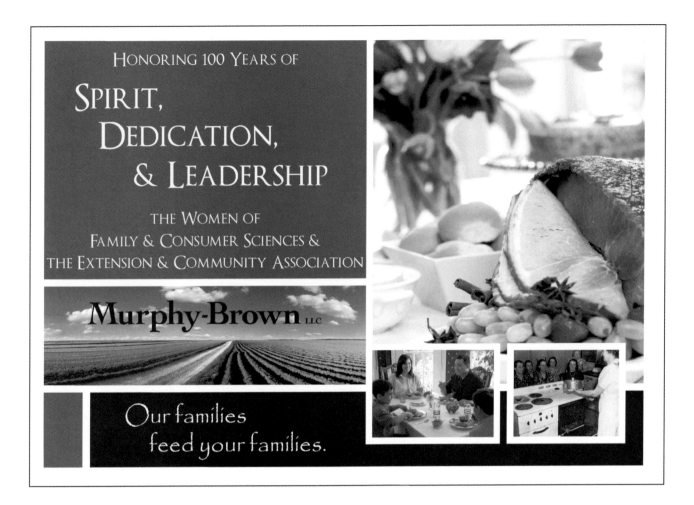

HONORING 100 YEARS OF

SPIRIT,
DEDICATION,
& LEADERSHIP

THE WOMEN OF
FAMILY & CONSUMER SCIENCES &
THE EXTENSION & COMMUNITY ASSOCIATION

Murphy-Brown LLC

Our families
feed your families.

Sallie Pearson Moore, Home Economics Teacher
   and Member, Randolph Extension Homemaker
   by Dr. Sarah Moore Shoffner
Our Past by I. F. Parker

Woodley Warrick by Wilma Hammett
Charlotte Womble by Wilma Hammett
Robert (Bob) N. Wood by Mary Lib Wood

GIVING LEVELS

Visionary Sponsor- $25,000
(Full Page Ad)

Legacy Sponsor - $10,000
(Half Page Ad)

Champion Sponsor - $5,000
(1/3 Page Ad)

Sustaining Sponsor - $2,500
(1/4 Page Ad)

Blue Ribbon Sponsor - $1,500

Butter & Egg Sponsor - $1,000

Cornerstone Sponsor - $500

Friends & Family Sponsor - $100

BLUE RIBBON SPONSORS

CAMDEN

Herman & Mamie Sawyer
by Dr. Pauline Calloway

CHOWAN

Betty Cox by Dr. Pauline Calloway
Jack & Trudy Parker
by Dr. Pauline Calloway
Frances Ward by Dr. Pauline Calloway

CUMBERLAND

Lisa Childers by Dr. Pauline Calloway

DAVIDSON

Davidson County Farm Bureau

FORSYTH

Forsyth County Farm Bureau

TOUCHING LIVES

The NC State Grange has been a proud partner with Family & Consumer Sciences and the Extension & Community Association since their beginning one hundred years ago.

The Grange salutes Dr. Jane S. McKimmon, Grange member, and the generations of women who have made our state thrive.

PROVIDING A **VOICE** FOR NORTH CAROLINA

FORWARD THINKING

Saluting the women of Family & Consumer Sciences and the Extension & Community Association for 100 years of acting as catalysts for change in North Carolina.

When electricity was just a hope for many North Carolinians, an extraordinary group of women dreamed the impossible ... and made it happen. Without you, rural electrification would have taken decades longer.

Today, we all benefit from your dare to dream big. Congratulations on an amazing milestone.

We look forward to your next big dream.

Duke Energy®

PERQUIMANS

Jewel Winslow by Dr. Pauline Calloway

RANDOLPH

Randolph County ECA Members Past and Present by Randolph County Farm Bureau Board of Directors

TYRRELL

Frances Voliva by Dr. Pauline Calloway

WAKE

Wake County Farm Bureau

GUILFORD

Guilford County Farm Bureau

HARNETT

Al & Wanda Hardison by Dr. Pauline Calloway
Catherine King by Dr. Pauline Calloway
Alice Thomas by Dr. Pauline Calloway
Jennifer Walker by Dr. Pauline Calloway

MARTIN

Ila Parker by Dr. Pauline Calloway

PASQUOTANK

Faytie Johnston by Dr. Pauline Calloway

Congratulations on 100 Years of Educating North Carolina Families.

MIDSTATE MILLS, INC.

PO Box 350
Newton, NC
828-464-1611
www.midstatemills.com

Family owned and operated since 1935

Manufacturer of:

Southern Biscuit.

TENDA·BAKE

Redi Mix.
Made With Southern Biscuit Flour

BIG M.

M Circle M Feeds

MAGIC QUALITY

Butter & Egg Sponsors

BEAUFORT

Beaufort County Cooperative Extension

BRUNSWICK

Brunswick County Farm Bureau

CARTERET

Carteret County Farm Bureau

COLUMBUS

Columbus County ECA Council

DUPLIN

Wanda C. Clay by Ed Emory
Jean Huey by Ed Emory
Alta Kornegay by Ed Emory
Mae H. Spicer by Ed Emory
JoAnn Y. Williams by Ed Emory

DURHAM

Durham County Farm Bureau

HOKE

Hoke County Cooperative Extension

JOHNSTON

Johnston County Farm Bureau, Inc.

MACON

Macon County Farm Bureau

PASQUOTANK

Pasquotank County ECA

ROBESON

Robeson County Cooperative Extension

ROCKINGHAM

Rockingham County Farm Bureau

WATAUGA

Frances Arnold by Sue Counts
Elaine Brookshire by Sue Counts
Dianne Brown by Sue Counts
Lillian and Oscar Danner by Sue Counts
Nancy High by Sue Counts
Rose McCann by Sue Counts
Betty Steelman by Sue Counts

WAYNE

Wayne County ECA

WILKES

Donna Edsel by Wilkes County ECA

Cornerstone Sponsors

ALAMANCE

Evelyn DeLoatch by Alamance County ECA
Frances Gerringer by Alamance County ECA
Judy Johnson Henderson by Alamance County ECA
Audrey Moore by Alamance County ECA
Donna Spangler by Alamance County ECA
Emogene Wallace by Alamance County ECA

ASHE

Orleta Demuth

BERTIE

Bertie County Farm Bureau

BRUNSWICK

Susan M. Morgan, Former FCS Agent
by Brunswick County ECA

women giving back

for a stronger community

Like North Carolina's pork producers, Family & Consumer Sciences and the Extension & Community Association have a long history of service to our communities. From spearheading the hot lunch program in schools to making bibs and blankets for hospitalized children, they have created a legacy of improving lives across the state.

Congratulations on one hundred years of making North Carolina a healthier place to live, work and play.

NORTH CAROLINA PORK COUNCIL

We bring a lot to the table.

BURKE

Burke County FCS

CABARRUS

Cabarrus County Government

CHOWAN

Chowan County ECA
by Chowan County Cooperative Extension

CURRITUCK

Currituck ECA

DARE

Dare County Farm Bureau

DURHAM

Bethesda Ruritan Club

GASTON

Past, Present, and Future ECA Members
by Gaston County ECA
Elaine Roux

GATES

Gates County Cooperative Extension

GRAHAM

Graham County Cooperative Extension

HALIFAX

Halifax County Cooperative Extension

HARNETT

Anonymous

HERTFORD

Hertford County Cooperative Extension and
    Hertford County ECA

IREDELL

Ken and Bertie Vaughn

JOHNSTON

Johnston County ECA

LEE

Hubert Lynn Blackmon by Ruby C. McSwain

Lee County Farm Bureau Past and Present Board
    Members by Lee County Farm Bureau

LINCOLN

Lincoln County Extension Center

MECKLENBURG

Mecklenburg County Farm Bureau

MITCHELL

Mitchell County ECA
    by Mitchell County Cooperative Extension

MOORE

Moore County ECA by Moore County Extension and
    Community Association

NASH

Ruth High Powell by The Kenneth Powell Family

PAMLICO

Pamlico County Farm Bureau

PITT

Pitt County Extension and Community Association

ROBESON

Robeson County Farm Bureau

Rosalind Redfearn, Anson County

RUTHERFORD

Rutherford County Farm Bureau

UNION

Union County Farm Bureau

VANCE

Vance County Farm Bureau

WILKES

Wilkes County ECA Members
    by Wilkes County Farm Bureau

WILSON

Wilson County Farm Bureau

YANCEY

Yancey County Cooperative Extension; Yancey
    County ECA Members and Eloise McIntosh,
    Long-time ECA Member

FRIENDS & FAMILY SPONSORS

ALAMANCE

Alamance County Farm Bureau Inc.
Evelyn D. DeLoatch
Frances Gerringer
    by Hulon Gerringer, Rance, Cheryl & Lisa
Hazel Iseley by Don and Phyllis Iseley
Audrey Moore by Don Moore
Emogene Wallace by Fred Wallace & Rachel Dowdell

ALEXANDER

Betty Church by Margo Mosley
Ella Mae Nichols
Colene Philmon by Alexander County ECA
Janie Shipley

ALLEGHANY

Alleghany County Farm Bureau
Anonymous

ANSON

Anson County 4-H
Anson County Cooperative Extension
Anson County Farm Bureau
Janine Rywak, County Extension Director
Pee Dee Electric Membership Corporation

ASHE

Ashe County Farm Bureau
Blue Ridge Electric Membership Corporation
Carolyn Shepherd
    by Skyline Membership Corporation
Ilene Stump by Robyn and Randy Stump

BLADEN

Bladen County Farm Bureau
Representative William and Brenda Brisson
Dorothy Boone
Cape Fear Propane
Four County Electric Membership Corporation
Dorothy McKoy
Dorothy McKoy, First African American State ECA
    President by Colly ECA Club, Bladen County
Jane H. Ross by Sandra R. Cain
Jane H. Ross

BRUNSWICK

Milton Coleman
Susan Morgan

BUNCOMBE

Buncombe County Farm Bureau

BURKE

Burke County Farm Bureau

CABARRUS

Cabarrus County ECA
William (Bill) and Martha Garmon
Ned and Dianne Hudson
Joyce Kluttz
Pat Misenheimer, Past President of County
    Neighbors by Aaron Misenheimer
Mt. Pleasant Lions Club
Mary Belle Johnson Overcash by Anonymous
Agnes Gold Overcash by Anonymous
St. Johns Grange
Wilmar ECA by Murray Nixon

CAMDEN

Camden County Farm Bureau

CARTERET

Betty Ward Motes by William Motes, Jr.

CASWELL

Grey Miles by Beverly, Donna, Sandra, Ervin, Susan
Piedmont Electric Membership Corporation
Solomon Lea ECA
Carolina Farm Credit, ACA

CATAWBA

Blackburn ECA Members by Sylvia King
Catawba Valley Cattlemen's Association
Glennie Daniels by Catawba County ECA
Glennie Daniels
Ruth Anne Livengood and Ann Miller
    by Fred and Debbie Miller
Miranda Pope
All Veterans by Hickory American Legion Fair

CHATHAM

Chatham County Farm Bureau
Chatham County FCS and ECA

CLEVELAND

Nancy Hairston Abasiekong, FCS Extension Agent
    by Cleveland County ECA
Cleveland County ECA
    by Cleveland County Fair, Inc.
Cleveland County ECA
    by Cleveland County Farm Bureau
Cleveland County FCS Extension Staff
    by Clevie W. Spangler
Cleveland County FCS Staff
    by Cleveland County Extension Center
Nancy Hardy Jones, Extension Agent FCS
    by Cleveland County ECA
Cleveland County ECA by Shelby Savings Bank
Clevie W. Spangler
    by Cleveland County Cattlemen's Association
Clarence S. Withrow by Sharon, Karen & Brian
    Withrow

CRAVEN

Joni L. Bass
Craven County ECA
Craven County Farm Bureau
Billy Dunham
Nelda K. Howell
Ila S. McIlwean by Ila Grey White
Mary H. McIlwean by Ila Grey White

CUMBERLAND

George and Pandy Autry
Cumberland County 4-H Foundation
Cumberland County Livestock Association
Cumberland County Master Gardener Association

CURRITUCK

Currituck County FCS Agents and Extension and
    Community Association of Currituck County
    by Jeffrey and Jessica Tice
Georgia U. Kight

DAVIDSON

Jane Lee Ebert
Mr. & Mrs. Charles Ray Fritts by Cathy Fritts Wilkins

DAVIE

Vicki Blackwelder
Davie County ECA Council by Davie County ECA
My Grandchildren, Dylan, Connor, Lydia, Logan, &
    Ella by Shelby Gregory

DUPLIN

Cape Fear Farm Credit
Duplin County 4-H
Duplin County Agribusiness Council
Duplin County ECA
Duplin County Farm Bureau
Four County Electric Membership Corporation
Tri-County Electric Membership
Mildred Turner Family

DURHAM

Bethesda Ruritan Auxiliary
Rougemont ECA
Dr. Frank S. Sargent

FORSYTH

Jane Davidson by Martha H. Isenberg

FRANKLIN

Franklin County Farm Bureau

GASTON

Sarah Nixon by Family & Friends
Quiltmakers Club
Gaston County Farm Bureau
Shirley Ferguson by Bel Heights ECA
Becky Withers, Helen Bess, and Margaret Spencer
    by Lucile Tatum

GATES

Mary G. Cowper by Paige L. Underwood

GRANVILLE

Jason and Cynthia Brand
Dr. & Mrs. August DeHertogh
Sarah Blackwell Downey
Granville County Cattlemen's Association
Granville County Farm Bureau
Iona Brooks James by Shirley Holliday
Penny Hill & Young Zion Greenwood EVA Clubs,
    Granville County
Joan M. Reid by Sandy Ruble

GREENE

Mrs. Jean Mainhart, ECA County President 2001-2007
    by The Greene County ECA Clubs

HALIFAX

Rose Massey by The Family of Marjorie & Leonard
    Allen
R. Douglas Phillips

HARNETT

Dr. Pauline Calloway
    by Lisa B. Childers and Wanda J. Hardison
Carolyn Greene

HAYWOOD

Haywood County Farm Bureau

HENDERSON

Past and Current FCS Agents and ECA Members
    by Henderson County FCS Program

HERTFORD

Hertford County Farm Bureau

IREDELL

Martha Kate Cashion Archer by Lucille Carter
Iredell County Farm Bureau
Union Grove Members ECA
    by Union Grove Homemakers Club

JACKSON

Jackson County Farm Bureau

JOHNSTON

Johnston County Cooperative Extension

LEE

Town of Broadway Board of Commissioners
Eunice Cameron by Cecil C. Cameron
Faye C. Cameron by Cecil C. Cameron
Central Electric Membership Corporation
Susan Condlin, County Extension Director/FCS
    Agent by Lee County ECA
Julia Alexander Hoyle, Home Demonstration Agent
    Nov. 1949 – June 1955 by Dick Hoyle
Geraldine Laws by the C. M. Laws Family
2011 Lee County Board of Commissioners
The Lee County ECA Leadership Team
Lee County FCS Program
    by Lee County Extension Advisory Council
Lee County Livestock Producers Association
Past & Present Lee County Home Demonstration,
    Home Economics, and FCS Agents
Sanford Lions Club

LENOIR

Alma Fields, Isabelle Fletcher Perry, Marguerite
    Whitfield, Past State Presidents
    by Classy Spirits ECA & Neuse ECA of Lenoir County
Anne Gaddis
Lorelei Jones by Iris S. Aldridge
Bill and Melda Lamm
Lenoir County Farm Bureau
Current Lenoir County Members by Alma Fields
Isabelle M. Perry by Lorelei Jones

LINCOLN

Melinda Houser, FCS Agent and Founder of the
    Lincoln County Apple Festival
    by Lincoln County Apple Festival
Sarah M. Nixon, Past State President 1987
    by Her Children, Cliff, Susan, Kathy & Murray

MADISON

Madison County Cooperative Extension

MARTIN

Ila Parker by Martin County ECA

MCDOWELL

McDowell County Farm Bureau

MITCHELL

Denise Baker by The Runion Family
Jane Cook by The Runion Family
Carolyn McKinney by The Runion Family
Mitchell County Farm Bureau
Helen Bowditch Runion by Her Daughters
Lois Williams by The Runion Family

MOORE

Mrs. Louise Blue by Robert T. Lea
Sam Ragan by The Pilot
Paige L. Underwood

NASH

Julia Bryant by Richard Bryant
Coopers Ruritan Club
Derrill Edwards
Nash County ECA
Nash County Farm Bureau
Nash County Master Gardener Volunteer
    Association
Nash County ECA Membership
    by Janice H. Latour, FCS Extension Agent,
    Nash County
Nashville Community Center
Oak Level Ruritan Club
Marie M. Rose by Brenda R. Vester
Mazell J. Vester by Hubert H. Vester, Jr.

NORTHAMPTON

Autrey Jenkins by Verlene Stephenson
Carrie Thompson by Cynthia Brown

ORANGE

Dr. Fletcher Barber Jr. by The Barber Family
Mrs. Bonnie B. Davis by Pearlene Foster Peace
Rose Walters Dunn
    by Wendy Burgess, Kim Scarlett, Jeannie Dunn
Orange County ECA
    by Orange County ECA 2009-2010 Outgoing
    Officers
Piedmont Electric Membership Corporation

PASQUOTANK

Jeffrey's Greenworld & Florist Inc.
Yvonne Mullen

PENDER

Four County Electric Membership Corporation
Pender County Farm Bureau

PERQUIMANS

Perquimans County ECA by Jewel L. Winslow
Perquimans County ECA

PERSON

Piedmont Electric Membership Corporation
Person County Cattlemen's Association
Person County ECA Members by Bess Hester-Whitt
Person County Farm Bureau

PITT

Sue B. May, My Mentor & Friend
    by Evelyn Spangler Brothers
Sue May

POLK

Home Economics Education Fund
Polk County Cooperative Extension

RANDOLPH

Talmadge S. Baker & Sara Baker
Carolina Farm Credit ACA
Doris Davis by Walter Davis
Phil & Carolyn Langley
Lynne Qualls
Randolph County ECA Liaison Agents Past and
    Present by Randolph County ECA
Randolph Electric Membership Corporation

RICHMOND

Earlene Waddell

ROWAN

Jean Lamb and Anne Zaffino
    by Rowan County Master Gardener Volunteer
    Association
Rebecca Lyerly

RUTHERFORD

Carolina Farm Credit serving Rutherford,
    Polk, and McDowell counties
Rutherford County CES and ECA

SAMPSON

Four County Electric Membership Corporation
Llewellyn Jernigan by Marshall and Jan Stewart
Sampson County Farm Bureau

SCOTLAND

Juanita Bowen, Scotland County ECA
    by Gloria L. Otis
Midge English,
    Central Friendship Club Scotland County ECA
    by Lynn Hannah-McDougald
Donna J. Faulk by Agnes Johnson & Randy Johnson
Candis Harrington, Central Friendship Club
    Scotland County ECA by Robert Malloy & Ida
    McGill
Mozelle Parker, Past State President 1986
    by Juanita Bowen
Ida Hicks Stewart,
    Central Friendship Club Scotland County ECA
    by Benny Stewart

STANLY

Anonymous
Ann M. Duckwall
Home Savings Bank of Albemarle
JK's Stained Glass
Hazel Ross Lee
    by Cassandra Stone & Jane Lee Watson
Frank Simpson
Sherrill Smith
Stanly County ECA
Stanly County Farm Bureau Inc.
Strategic Investment Advisors Inc.

STOKES

Lawsonville ECA
Stokes County Farm Bureau

TYRRELL

Ken & Terri Cherry
Bryan Foster
Wesley Foster
Green Valley Farms
Bobby and Frances Voliva

UNION

Charles and Gloria Baker
Hope Hunt, FCS Agent
Sally Eller McNeill, FCS Agent, Union County
Richard Melton, Union County Extension Director

VANCE

Annie Mae Royster By Her Daughter, Lois R. Williams

WAKE

Needmore ECA of Wake County
Sue H. Myatt
Wil-Pine ECA of Wake County

WARREN

Dr. Robert & Rachel Monteverdi

WASHINGTON

Sandra Brown
    by Washington County Cooperative Extension

WATAUGA

Alfred and Daisy Adams
  by Wachovia Bank, NA, a Wells Fargo Company
Carolina Farm Credit
Sue Counts
Sue Counts By Her Children, Lisa and Heather
Lillian H. Danner
Woodrow "Woody" Richardson by Diane Deal
Robert and Agnes Shipley
  by Agnes Shipley Moore, Bob Shipley, Jr.,
  Janie Shipley
Town and Country ECA
Watauga County ECA
Watauga County Farm Bureau

WAYNE

Evelyn Raper & Sandra Head
  by Wayne County ECA
Hansford T. Ricks
  by Charlotte Ricks Jenkins and Phillip Ricks

WILKES

Betty Knight by County Staff

WILSON

Mrs. Elgia S. Farrior
  by Her Daughters, Vicky F. Barnes, Ann F. Cooper,
  Tenna F. Smith, Sharon F. Gurley
Kathleen Scott by Wilma & Larry Hammett
Kathleen Scott by Kay, Dale & Kat Saville
Mozelle F. Scott
  by Howard Scott, Rachel Scott Crawford,
  Judy Scott Pate
**Wilson County ECA Members (Past, Present,
  Future)** by Candace L. Murray, Extension Agent,
  Wilson County

YADKIN

Olivia S. Simpson by Marilyn Wells
Yadkin County Farm Bureau

Memorial Gifts Designated by County

Blue Ribbon Sponsors

CURRITUCK

Liz Sanderlin by Dr. Pauline Calloway

HYDE

Iberia Roach Tunnell
  by Dr. Pauline Calloway

WASHINGTON

Frances Darden by Dr. Pauline Calloway

Butter & Egg Sponsors

DUPLIN

Lois G. Britt by Ed Emory
Floy G. Garner by Ed Emory
Judy H. Wallace by Ed Emory

EDGECOMBE

Ruby Powell Goff by Her Loving Family

SURRY

Elaine Whitaker by Surry County Farm Bureau

WATAUGA

Ruth Petrey by Sue Counts
Allene Sykes (Sue's Mother) by Sue Counts
Paris Winebarger by Sue Counts

Cornerstone Sponsors

CATAWBA

Ethel Lutz by Catawba County Farm Bureau

CUMBERLAND

Dorothy Farrell Kitchen by Hubert Bullard

LENOIR

L. O. Moseley – Student at A&M (early NC State) my father by Isabelle M. Perry

Friends & Family Sponsors

ALAMANCE

ALAMANCE

Roberta W. Pritchett by Edgar & Bonnie Pritchett

ANSON

Mrs. Maude S. Braswell, (Mother) by Ada Dalla-Pozza
Mrs. Rosalind Redfearn, Anson County's 1st Agent by Ada Dalla-Pozza

AVERY

Connie Greene by Avery County Cooperative Extension

BLADEN

Margaret Singletary Campbell (Mother) by Charles Lee Campbell, Jr.

Velma Hatcher Ellis (Mother) by Goldie Ellis Campbell

Mrs. Thomas Boston Harrelson by Fleta L. Harrelson

Eunice and Leo Nance by Linda Rivenbark

CABARRUS

Channing Hilliard Fries by Marcia K. Lyerly, Joseph Fries, Jean Beasley, Robert Kluttz
Channing Hillard Fries by The Children of Mildred Fries Wiseman

Edith McGlamery by Doris Rogers

Dorothy Simpson, Past President of County Neighbors and ECA Council Officer by Aaron Misenheimer

CARTERET

Blanche S. Gillikin by Dolena Ball

CASWELL

Josie S. Foster by Blanche Page

CATAWBA

Blackburn ECA Members by Sylvia King
Nancy Myers by Nancy Murray
All Veterans by Hickory American Legion Fair

CHOWAN

Gladys B. White by Frances Ward

CLAY

E. D. Bowditch, 1ˢᵗ Clay Agent
by His Children and Grandchildren

CLEVELAND

Lillian W. Bridges by Shirley Bridges
Elizabeth Roseman Carver by First National Bank
Hattie Bingham Edwards
by Garry Tillman, Loretta Justice, Forrestine Teague
Wilma M. Hoyle by Jane H. Hoyle
Edith Ledford Lutz by Mary Jane Seagle
Ethel Norman Lutz by Jean Ann Privett
Thelma E. McVea By Nancy & Aniedi Abasiekong
Ima Carpenter Seagle by Mary Jane Seagle
Annie L. Warlick by Sue Warlick Boles
Annie L. Warlick by Ostine Warlick West
Bettye Jamerson Withrow
by Sharon, Karen & Brian Withrow

COLUMBUS

Adell S. Noble by Elaine N. Blake

GIVING LEVELS

Blue Ribbon Sponsor - $1,500

Butter & Egg Sponsor - $1,000

Cornerstone Sponsor - $500

Friends & Family Sponsor - $100

CUMBERLAND

Elizabeth Bright Brown by Willie E. Loftin

CURRITUCK

Bertha Perry by Moyock ECA Club
Elizabeth Sanderlin
by Currituck Extension Foundation
Elizabeth P. Sanderlin by Faytie C. Johnson

DUPLIN

**Mrs. Carl (Omega) Britt, Maysville Home
Demonstration Club; Mrs. Bruce (Helen)
Beavers, Oak Ridge Community Development
Club** by Keith & Glenda Beavers
Ethel Register & Mildred Turner
by Nancy Lanier & Kathy Weeks, Her
Granddaughter & Daughter
**Nellie Grey Carr Williams and Fannie Johnson
Owen** by S. Franklin and Paula Owens Williams
Bertha Hardee Wilson by Snodie & Nancy Wilson

DURHAM

Estelle Nixon by Cheryl LeMay Lloyd

FORSYTH

Dewey and Debbie Davidson by Jane Davidson
Carolyn Scott Flynt
by her Granddaughters and Great Granddaughters
Mamie Wilson Scott
by Her Granddaughters and Great Granddaughters

GRANVILLE

Evelyn Satterwhite Brooks by Rebecca Faulkner
Johnsie C. Cunningham by Sandy Ruble

HALIFAX

Marjorie Jenkins Allen
by Her Children and Grandchildren
Georgia Wade Butts by Sarah Ann Butts Sasser

HENDERSON

**Jean Miller, former FCS and 4-H Secretary in
Henderson County** by Henderson County 4-H

HERTFORD

Jane Taylor by Autrey Jenkins

IREDELL

Joe L. and Hazel Gaither by Ann Simmons

JACKSON

Nannie Childers by Jean Childers

LEE

Ruth McCain Cameron by Boyce & Carol Cox
Florence G. Gilliam
  by Lynda G. Bowers & Barbara G. Alphin
My Mama, Lydia Nutt Gladney by Ann G. Clarke
Elizabeth Matthews by Willena M. Warren
Allean Meador by Dewey & Lou Roberts

LENOIR

**My Mother, Adell Faulkner & Previous Lenoir
  County Members** by Alma Fields
Mrs. Ruth Johnson
  by Classy Spirits ECA & Neuse ECA of Lenoir
  County

LINCOLN

Louise Harris by Dorothy Harris
George Stoudemire by David Choate

MACON

Bessie Cabe Gray by Eugene and Shirley Gray
Florence Sherrill by Jessie Cabe

MADISON

E. D. Bowditch, 1ˢᵗ Madison Agent
  by Helen B. Runion
Eileen M. Hensley (Mother) by Joy H. Frauson

MARTIN

Maude Bennett Crutchfield by Beluah Bennett
**Elizabeth Parker Harrison, Vivian Morris and
  Helen Hoskins and past members of Martin
  County ECA** by Martin County ECA
Ruth Roberson by Irene Wynne
Helen B. Wynne by Tanya Wynne

MITCHELL

E. D. Bowditch, 1ˢᵗ Mitchell Agent
  by His Children and Grandchildren

MOORE

Jessie Crouse by Carolyn C. Register
Mrs. Eva Brown Griffin by Craven F. Hudson

NASH

Mrs. Ella Baker Barnes
  by Barnes Farming Corporation
Ruth H. Powell by Daughter, Carolyn P. Joyner
Ruth H. Powell by Joe Powell
Estelle T. Strickland
  by Clay Strickland & Violet Weathers
Hazel A. Valentine
  by Nashville Business & Professional Women
Hazel A. Valentine by Tim Valentine and Family

NORTHAMPTON

Mattie M. Harris
  by Raye H. Gay and Jean H. Kirkland

ORANGE

Arlene "Muffin" Brosig by Robert Nutter
Alma L. Dorsett by Elaine G. Dorsett
Dr. Gerald W. Fernald by Marjorie L. Fernald
Parthenia W. Johnson by Rutha Brooks
Lettie Liner by Hugh & Mary Liner
Mrs. Martha Jane Lloyd
   by Mr. & Mrs. Carl B. Lloyd, Sr.
Mrs. Mary Catherine Lloyd
   by Dr. & Mrs. (Susan A. Lloyd) Christopher
   Lochmuller
Florence Mohler by Hugh & Mary Liner
Elizabeth Cheek Neville by Gordon and Pat Neville
Juanita M. Pritchard by Wendy P. Curtis
Billie Walker
   by Iva Walker, David Walker, Michael Walker
Lucille Walters
   by Wendy Burgess, Kim Scarlett, Jeannie Dunn,
   Rose Dunn
Martha Walker by Rebecca W. Smith

PAMLICO

Ada Whorton Mayo by Ralph and Barbara Warren
Ruth Whorton Mayo by Mrs. Laura Warren
Mother by Fonrose G. Rice

PERSON

Sue Duncan by Elizabeth N. Burke
Sara Warren Hester by Robert & Sara Hester LLC
Tempie W. Jeffers by Greta Jeffers
Past Person County Home Demonstration,
   Extension Homemakers, ECA Members
   by Person County ECA Council
Past Piedmont Club Members by Piedmont ECA
Effie Warren by Ralph and Betty Warren
Dorothy Williford by Victor Williford, Jr.

PITT

Miss Addie Gore, Pitt County Extension Agent
   by Dr. Bernadette G. Watts

RANDOLPH

Janette Richardson Gatlin by Sammie Garner

ROCKINGHAM

Mary B. Randall by Joyce Randall Spear

ROWAN

Channing Hillard Fries
   by The Children of Juanita Fries Kluttz

SCOTLAND

Elizabeth Teal Blake by Norma Blake Jones
Lillian S. Buie by Celeste Buie Lewis
Marie Harding by Juanita Bowen
Mary L. Harding by Willie F. Harding
Juanita H. Perkins by Khan V. Perkins

VANCE

Johnsie C. Cunningham by Susan Rowland Brame
Maude Nelson Harris by Her Daughters
Frieda B. Haun,
   "The Extension was my higher education"
   by Her Children Ericka, Betsy, Harold, and Ronnie
Rose Mabry Jackson by Jean Jackson
Hattie F. Plummer, 1st Home Demonstration Agent
   in Vance County, 1914
   by Her Granddaughters, Ann Rowland Nicholson
   and Barbara Rowland Adams
Jeanette Rogers by Her Family
Mable P. Williams by Her Children, Mary Roper,
   Patricia Priest, Sandra Parham, Joselyn Williams,
   Garry Williams, Michael Williams

WAKE

Winnifred Weeks by Wanda Denning
Willow Springs ECA by Wanda Denning

WASHINGTON

Frances Darden by Washington County Cooperative
   Extension

WATAUGA

Geraldine P. Hyatt by Lillian H. Danner,
   Roger P. Hyatt, Joseph M. Hyatt
Kate Reese by Clint Reese
Nora Wilson by Lillian Danner

In the tradition of Home Demonstration and Home Economics, Family & Consumer Sciences continues to bring relevant and timely programming to the citizens of North Carolina with the help of its Extension & Community Association volunteers.

We are in awe of your commitment to our families and communities, and of the powerful voice you lend to the betterment of our state.

We stand on the shoulders of your greatness. Thank you for one hundred years of history to build upon.

you are the **CORNERSTONE** of our **FOUNDATIONS**

Ordinary Women, Extraordinary Service

Family & Consumer Sciences
FOUNDATION NC State University

North Carolina Extension & Community Association
FOUNDATION
Leadership ⚛ *Education* ⚛ *Community*

WILKES

Mary Brookshire by Betty Knight
Sue Walsh Shew by Claude and Vickie Shew

WILSON

Walter and Pearl Blalock by Dr. T. C. Blalock
Walter and Pearl Blalock
　by Maroney Family Living Trust
Walter and Pearl Blalock by Sara B. Munford
Walter P. Farrior, Jr. by Elgia S. Farrior
Mary Gay by Kathleen Scott
Cora Scott Kirby by Rachel Thomas

Mrs. Ivey A. Lamm, Sr., a 1934 Charter Member of
　Lucama Home Demonstration Club
　by Sylvia Lamm
Alma Barnes Scott by Her Children
Frank W. and Victoria Kirby Scott by Elgia S. Farrior
Linwood H. Scott & Myrtle B. Scott
　by Mr. & Mrs. Linwood Scott, Jr.
Linwood and Myrtle Scott by Scott Brothers Inc.

YADKIN

Addie L. Heckard by April B. Dillon
Martha Shore by Susan S. Steelman